Hedge
FUNDS

Hedge FUNDS

FOR CANADIANS

NEW INVESTMENT STRATEGIES
FOR WINNING IN ANY MARKET

Peter Beck • Miklos Nagy

John Wiley & Sons Canada, Ltd.

National Library of Canada Cataloguing in Publication

Beck, Peter, 1955-
    Hedge funds for Canadians : new investment strategies for winning in any market / Peter Beck, Miklos Nagy.

Includes index.
ISBN 0-470-83284-3

    1. Hedge funds--Canada. I. Nagy, Miklos, 1959- II. Title.

HG5154.5.B42 2003   332.64'5   C2003-902079-7

Production Credits
Cover & interior text design: Interrobang Graphic Design Inc.
Printer: Tri-Graphic Printing Ltd.
Printed in Canada
10 9 8 7 6 5 4 3 2 1

For my Mother, who would have been very proud.
Peter Beck

For my children Phillipp, Sebastian, and Pierre.
Miklos Nagy

Contents

Introduction

The kitchen! The nucleus of all housewarming parties. It seems that eventually everyone gravitates to this spot. It is the place of the most interesting conversations, discussions, and storytelling. Maybe it's the proximity of food and drinks that acts as a magnet.

At a particular party on a Saturday night in April 2002, I became a minor celebrity in the kitchen. Not for my cooking abilities (although they ranked at the top of the list when my wife considered my proposal to marry her), but for the two television appearances I had made the day before.

I had appeared on CBC in the morning and on CityTV in the afternoon, talking about hedge funds. It seemed that a number of individuals recognized me as I was reaching into the fridge for the champagne that I had hidden behind a large bowl of pasta salad. And so the questions began. An hour and a half later when Sondra, my wife, came to my rescue, I was still answering questions about hedge funds.

By that time almost all the participants of the party had spent some time next to the fridge where I happened to set up my information session, listening to the ins and outs of hedge fund investing. One request that kept coming was for a recommendation for a book on the subject. Every time I had to give the disappointing answer: "There is no such a book in Canada. There are a number of books written on U.S. hedge funds, but their relevance is rather limited due to the different rules that apply in Canada."

So, when three days later my good friend Miklos called me and suggested that we write a book about hedge funds, the only thing that came to mind was the famous "Why didn't I think of that?"

Miklos, who had launched CanadianHedgeWatch.com, Canada's number one hedge fund information site, had been getting e-mails asking about books on the subject. It did not take him long to come to the conclusion that if there is no book, and people want it, *it has to be written*. The rest, as they say, is history.

The good people at John Wiley & Sons were enthusiastic about the idea. They immediately recognized the need for a book on the subject and helped us tremendously.

Our goal is to give a comprehensive introduction to hedge funds in Canada. After looking at the history of the industry, we highlight the differences between hedge funds and mutual funds, examine the wide variety of hedge fund styles, and demonstrate the advantages of holding hedge funds in your portfolio. To aid you in picking the right hedge fund for your needs, we've provided a "ranked" list of the top 50 hedge funds in Canada today, spelling out their characteristics, their returns, and their risks.

Bon chance, and happy investing!

—Peter Beck and Miklos Nagy

CHAPTER ONE

The History of Hedge Funds

ALFRED WINSLOW JONES

Unlike most investment strategies, which have evolved over many years and through many different theories and practices to their current forms, hedge funds can be traced to a single and truly remarkable individual. The son of an American father, Alfred Winslow Jones was born in Melbourne, Australia, in 1901 and moved to the United States with his family at the age of four. As an adult, a long series of career changes and adventures led him to the ripe old age of 48, when he founded what is now recognized as the first hedge fund.

After graduating from Harvard in 1923, Jones had travelled the world as a purser on a tramp steamer and in the early 1930s served as vice consul to the United States Embassy in Berlin while the rise of Hitler and Nazism was in full swing. During the Spanish Civil War, he reported on civilian relief for the Quakers; in 1941, he completed a doctorate in sociology at Columbia University. His thesis, "Life, Liberty and Property," became a standard sociology text of the time.

It was during the forties, however, that Jones developed the financial strategies that made him famous. He became an associate editor of *Fortune* magazine (as well as writing for *Time* and many other non-business periodicals), and it was while researching for an article entitled "Fashions in Forecasting" that Jones became well acquainted with many Wall Street analysts, technicians, and forecasters. His research and conversations led him to formulate an entirely new kind of investment strategy. By the end of 1949, he had raised $100,000 (of which $40,000 was his own) and began a general investment partnership to test his theories. It was the beginning of a new and innovative industry; one that was to fundamentally change the way investors thought about their business. But it was 17 years before it was brought to light.

TRADITIONAL INVESTMENTS: THE PROBLEMS WITH "GOING LONG"

Jones realized that one of the fundamental problems with traditional investment strategies was their vulnerability to the unpredictable declines of the stock market. Mutual funds, for instance, bought securities, held on to them until the price of the securities went up, and then sold them for a profit. This is the "traditional" model of investing, often referred to as a "buy and hold" strategy, or "going long." The flaw that Jones found in this was simple: *stock values simply don't always go up*. When markets go down, stock prices go down, so funds that invest in stocks go down as well. This means that investment funds, such as mutual funds, are directly correlated to the directions of the markets.

The history of investment management in the United States dates back to the beginning of the 19th century; it was founded on the three major principles of fiduciary responsibility, or acting solely in the best interests of the client: the *preservation of capital*, where the primary goal was to make sure that the initial investment was secure, and *prudence*, which demanded that a fiduciary (money manager) should gain a reasonable return *without speculation* (taking a risky gamble on a stock). Upholding all three principles is extremely hard to do when markets are declining, as the only way to make returns is to be a brilliant stock picker—in other words, find the few securities that are gaining in a downward or "bear" market. Speculation was severely frowned upon, as it was thought to be against the moral responsibilities of money managers.

The mutual fund industry was actually the first notable departure from these original tenets, in that mutual fund managers sought to *multiply* capital, and not just *maintain* it. These new "performance-oriented" funds brought a new and more aggressive approach to investing. Where investing had originally been more a side project for banks and insurance companies, mutual funds managers did it *full-time*. And more importantly, they were paid specifically for managing money, and the more money they managed, the more they were paid. Using full-blown marketing campaigns, they promoted themselves as money *makers*, not capital *preservers*. The industry exploded, to say the least, and the foundations of today's mutual fund industry were laid. Chapter 2 will go into more detail on the history of mutual funds. For this chapter's purposes, however, we just need to realize that *long only* (buy and hold) when used as a sole strategy will always be correlated to whether the markets are going up or down. Thus investments such as mutual funds provide returns that are *relative* to the current market trend.

JONES'S SOLUTION

Jones saw two main objectives for his investments. First and foremost, he wanted to get rid of market correlation in order to reduce the risk of losing money in a down market. Second, he wanted to make profits (as is the goal of all investors) even in down markets. His solution was simple and brilliant.

By combining two separate techniques, *short selling* and *leverage*, and maintaining long positions as well, Jones was able to "hedge" his bets against market downturns, while still making profits from rising ones. In short, he could be profitable no matter what the markets were doing. How was this possible? To understand it, we need to start by defining the two techniques.

Short Selling

Short selling is the act of borrowing a stock and selling it in anticipation of being able to *repurchase* it at a lower price, at or before the time it must be returned to the lender. This may seem confusing at first, but the idea is fairly simple. A short analogy can help.

A high-tech video game player is the hottest new thing on the market. Everyone wants one. The player retails for $179, but because of the high demand (and because stores can't keep them in stock), people are prepared to pay ridiculous prices for them. Your brother, in fact, has just purchased one for a whopping $300. Being a little more market savvy than your brother, you analyze the situation and realize that this is a vastly overblown price. You are sure that as soon as the fad is over, prices will drop, because a newer, more advanced video game player will show up on the market and become the next hot item. With this in mind, the short selling analogy goes like this:

1. You propose to borrow the video player from your brother, give it back in a month, and buy him a new game cartridge for it as payment. He agrees, and you take the player home.

2. The next day, you sell the player to a desperate buyer for $300, who figures it's a pretty good deal, since the few of them that are even on the market are now going for more than that. You put the money in your pocket.

   Over the next three weeks, your prediction comes true—in spades. A rival company produces a video player that vastly outperforms the existing one, and everyone is jumping in to buy the new players and trying desperately to sell the old ones.

3. Down at the local computer store, the old players are now on sale for $150, because there is no more demand for them. You pull out your $300, buy a player for $150 and a game cartridge for your brother for $25 (they're on sale now too!). You take the cartridge and the player back to your brother, thank him for the loan, and go home.

You've just made a net profit of $125, or $300 − ($150 + $25).

Securities can be handled in the same way. A trader can borrow securities—there are many ways to do this—that he or she believes are overvalued (worth less than they are selling for) and then sell them in anticipation of the security losing value before the promised date of return. The profit is gained from repurchasing the security at the lower price. The chart below can help illustrate this. Assume that an investor sees a reason that shares in Company X will decline in value over a

FIGURE 1.1

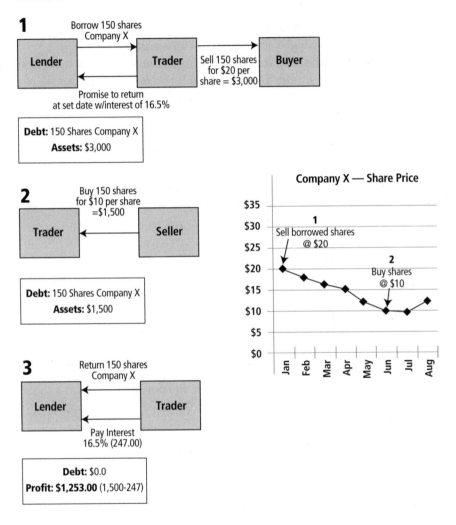

period of time. This could be due to any number of factors, depending on what Company X does and what the market conditions are.

By using short selling, it is therefore possible to make money on losing shares, and in an overall declining market, this technique can be used to make profits (it must be noted here that predicting whether a share's price will go down is just as difficult as whether it will go up).

Leveraging

Leveraging is the act of borrowing money to amplify an investment's return. Again, analogies are useful:

Let's say you live next door to a prosperous strawberry farm. You find out that the farmer is willing to sell you strawberries for $1 per pint (lower than market price, because he doesn't have to do any shipping or marketing). You also find out that the small grocery store down the road is willing to buy strawberries for $1.50 a pint. This looks like an ideal way to make a profit. You can buy a pint of strawberries for $1 and sell it for 50% more—all that's involved is transportation! If you have $10 to spend, you can make $5 profit.

With this in mind, the leveraging analogy works like this:

1. You have $10. That's all there is in the bank. With $10, you are guaranteed a $5 profit, by buying $10 worth of strawberries and selling them for $15.

   You *borrow* $90 from your brother and promise to pay it back the next day and buy him an ice cream for his trouble (interest, in essence).

2. You take the $100 (your $10 and your brother's $90) and purchase 100 pints of strawberries from the farmer.

3. You sell the 100 pints to the grocery store for $150.

4. You return the $90 to your brother the next day, buy him a super double-dip jumbo ice-cream cone for $2.75, and go home.

You have just made a net profit of $47.25—$150 − ($90 + $2.75)—which is $42.25 more than you would have made using your own money.

Leveraging is a common instrument in investing. In essence, it amplifies the amount of return you receive. Using our Company X from the short selling description, we can represent this process.

It should be noted here, though, that leveraging is a dangerous business, as it also amplifies *losses* if you make a bad decision. For instance, if your 100 pints of strawberries turned out to be sour and the grocery store refused to buy them, you would not only lose your own $10, but would be in debt to the tune of $92.75, or the cost of the ice-cream cone *plus* the borrowed $90.

FIGURE 1.2

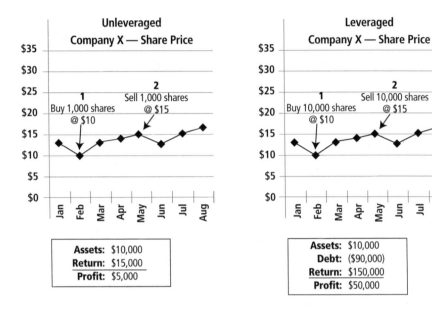

Hedging

By having long investments on stocks Jones felt were undervalued (worth more than he paid for them), and short positions on stocks he felt were overvalued (worth less than he sold them for), he was able to balance his investments and make money in both advancing and declining markets.

We can demonstrate the way these techniques can combine to produce superior returns with a hypothetical example using events from recent history.

In Figure 1.3, a hedge fund manager in 1994 goes "long" on Microsoft stocks—that is, betting that they will increase in value. This position was taken based on a gamble that Microsoft was becoming the largest player in the computer market and would continue to grow—a pretty safe bet. At the same time, however, the manager goes "short"—betting the price will drop—in Novell Inc. This position was taken because Microsoft had just introduced Windows 95, which integrated a network application into its operating system. Novell sold the network application for its platform separately. Who would want to buy two separate pieces when you could get both in one package?

FIGURE 1.3

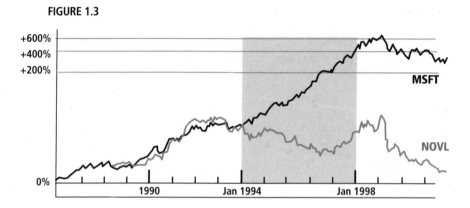

It turned out to be a good gamble. From January 1994 through January 1998, Microsoft stock increased its value by 600%, a tidy profit. During the same period, Novell stocks lost 70% of their value. Once again, the manager turns a hefty profit, having sold the shares previous to the decline.

This is a win-win scenario. The hedge fund strategy is actually twofold and is designed to not only make money in declining markets, but to minimize risk, so that losses on one side can be offset by gains on the other. Should Novell Inc. have gained rather than lost (by introducing a different popular software package, for instance), any subsequent return loss would have been more than adequately negated by gains on Microsoft—you would have bet on *both* sides of the table, so the only assets on one side you can "lose" are those which are not offset by assets "winning" on the *opposite* side.

To further understand Jones's system, we can use another example. Let's say you start out with $10,000 in capital. Using Jones's model, you would borrow money (leverage your position)—let's say you borrow $1,000, so you could buy $11,000 worth of shares. Then, you would *short* shares (borrow them hoping they decline in value) valued at $5,000. While the total amount you have invested is $16,000 (the $11,000 long and the $5,000 short positions), your *net market exposure* would only be $6,000 ($11,000 long minus $5,000 short). Jones would then say that your portfolio was 60% "net long," meaning that only 60% of your money is subject to decline in a downward market. His formula was as follows:

Market Exposure = (Long position – Short position) / Capital

This position is strengthened further by the fact that in an over-all market decline, your short positions will *gain in value*, offsetting your losses on the *long side*.

Active Management

As we can see, the strategy requires a little more work than the traditional "buy and hold" model. It requires that the fund be *actively managed*, to take advantage of market swings and make sure that the investments are properly balanced.

So when the markets were down, Jones could shift a larger portion of his portfolio to the short side and, when they went up, shift back to the long side. And by applying leverage, he was able to greatly amplify his returns. Far from the traditional "buy and hold" strategy, Jones actively managed his capital, getting in and out of short and long positions to guard against swings in the market and make profits in every market climate. And amazing profits they were.

THE JONES THAT NOBODY KEEPS UP WITH

Jones operated in almost complete obscurity from 1949 until 1966, when an article in *Fortune* by Carol J. Loomis entitled "The Jones That Nobody Keeps Up With" profiled his partnership. The article detailed Jones's unique investment strategy and revealed that his fund had outperformed the best performing mutual fund by an impressive 44% and the best five-year mutual fund at the time by a staggering 85%, *net of all fees*.

> In effect, the hedge concept puts Jones in a position to make money on both rising and falling stocks, and also partially shelters him if he misjudges the general trend of the market. He assumes that a prudent investor wants to protect part of his capital from such misjudgments. Most investors would build their defenses around cash reserve or bonds, but Jones protects himself by selling short.

To those investors who regard short selling with suspicion, Jones would simply say that he is using "speculative techniques for conservative ends." As illustration, he is given to contrasting his methods with those of an investor who has, say, $100,000 and elects to invest $80,000 of it in stocks and the rest in "safe" bonds. Jones would use the $100,000 to borrow perhaps another $50,000.... Of the $150,000 total, he might put $110,000 into stocks he likes and sell short $40,000 worth of stocks he thinks are overvalued. Thus he ends up with $40,000 of his long position hedged—i.e., offset by a short position—and the remaining $70,000 fully exposed.... His problem, therefore, is to buy stocks that will rise more than the general market, and sell stocks short that will rise less than the average (or will actually fall). If he succeeds in this effort, his rewards are multiplied because he's employing, not just a portion of his capital, but 150 percent of it. The main advantage of the hedge concept, then, is that the investor's short position enables him to operate on the long side with maximum aggressiveness. (Loomis, *Fortune*, April 1966)

Incentive Fees

The *Fortune* article attracted much attention from investors and managers alike. Investors, because of the remarkable returns, and managers, because of another unique twist in Jones's approach. He had introduced an *incentive fee* as managing partner in 1952 (after transforming the general partnership into a limited partnership), of 20% of all profits from the fund. This was an extremely attractive package for other fund managers, who were more than happy to give up large salaries in favour of profit participation in the portfolios they managed, as it created an opportunity to earn 10 to 20 times as much compensation (compared to long-only management) while managing smaller amounts of money.

Combined, these factors produced a minor explosion in the hedge fund industry, and from 1966 to 1968, nearly 140 new hedge funds were launched in the United States.

THE DOWN YEARS

Unfortunately, many of these new hedge fund managers weren't really "hedging" at all and didn't follow Jones's model for minimizing risk. For the most part, this was because of the stellar performance of the markets in the mid to late 1960s. As we have seen, when markets are up, hedge funds balance their returns by placing a larger portion of capital on the long side. Many of the equity markets rose by as much as 50% or more through 1967 and 1968. Under these conditions, the army of new and largely inexperienced hedge fund managers began realizing that shorting even a portion of their portfolios was becoming time consuming and costly. Most of them virtually stopped shorting at all and fell deeper into the more attractive (but inherently dangerous) strategy of high-leverage, long-only positions.

This was to be their downfall. Between the beginning of 1969 and the end of 1974, there were two very powerful downturns in the market. Most people are more familiar with the 1973-74 bear markets (remember the lineups at the gas stations?), but the previous market crash in 1969-70 was the most damaging to the new hedge fund industry. The savage conditions of 1973-74 finished off most of the already crippled hedge funds, and after the dust settled, only a scant 68 hedge funds were left, with assets under management by the largest 28 funds declining by more than 70%.

THE COMEBACK

The period between 1974 and 1986 was one in which only the shrewdest of managers survived, among them some of the biggest and most well known today: George Soros (who began his Quantum Fund in 1969), Michael Steinhardt (Steinhardt Partners in 1967), and, not surprisingly, Alfred Winslow Jones himself. Most importantly, this period saw the development of a new breed of hedge funds—funds that employed strategies and used tools unavailable to Jones and his disciples. Among the most successful, Julian Robertson and his Tiger Fund Management, created in 1980, eventually became the poster child for the hedge fund revival in the late eighties and helped to establish a new and much larger milieu for the industry.

Tiger Fund Management applied the traditional "hedged equity" model to its $8 million in assets under management, and soon the financial world began to take notice, as Tiger posted a 24.3% gain in 1981, against a 5% drop by the Standard & Poor's 500 index—an average of the returns for the top 500 performing stocks. Over the next 18 years, Robertson averaged an annual return of 29%, better than anyone else at the time. With few hedge funds operating at the time, he soon began piling up assets as more and more investors scrambled to get on board. This is when he was forced to diverge from the traditional "Jones" model. Why was this?

Picking stocks and working both the long and short sides of the market, it becomes very difficult to find enough strategies and ideas to handle large amounts of capital without disrupting the markets. This is because any large volume movements in a stock (caused by a large buy or sell order, for example) will most likely have an effect on its price and can alter the whole strategy of a fund. Imagine you hold stock in a company, and all of a sudden a hedge fund sells a million shares. What would you think? You'd assume that the manager knew something that you didn't, and you'd sell your shares before they started losing value—and so would everyone else. So when the Tiger Fund suddenly found itself with over $3 billion in assets, the hedged equity approach (Jones's model) became too cumbersome to manage, and Robertson turned to a style called "global macro" that he is well known for today (and indeed this is the style that both the media and the public have come to think of as "hedge funds" even though they represent less than 7% of the hedge fund industry—we'll discuss this later).

Global macro managers try to generate returns by recognizing differences between the price and the underlying value of stocks across a wide range of markets. Robertson's first "global macro play" was early in 1985, when he bet that the U.S. dollar would decline against the Swiss franc, deutsche mark, pound sterling, and yen. Spending $7 million on instruments known as "foreign currency call options," he managed to increase profits over a few months in excess of 200% of the capital risked. Investors began to sit up and take notice.

In 1986, *Institutional Investor* published an article that eerily mirrored Loomis's in *Fortune* from 20 years earlier. "The Red Hot World of Julian Robertson" appeared in the May issue of that year and began another wave of interest from investors and managers alike. Bolstered by such swashbuckling hedge fund superstars as George Soros and his international bets (he made almost $2 *billion* betting that the English pound would fall), hedge funds were transformed from Jones's "speculative instruments for conservative purposes" to what the media touted as (and the public have come to know as) "freewheeling global playgrounds for the super rich."

This and other controversial events of the nineties aided in creating a worldwide skepticism of hedge funds. This mistrust was further amplified in 1998 by the Long-Term Capital Management scandal, when a multi-billion-dollar bailout was organized by the Federal Reserve to avoid what the press was touting as a possible "global economic meltdown."

Literally hundreds of hedge funds with highly specialized strategies bearing no resemblance to Jones's original model have been created since 1980. The term "hedge fund" itself has been expanded to include any incentive-based investment vehicle employing non-traditional methods. Like ivy left unpruned, the industry, under the name "hedge fund," has grown and insinuated itself into virtually every part of the market. And it is the long periods of unchecked growth, the "gaps" between the media and the public's attention, that have allowed the industry to experiment with and exploit the many inefficiencies left open by more traditional investment vehicles.

THE MYTHS AND FACTS ABOUT LONG-TERM CAPITAL MANAGEMENT

One of the most infamous hedge fund stories is the relatively recent tale of Long-Term Capital Management (LTCM). The Federal Reserve's organized multi-billion-dollar bailout in 1998 of this large global macro fund has given large financial institutions cause to rally behind renewed support of traditional investment vehicles and has caused investors to shy away from hedge funds and banks to become much more cautious in lending money to hedge funds. This is arguably a mistake.

Established in February 1994 and limited to investors who could afford a minimum of $10 million, Long-Term Capital Management generated billions of dollars in profits, logging astounding annual returns of nearly 30% in 1994 and more than 40% in 1995 and 1996. By the end of 1997, LTCM had nearly *tripled* its investors' money. Two of the firm's partners, Robert Merton and Myron Scholes, shared the Nobel prize for economics in 1997 for their work on the pricing of options and other sophisticated financial instruments (which formed the basis of LTCM's investment strategies).

LTCM's strategy was a fairly traditional "Jones" style, aiming to make money no matter the direction of the markets, by buying assets that seemed cheaper than they should be and simultaneously short selling assets that seemed too expensive. Using complex computer models, LTCM believed it had a nearly foolproof strategy that found and then exploited temporary price "distortions" between the price of U.S., Japanese, and European bonds whose relative price had reflected a historical pattern of consistency ("undervalued" and "overvalued" securities). The theory was that over time, the value of these bonds would tend to become identical (the "spread" between the bonds would return to its historical level). While the two values remained "distorted," however, a profit could be realized by capturing the difference. We'll explain in more detail how this works in Chapter 4.

The plan worked spectacularly well, until the Asian economic crisis hit and the Russian government defaulted on its domestic debt in August and September 1998. Suddenly, there was a worldwide "flight to safety" (where investors quickly try to safeguard their capital by investing in "safer" vehicles), and historical patterns were completely abandoned as panicked investors sold Japanese and European bonds to buy U.S. bonds (traditionally a "safer" investment). The temporary distortions between the bonds, instead of narrowing as in the past, actually ballooned. Rather than making a profit on a narrowing gap, LTCM incurred huge losses on both sides of their bets.

THE MAIN PROBLEM: LEVERAGING

Not only did Long-Term Capital bet the wrong way on both sides of their "hedge," but because the difference in the price between the bonds they were trading was minute, they had also leveraged themselves heavily (to amplify returns) and had borrowed that money from the largest banks and brokerage houses in the world. This endangered a world banking system that was already shaky from the huge losses in Russia and Asia. The fund had less than $2.5 billion in capital, which it used as collateral to purchase as much as $125 billion in securities. Using these securities as collateral, the firm was able to engage in complex financial transactions that affected as much as *$1.25 trillion* in securities worldwide. Because of the hedged positions, many of these transactions offset one another (Jones's "market exposure"), so Long-Term Capital's collapse would not have resulted in total losses anywhere near this size. However, the U.S. federal government was worried that if the fund were forced to "unwind" all its positions (sell off assets) over a very short time period, the entire global financial system might have been in trouble— you will remember our discussions about how difficult it is to move large blocks of shares without disrupting the markets.

Which is why, in September 1998, the president of the Federal Reserve Bank of New York called a meeting of the chief executives of some of the world's biggest commercial and investment banks. Using its position, the Fed successfully organized a massive private-sector rescue of Long-Term Capital Management by demanding that most of the banks contribute $300 million each to a $3.5-billion rescue fund.

A RARE CASE

Hedge funds, contrary to popular belief, do not speculate wildly, but rather see themselves as "arbitrageurs," meaning that they look for assets with prices they believe are temporarily higher or lower than their fundamental value. By taking one side of a trade that everyone else doesn't want, speculators improve *liquidity*, or the *amount* of stocks and bonds that are traded regularly. This keeps the markets "moving."

In truth, the LTCM failure is an isolated and rare case. The carefree late nineties' bull-market boom of hedge funds quickly changed to concern and pessimism as people started wrongly blaming hedge funds for the economic turmoil that, in fact, brought them down as well. The relative secrecy of their operations, the charismatic and entrepreneurial nature of their managers, and the speculations concerning their involvement in manipulating markets worldwide combined with a scant few examples of funds borrowing (leveraging) heavily to amplify their bets to create an overall skepticism that seriously tarnished their reputation.

The combination of a low-risk strategy with enormous leverage is indeed rare, and other market-neutral funds earned an average of 14% returns over the five years leading up to 1998, compared to the incredible 40% a year for LTCM during the same period. This alone indicates that LTCM was a unique case.

It is also important to note that leveraging heavily is not only limited to so-called alternative investments. Many large banks regularly leverage their trading arms by as much as 20 to 1, and on a much larger scale. Some reports say that where LTCM had an exposure of $80 billion in the U.S. Treasuries, the banks had *$3 trillion* tied up in similar bets.

This was the reason that the banks felt they had to rescue LTCM. Had the fund been allowed to collapse, and all of its positions been liquidated, it would have drastically and negatively affected the banks' similar bets.

In truth, almost a third of all hedge funds don't borrow at all, and more than half borrow no more than the amount investors put into them. The rest rarely leverage more than 10 to 1, and only on certain positions.

HEDGE FUNDS IN CANADA TODAY

The public perception of hedge funds as the new millennium began was dismal. In the events of the past few years leading up to today, however, we can see the rebirth of interest in hedge funds. Between 1995 (when there were fewer than 15 funds in Canada) and 2000, the hedge fund industry grew slightly in this country, but in the second half of 2000, it began a boom that continues today. There are currently around 180 active hedge funds in Canada, and every indication is that this is just the beginning. There has been a consistent growth in the industry since 2000, with around four to eight new hedge funds being launched each month. It seems obvious that the heavy losses suffered by investors in traditional long-only mutual funds and other vehicles during the bear market that began in 2000 have created an increasing interest in alternatives.

The hedge fund market in Canada is still relatively small, representing only about 1% of mutual fund investments (around CDN$4 to $5 billion). By contrast, the United States boasts around 5,000 hedge funds, accounting for about 7.5% of mutual fund assets. Even U.K. and Netherlands investors have around 3.5% of their capital in hedge funds.

The Canadian hedge fund market clearly has some growing to do. The following chapters lead you through a more in-depth look at the current state of the investment industry in Canada, describe the various styles of hedge funds today, and talk about how investors should apply hedge funds to their existing portfolios. With the state of the markets at the time of this book's publishing, this information is essential to the prudent investor's goal of finding vehicles to continue portfolio growth through these and any future volatile times.

CHAPTER TWO

The Difference Between Hedge Funds and Mutual Funds

A SHORT HISTORY OF MUTUAL FUNDS

Mutual funds have been on the financial landscape for longer than most investors realize. The industry is usually traced back to Great Britain, where the Foreign and Colonial Government Trust, formed in London in 1868, is widely considered to be the first example of a "mutual-fund style" investment. Some would argue, however, that this kind of investing had been introduced almost a century prior to this in Holland, when a Dutch merchant named Adriaan van Ketwich invited investors to form an investment trust under the name of Eendragt Maakt Magt (loosely translated to mean "Unity Creates Strength") in 1774. The purpose of the trust was to let small investors diversify without a large investment. This diversification, or "risk spreading," came from foreign bond investments in countries such as Austria, Denmark, Spain, Sweden, and Russia, as well as some European-owned plantations in Central and South America. With an initial capitalization of 1 million guilders (around US$500,000 today), the fund invested in 10 different groups of bonds and diversified its assets across these groups. The fund promised a 4% per year dividend, which was slightly *below* the average interest rate on the bonds in its portfolio. What this meant was that as long as the bonds did not default, investment income would be more than the promised dividend payments—creating a surplus. The interesting twist was a form of lottery embedded in the process to attract investors. The difference between the promised 4% return and the actual interest rate of the bonds was placed in a cash reserve. This reserve was then used to "retire" a specified number of fund shares each year at 10% more than their face value. The dividends for the retiring shares would then be split between neighbouring shares; when share number 67 was retired, for example, its 4% dividend would be split between shares numbered 66 and 68, which would then earn 6% (obviously, by today's standards, this was a highly suspect practice).

Other investment vehicles followed Eendragt Maakt Magt, with similar success and equally interesting names such as Voordeelig en Voorsigtig (Profitable and Prudent) in 1776, and a second by van Ketwich himself called Concordia Res Parvae Crescunt (Small Matters Grow by Consent) in 1779. The success of these ventures was, it is assumed, based on modest capital gains and not on creative nomenclature.

The Foreign and Colonial Government Trust in England some 90 years later had a similar mandate. It promised the "investor of modest means the same advantages as the large capitalist ... by spreading the investment over a number of different stocks." Like its Dutch counterpart, it offered *diversification*, one of the few ways to minimize risk in a long-only investment (losing smaller amounts by spreading out the capital among a variety of vehicles). Most of the early British investment companies (including the early Dutch investment trusts) and their American counterparts resembled today's "closed-end" funds and sold a *fixed number of shares* (raising a certain amount of money to invest), with the price of those shares being determined by supply and demand (as a source for this section, see Investment Company Institute [ICI}, *Mutual Funds Fact Book* 1997).

The first "modern" mutual fund is widely considered to be the Massachusetts Investors Trust, which was introduced in Boston in March 1924 with a modest portfolio of 45 stocks and $50,000 in assets. It was the first so-called "open-end" mutual fund and introduced a concept that revolutionized the fund industry: a continuous offering of new shares, thus continuously raising money to invest. These shares were redeemable at any time, based on the current value of the fund's assets (the fund is still in existence today, and information about it can be found on the Internet at www.mfs.com).

The growth of the early mutual fund industry was hampered by the 1929 stock market crash and the Great Depression. With long-only portfolios, even the sharpest investors couldn't beat the staggering losses during this period. The result was that mutual funds began gaining popularity only in the forties and fifties, when the markets started to boom. In 1940 there were fewer than 80 funds in the United States, with total assets of $500 million. Twenty years later, there were 160 funds and $17 billion in assets. The industry truly exploded when huge amounts of money began flowing into mutual fund coffers in the mid-1980s, and by the end of 1999 more than 8,000 mutual funds were managing close to $7 trillion in assets.

The first mutual fund in Canada, the Canadian Investment Fund, was founded in 1932. Mutual fund growth in this country mirrored U.S. trends over the 50 years following this, but the actual explosion in the Canadian mutual fund industry happened slightly later, in the 1990s, with assets increasing from $25 billion in December 1990 to $417 billion by June 2002. Today, approximately 4,200 investment funds are available in Canada, offered by a variety of fund and insurance companies. Interestingly, the Canadian government's Department of Finance Web site (www.fin.gc.ca/fin-eng.html) states that there are approximately 50 million unit holder accounts in Canada. Since there are only around 30 million people living in this country and some of them are too small to even say "mutual fund" (never mind holding units in one), it is obvious that most investors have units in multiple funds. This is a good demonstration of the huge popularity of these investment vehicles in Canada today.

What has happened recently? Anyone can look at the business section of a newspaper and tell you that mutual funds have been seriously declining in value over the two years leading up to the end of 2002. There are two main reasons: one, mutual funds, because of their long-only positions, are correlated to the markets (and thus provide returns that are relative to them), and two, the rules they must abide by *prohibit them from doing anything else*.

RULES FOR MUTUAL FUNDS

The United States Investment Company Act of 1940 regulates the do's and don'ts of mutual funds. The Canadian counterpart to this is the National Instrument 81-102, which regulates the funds under the Department of Finance's definition:

Mutual Fund

A company that uses its capital to invest in other companies. Its capital is a pool of funds gathered from a number of investors and placed in securities selected to meet specific criteria and goals. Mutual fund companies fall under the jurisdiction of the provincial securities commissions.

Two fundamental guiding principles govern the investment techniques of mutual funds: *safety* and *liquidity*. Safety refers to the fact that fund managers are not allowed to invest in instruments that have very high risk, and liquidity means that they must invest in instruments that are easily sellable (so they can provide cash in case the investor redeems his or her shares). Both these tenets are a result of the fiduciary responsibility, preservation of capital, and prudence principles (discussed in the previous chapter) put in place to protect the investor from the risks of speculation and to satisfy government regulators who are concerned with the integrity and stability of the markets. Let's look more closely at these two principles.

Liquidity

Liquidity is essentially a measurement of how easy it is to liquidate (convert to cash or equivalent) an investment. We can use a fairly common example to demonstrate the inherent risks in illiquid (or not easily convertible into cash) investments:

Jim, a young professional, inherited $250,000 from a distant aunt, who died in Germany. He paid off some bills, bought some clothes, and took an extravagant European vacation, so by the time all was said and done he had about $200,000 left. He decided to invest his newly found wealth.

It was the spring of 2000, and Jim believed the stock market was showing signs of serious decline, so he figured that real estate would be a more solid investment (even though he also believed that some of the fibre optic companies looked like they might get better in the next few months). He purchased a small condominium downtown and rented it out to a couple who were more than happy to sign a two-year lease. After paying expenses, Jim was making a 5% return on his investment and betting that the condo would appreciate 6 to 7% every year until he sold it.

As fate had it, though, Jim met Cathy shortly after his transactions. It was love at first sight. Three weeks later he proposed to her, and in the summer of 2000 they were married. Two months after the wedding they were house hunting, as Cathy was pregnant and they could not imagine raising a child in Jim's small midtown condo (which they were living in at the time).

Jim put both condos on the market—the one they were living in, and the one he had purchased for investment purposes. By selling both of them, he figured they would have a large enough down payment for a nice house in a good neighbourhood. In a short six days, he had an offer for the unit they were living in, for *more* money than it was listed for. Jim was happy to sign. However, the other condo was a different story. There were many interested parties, but once potential buyers found out that there was a lease on the condo for another year and a half, they shied away. They wanted to move in, not sit on the property for investment purposes.

Three months later the unit still had not sold, and Jim had reduced its price to well below what he paid for it. In the meantime the deal on their other condo had closed, and Jim and Cathy had to move into a rental, since they didn't have enough money for the down payment in the area where they wanted to purchase. Time was *definitely* not on their side. Finally, at the end of January 2001, they received an offer for the rental unit. Once the deal was done, and commissions and legal fees were paid, Jim calculated that he had lost $37,000 on the deal. Though in the end Jim and Cathy managed to get enough money together for the down payment on their dream house, it was an agonizing experience living in limbo for months on end.

Jim's alternative, as he saw it, would have been to invest in a number of fibre optic stocks. Not only would he have made money during the summer of 2000 (due to the boom in technology stocks), he would have had no problem getting back into cash, or liquidating the shares—a call to his broker would have done it, and a small commission (small compared to what real estate agents get) would have been all it cost.

Stocks, for the most part, are very liquid instruments. Buyers and sellers can always be found on the major stock exchanges, so it is relatively easy to get a match for your needs (as long as your block of shares isn't too big!). This is why mutual funds are obliged to invest in instruments that are highly liquid—if you have to get your money back, they can just sell some of their holdings quickly and redeem your units.

Safety

The safety of an investment is the second major consideration. In the previous chapter we described what short selling is. Short selling involves borrowing a stock and selling it in anticipation of being able to repurchase it at a lower price, at or before the time it must be returned to the lender. But what happens if the price starts going up after you have made the commitment and borrowed it? By definition, you lose money. If you buy a stock, the most you can lose is the price you paid for it (i.e., the stock's value cannot go below zero), but on the short side the losses can be unlimited, since (theoretically) prices can continue to rise indefinitely. There is no limit to how much money you can lose. This is where safety comes in. The rules of mutual funds prohibit investing in a short position, thereby protecting the unit holders from the theoretically unlimited losses.

A number of other prohibitions exist, such as strict guidelines on the percentage of the fund's holdings that can be in one stock (or type of stock) and the percentage of stocks of a particular company a fund can hold. Both these rules are in place to minimize potential losses to the fund by forcing it to diversify its holdings and spread out risk.

Mutual funds can therefore *hold only a diversified long portfolio*. These regulations serve as safeguards to protect the public's interest, but as we will see, they can become a hindrance under certain circumstances.

RELATIVE PERFORMANCE AND WHY MUTUAL FUNDS ARE MEASURED BY IT

Mutual fund performance is generally correlated to market performance, due to the buy and hold (long) strategy. Therefore, mutual funds are measured in light of that performance. This measurement is obtained by comparing their performance to the overall performance of various averages and indices, or amalgamations of top-performing securities ("blue chip" stocks) in the market.

In North America, there are four major stock markets: the New York Stock Exchange (NYSE), the American Stock Exchange (AMEX), the National Association of Securities Dealers Automated Quotient (NASDAQ), and the Toronto Stock Exchange (TSX). All these exchanges have an index that is one way or another tied to the performance of the stocks listed on the exchange.

The NYSE has the famous Dow Jones Industrial Average index, which reflects the price of 30 major stocks in important industry sectors, 28 of which are listed on the exchange itself and two, Intel and Microsoft, which are actually NASDAQ stocks. The NASDAQ has the NASDAQ 100 index, which tracks the prices of its 100 top securities. The AMEX Composite Index is a similar index. In Canada, what was the TSE 300 Composite Index (or an average of the top 300 stocks on the old TSE) was recently converted to the S&P/TSX Composite Index, reducing the number of stocks averaged to 60 (this was largely because of the dot-com crash in 2001).

These indices, while useful for specific industries in specific places, are limited in scope when compared to the broader markets (since they measure only a few stocks). To measure the performance of broad markets, there are the so-called broad market indices. The most famous of these is the S&P 500. The Standard & Poor's corporation of Chicago publishes this index, which covers the 500 largest corporations in America, regardless of their home exchange.

Because of the large number of stocks it covers, the S&P 500 is the most representative of the general markets of the United States, and as such, it serves as the "benchmark" for many mutual funds. This means that the performance of a fund is measured against the S&P 500 Index.

So, if in a given year a fund that uses the S&P 500 as its benchmark gains a 15% return while the index gains only 13%, we would say that the fund *outperformed the index* by 2 percentage points. In declining markets, if the index drops by 19% and the fund drops by only 14%, we would say that the fund *outperformed the index* by 5 percentage points.

This is what is called *relative* performance (relative to the index that is used as the benchmark for the fund). However, not all funds use the S&P 500 as their benchmark. Funds that invest in Canadian stocks, for instance, would use S&P/TSX or the Toronto Stock Exchange's tracking index.

Why are mutual funds measured relative to the broad market indices? The practice is a combination of history and economic theory.

Modern Portfolio Theory

Mutual funds started to gain popularity in the 1950s when stock market performance was robust. After World War II, thousands of soldiers returned home to start families, enter the civilian workforce, and spend their money. The "baby boom" hit quickly, and the economy was fuelled by a need for everything from new and larger housing to new technologies.

This period also coincided with the evolution of new financial thinking in academia and the development in the 1950s of the modern portfolio theory by Harry Markowitz and William F. Sharpe, professors of economics at the University of Chicago. The theory was based on the observation that asset classes (securities in specific industries) all had different degrees and types of risk associated with them. Markowitz and Sharpe suggested that by analyzing these varying degrees and types of risk and quantifying them, one could put together a diversified portfolio that gave a return directly related to the amount of risk. This construction of the portfolio was done by carefully combining asset classes, so that they were not correlated to one another and they responded with different patterns to different market conditions. The relationship between the oil and gas industry and the oil and gas *service* industry would be correlated, for instance. When the oil industry is hurt because of a particular event, the service industry is hurt at the same time and to a greater or lesser degree (this also applies to a number of other industries such as tourism and airlines). Thus a portfolio containing stocks in both these classes would be more exposed to risk (of declining in value) in the event of a disaster in the industry.

Before this theory was put forward, investors had relied on one of two strategies in making stock choices: *technical analysis* or *fundamental analysis*. Technical analysts carefully examine historic market data, looking for patterns in the movements of particular stocks and investing in the hopes that the patterns will repeat themselves. Fundamental analysts analyze particular businesses and their prospects for growth based on factors within the industry, investing in companies they feel either were on the verge of growing faster than the economy or appeared undervalued.

In the 1960s, researchers began to use computers for the first time to analyze historical data and pick apart the daily price movements of every stock listed since 1926. What they discovered changed investing yet again. They found, through their analysis, that stock prices, rather than having recurring patterns, were affected by *events*. Events are, by nature, random, so technical analysis—looking for repeating patterns—was worthless and even impossible. The researchers also concluded that the markets were highly efficient, meaning that any information affecting a stock's price (world events, accounting scandals, takeovers, etc.) was reflected immediately. This threw out fundamental analysis as well, for it was evident that investors were all using the same information from the same sources and would all arrive at the same conclusions.

The overall conclusion was that picking winning stocks was impossible, and investors should focus more on being in the right *asset class* (such as energy or high tech) and not just the right stock. The key was to formulate an asset allocation policy (based on risks and returns) and construct a portfolio based on the policy's objectives. Asset allocation attempts to diversify holdings (the portfolio) so that no one industry downturn or collapse will hurt the portfolio too much. The idea is to find asset classes that are uncorrelated to one another. Almost all large institutions began using asset allocation as their main strategy, so much so that money managers in these institutions began specializing in particular asset classes and focusing their efforts in tightly defined styles.

All of this was combined with a raging bull market through the fifties and sixties, when companies in virtually every sector were booming. In this climate, the buy and hold strategy was extremely profitable, and mutual fund sales were driven by *performance*. Stock market analysts at the time were claiming that the general stock market gave higher returns over time than anything else, implying that investing and waiting would eventually pay off, and a couple of losing years were simply the price to be paid to achieve superior returns in the long run.

In this environment, the yardstick used by investors and advisers alike is the comparison of *relative* performance among available funds. To do this comparison, they adopted benchmarks such as the Dow Jones and the S&P 500.

HOW HEDGE FUNDS
DIFFER FROM MUTUAL FUNDS

- *Hedge funds seek "absolute" returns.*

  Unlike mutual funds, hedge funds seek to benefit from both increasing and decreasing stock prices, while mutual funds make money only if the underlying investments they hold increase in value. Hedge funds have investments in long positions (investments that go up in value if the underlying asset goes up) and short positions (investments that go up in value if the underlying asset goes down). By combining "longs" and "shorts" in a portfolio, hedge funds are able to reduce risk because in a falling market, short positions will offset or even reverse losses accumulated on long positions.

  Hedge funds do not fully subscribe to the old idea that stocks are superior performers over the long term. Rather, they aim to reduce the risk usually associated with investing in stocks (whether they will gain or lose value depending on events). Because their structure has the potential of making money in any market condition, hedge funds seek to make positive returns every year rather than merely outperforming the market index. Hedge funds simply have more tools at hand to make money than mutual funds, and because of this, their goal is to achieve absolute (positive) returns, uncorrelated to the market.

- *Mutual funds are highly regulated.*

  Mutual funds are restricted from using short selling and other hedging techniques. As we have seen, these rules were put in place many years ago to protect investors from the risks associated with what were deemed to be "speculative" investments. These regulations can, however, serve as a kind of straitjacket, making it more difficult to outperform the market and to protect the assets of the fund in sliding (down) market conditions. Any kind of restriction means potentially less return. This is especially true in a falling market when, as more stocks lose ground, mutual fund portfolios are likely to decrease in value as well—how can you make money when your benchmark is negative? In this type of market only managers of superior insight can make money, and that has so far proved to be a very tall order.

- *Hedge funds are less regulated than mutual funds.*

  Hedge funds are much less regulated than mutual funds. Less regulation means more options, which in turn leads to potentially better performance. Hedge funds also generally have higher than usual minimum investment thresholds. Because their investors are usually more knowledgeable about their investments, hedge funds are granted the option to pursue strategies and techniques not available to mutual fund managers.

- *Remuneration (payment) of mutual fund managers is based on a percentage of the assets under their management (AUM).*

  Mutual fund managers are paid according to an annual management fee based on the value of assets under their management (AUM). The fee is usually 2 to 3% of AUM per year, and is *not dependent on the fund's performance*. This fee structure means that mutual fund managers are *not penalized for negative or worse than average performance*. While logic might dictate that poor performance would slow the growth of a mutual fund's AUM (by failing to attract new investors), this fee structure provides little or no incentive for managers to perform, but rather encourages them to stick to their benchmarks and be "middle of the road."

• *Hedge fund managers typically receive a performance-related fee.*

From Chapter 1, you will remember that hedge fund managers receive an incentive fee on top of the annual management fees (which are similar to mutual funds' management fees). This is because hedge fund management is more demanding and requires greater knowledge, skill, and talent. And it is because of this differing fee structure that hedge funds are able to attract the best talent in the market. Hedge fund managers also most often have a significant amount of their personal wealth invested in the funds they manage.

This "incentive" or "performance fee" is usually 20% of the fund's performance in a calendar year. Simply put, posting a high positive return is financially much more rewarding for a hedge fund manager than for the manager of a mutual fund. The following example shows the effect of the incentive fee:

TABLE 2.1

	Hedge Fund A	Mutual Fund A
Size (start of year)	$150 Million	$150 Million
Management Fee	2.0%	2.5%
Performance	20%	10%
Performance Fee	20%	N/A
Total Fees	$9.0 Million	$4.5 Million

The performance fee model of remuneration (or payment) used by hedge funds transfers the pain of incurring a loss to the manager by depriving him or her of potential compensation (which is in many cases equal to or greater than the management fee).

- *Mutual funds cannot effectively protect portfolios in declining markets other than by going into cash.*

In a falling market the value of mutual funds will probably decline since most of the stock in their portfolios will parallel the general market direction (that is, a relative return). Even if a mutual fund manager anticipates further drops in the market, regulations restrict mutual fund investments to long positions only (which will reflect the market trend). The only safe bet in this situation would be to liquidate losing investments into real money, or cash. Managers rarely take the action of going to cash, however, for three reasons:

1. Each mutual fund has a mandate to be in a specific sector of the market, or *asset class*. It is not the job of a mutual fund manager to deviate from this mandate by moving into cash, as each manager's asset class is often an integral part of an overall diversified portfolio. Thus the mandate to stay in their asset class is far more important than the safety of the investor's capital within that class.

2. Mutual funds are rated by their relative performance, therefore a negative performance by itself is not considered detrimental, as long as losses are comparable to other funds and their benchmarks.

3. The broad market increases about 60 to 70% of the time (increases rather than declines), and a cash position has only a 30 to 40% chance of outperforming funds relative to this. If a manager is wrong, and underperforms compared to other fund managers, the penalties of possible job loss and/or a reduction of assets under management outweigh any prospective gain.

- *Hedge funds use various "hedging" strategies to make money on the downside.*

Because of their regulations and aims, hedge funds actively use techniques that have the potential to realize increased value in a falling market. By combining long and short positions in a portfolio, most hedge funds reduce their dependence on market direction in order to perform. It should be noted, however, that some funds that are termed hedge funds do not actually "hedge" against risk. For example, a global macro fund (see hedge fund strategies in Chapter 4) may speculate on changes in economic policies that have an impact on interest rates, while using high levels of leverage. Returns for these funds can be impressive, but so can their losses. In reality, they account for less than 5% of all hedge funds.

- *Performance of mutual funds is dependent on the direction of the equity markets.*

As noted earlier, mutual fund managers will likely perform positively only if their benchmark market does the same. This is because they are limited to long positions and their investment levels are usually close to 100%.

Many hedge fund strategies are not dependent on market direction. Accordingly, they have a very low correlation to traditional equity markets as well as to each other.

Because hedge funds may hold long and short positions at any point in time and because their relative share (compared to each other) can also be frequently changed, hedge funds are much less reliant on market direction than mutual funds. Due to this ability, hedge funds depend much more on the stock-picking abilities of their managers than on positive performance, a benchmark, or the market.

- *The mutual fund industry is homogeneous.*

There is a high correlation among mutual funds, so diversification among equity mutual funds will only slightly change the overall risk of the portfolio. Because of their more limited choices, and because most of them are 90 to 95% invested in widely diversified, long-only positions in their respective markets, similar mutual funds exhibit very similar performance results. They are therefore *homogeneous*. As a result, diversification in similar types of mutual funds adds little to a portfolio's risk reduction. The problem is that many Canadians seek to diversify by spreading investments over several mutual funds, yet because of their homogeneity, most mutual funds are invested in the same companies. It is an "apples to apples" comparison and simply does not result in an effectively diversified portfolio.

- *The hedge fund industry is heterogeneous.*

There is a low correlation among hedge funds. Diversification among hedge funds therefore results in substantial reduction of risk. They are therefore *heterogeneous*.

Hedge funds are a very diverse group of investment vehicles. Even similar types of hedge funds exhibit widely different results with regard to both risk and performance. As a result, hedge funds have low correlation with each other and to mutual funds. This is because

1. Hedge funds have significantly more choices in products and strategies than mutual funds.

2. Hedge funds are allowed to have a more focused portfolio because, unlike mutual funds, they are not restricted by a limit of 10% exposure to any one financial investment vehicle.

Because of their heterogeneity, hedge funds can provide excellent diversification benefits by investing in different hedge funds (or in a "fund of funds" hedge fund—see Chapter 4) within an individual portfolio.

We have seen that mutual funds, by their nature and history, are highly regulated instruments. The industry is founded on a buy and hold strategy, which correlates performance directly to the increases and declines of the broad markets. With trillions of dollars under management, mutual fund companies basically use themselves as benchmarks for returns, a policy that has created a culture that can see a loss as positive, as long as that loss is relatively less than the markets or that of other mutual funds.

Conversely, hedge funds are largely uncorrelated to the markets and are free to employ strategies and techniques for investment unavailable to mutual funds. This allows hedge funds to actively seek positive, absolute returns every year, by remaining uncorrelated to both the broad markets and other hedge funds.

HEDGE FUNDS	MUTUAL FUNDS
Private investment vehicles	Regulated investment vehicles
Limited use of leverage	Use of leverage is not permitted
Manager may short sell	Prohibited from short selling
Manager is compensated on performance	Manager is paid a salary and bonus
Manager invests own capital in fund	Manager does not invest own capital in fund
Liquidity varies from daily to yearly	Daily liquidity and redemption
Offered by offering memorandum	Offered by prospectus
Flexibility in investment strategies	Relatively inflexible
Seek to make positive returns (absolute returns)	Seek to outperform known market benchmark

In today's volatile markets, being able to manipulate investments to decrease risk and take advantage of any opportunity for positive returns is paramount. In Canada today, there is an obvious and growing need for these kinds of alternatives.

CHAPTER THREE

Why Canadians Need Hedge Funds

MUTUAL FUND PERFORMANCE

In the first two years of the new century, the performance of mutual funds was disappointing, to say the least, with return levels of the average equity mutual fund in Canada declining from 11% in 2000 to 4.1% in 2001. Statistics for 2002 are even worse, with the average Canadian equity fund losing a painful 12%. This alone has made many Canadian investors not only concerned but inclined to actively seek at least stable, and at best profitable, investments. As a case in point, almost $6 billion was taken out of mutual funds in Canada from June 2002 to January 2003.

The reason for this was that the overall market declined during the same period. As discussed in the previous chapters, mutual funds provide relative performance, and thus their volatility is parallel to the performance of the general markets. When the markets are down, mutual funds are down, too.

Table 3.1 shows the performance of the S&P 500 Index (generally representing U.S. stock markets), the TSE 300 Index (Canadian equity markets—now the TSX), and the Canadian and U.S. bond indexes.

TABLE 3.1

	2000	2001	2002
S&P 500	-6.10	-6.30	-23.10
TSE 300 - S&P/TSX	+7.40	-12.60	-12.40
U.S. 90-Day T-Bills Bonds	+5.80	+3.60	+1.60
Scotia McLeod Short Term Bond Index	+8.29	+9.40	+6.30

All values expressed in Canadian dollars.

We can see from this information that in order for the relative performance-oriented mutual funds to get back to the stellar numbers of the nineties, there must be a bull market that matches the general market numbers of the same time frame. History shows us that there is simply no way to predict these swings or how long a particular trend will last.

THE ROLLER COASTER EFFECT

The outstanding performance of the markets for the last years of the 20th century was the result of a booming technology sector. Prices skyrocketed daily as both institutional and private investors bought up stocks at a feverish pace. The NASDAQ, where most tech stocks trade, ballooned well into the 5,000s (5,132, in fact, was the all-time high during trading on March 10, 2000. At market close on that day the NASDAQ stood at 5,048).

What happened to all that stock after the collapse in 2000? As the NASDAQ plunged more than 2,000 points over a four-week period through late March and April, why did people hold on to their investments? The answer is *hope*. Investors hold on to their overpriced stocks, hoping desperately that the prices will climb again and they can get out without huge losses.

Look at Figure 3.1 and imagine that you invested in Nortel in October 1999. On the first of that month, you would have purchased the stock at US$28.38 (adjusted price). This was $20.62 or almost *four times more* than it was at the same time in 1998. Still, everyone was saying that it would continue to climb, with no end in sight.

FIGURE 3.1: Nortel Stock Prices, October 1999 to July 2002

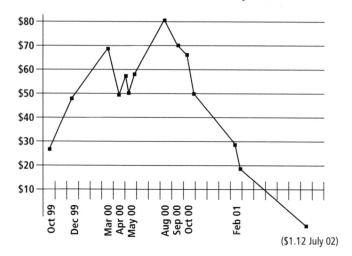

($1.12 July 02)

Sure enough, by the end of December 1999, your shares have grown to an astounding $50.35, a 56% return in only *three months*. Eureka! You've hit the jackpot. You're telling everyone about your incredible market skills, liquidating other investments to put more money into Nortel, and urging all your friends and family to buy it as well and enjoy the ride with you.

Three months later, the stock is at an incredible $70.42, almost a *110% return in six months*. You're planning early retirement as you sit and scan the Saturday morning business section. Like a gambler on a lucky streak, you just "let it ride."

But wait. The stock drops radically for a few weeks, and it stands at $51.10 on April 17. What's happening? Not to worry; it will come back. Sure enough, it's back to $58.23 on May 1. Whew. But then it tanks again to $51.60 the next week. Should you sell? No. No one else is selling. They must know something. Your hunch is correct; it's back to $59.88 on May 30. Not only that, it shoots up over the next three months to $82.51! The train is on the tracks again, and you're sitting on a stock that is worth almost *three times more* than you paid for it. Now it's not just early retirement, but you're eyeing the aging Buick in your garage and thinking about a BMW, or maybe *two*.

September comes with a bit of a jolt, though. The stock goes down to $72.47 on the fourth. No problem; you've seen this before. Heck, it went all the way down to $51 and change back in April. By October 16, it has dropped to $68.11. Still nothing to worry about; it's been worse. No problem.

The next week, however, it plunges over $25 to $42.44. Should you wait it out? Yes. It can come back from that, can't it? Only a year ago, it was worth a mere $28.38. This is a glitch.

The next three months are nail-biters. The stock goes up a little one week, only to lose again the next, on a small but steady decline. Nervous, but still confident in an upswing, you wait it out until the first part of February, when it suddenly dives $5 in a week and stands at $30.50. Now you're *really* scared. You bought the stock for $28.38, so you're dangerously close to being right back where you were. So much for the BMW, you think. There's still a spread worth keeping though, and the stock hasn't been *really* volatile. A few bucks here and there; you can afford to wait until it's a little closer to your original purchase price.

Too late! The next week the stock nose-dives to $20. Now you're in a *losing* position. How can this have happened? What was I thinking? One thing is for sure, though; you're not going to sell it and lose money. No sir. Not until you're *sure* it won't come back.

The rest, as they say, is history. A long and steady decline in Nortel's stock price brought it to an unbelievable low of $0.44 on October 10, 2002. After being up almost 300%, your stock is now worth a mere 1/30th of its original purchase price. In hindsight, of course, you should have sold. The culprit here was a combination of hope and greed. Once a winning investment becomes a losing one, it is incredibly hard to sell. Most people will simply stand sadly by and watch the ship sink.

So when does it end? It doesn't. When markets do finally begin coming back up, it creates the same momentum. People think, "Aha! The stock is coming back, and I can buy it really cheap right now!" and on the other side, investors who've been burned by the stock's collapse are looking to "dump it" and recoup their losses. This creates selling pressure, and once again, the buying frenzy will over-inflate the stock's value, and the subsequent selling will eventually begin to drive the market down, and so on, and so on.

This roller coaster effect is expected to be the trend of the first part of this decade, and with these kinds of market conditions, it will be almost impossible for mutual funds to provide a consistent positive return. So the average investor, without spending considerable time on research and trading, will have an extremely difficult time making a reasonable return on his or her investments.

What can be done to protect investments from this roller coaster ride? Again, the answer is simple: invest in instruments that are *not correlated to market performance*. These are often referred to as *alternative investments*.

ALTERNATIVE INVESTMENT VEHICLES

Broadly defined, an alternative investment strategy is anything outside the traditional investments of stocks, bonds, and cash equivalents. This means it is defined by the fact that it is not correlated with the stock and bond markets. The simplest of these vehicles is leaving your money in a bank account or GIC. You receive an *absolute return* (the amount of interest guaranteed by the institution you entrust your money to), and the security that comes with it. At the writing of this book, however, a 12-month GIC will provide you with only a 1.6% interest income. This is hardly a handsome return and, in many cases, won't even keep up with the rate of inflation. Some other vehicles offer better returns, but come with added risk and many complications.

Real Estate

You will recall the story of Jim and Cathy from the previous chapter. When you take into account the time, money, and transaction costs (typically between 6 and 10% of the property's sale price as opposed to 1% on mutual funds or 2 to 4% on other investment vehicles), real estate can be a much more risky investment today than in the past. The average price of a resale home in Canada in 1989 was $143,846. In 2001, that same home would have sold for $171,910. Once the inflation rate is factored in, this amounts to a *17% loss*. Even adding in possible rental income, there is still renovation, maintenance, tenant turnover, and numerous other management issues. Despite the draw-backs to real estate, however, there are some benefits to including it as part of a diversified portfolio. Real estate's low correlation and typi-cally modest returns can provide a valuable cushion when markets are down. Some advisers recommend allocating up to 10% of a portfolio to real estate. In most cases, it can serve as a potential hedge against inflation and deflation due to the relative predictability of long-term returns (if Jim had been able to wait a few years, he most likely would have seen his property increase in value).

Much like the stock market, it is the intelligent and informed pick-ing of real estate ventures that offers the greatest possibility for posi-tive returns. Recognizing an undervalued piece of property can be highly profitable, if you're willing to wait. However, if you guess wrong, it can be disastrous. Industry closures, water contamination, highway construction—property can depreciate in many ways, most of them unpredictable. Some real estate ventures are private sales—that is, individuals buying and selling properties. People who prefer to leave the property picking to more informed professionals can turn to real estate investment trusts, or REITs. These are a form of income trusts, another alternative investment vehicle.

Income Trusts

Income trusts have been rapidly growing in popularity over the past few years. In fact, they hold more than $40 billion of Canadians' money at the writing of this book (2002), more than twice the amount they held just two years previously in 2000.

Income trusts have been growing in popularity because for many Canadians they are a lower-risk alternative to stocks, while offering a significantly better return than bonds, with returns averaging any-where from 8 to 14%. With the volatile and unpredictable markets, this has meant a boom for this relatively small class of investments—there are more than 200 income trusts in Canada in 2002, almost dou-ble the amount in 1998. Although income trusts have generally operated in the energy and real estate sectors, the offerings have expanded to include everything from cold storage facilities to pizza parlours. But while income trusts are a good investment option to help diversify a portfolio, keep in mind that they are not all created equal: they are best suited for businesses that don't need a lot of capital, since they pay out most of their profits to investors.

One of the most popular types of income trusts is the Real Estate Investment Trust (REIT). A REIT is a security that uses investor capital to purchase or manage real estate, either by buying properties or securing mortgages. REITs operate just like stocks and are traded on major exchanges. They work by selling units to investors, who then receive regular and stable cash returns from the company's real estate holdings.

Some of the advantages of REITs include affordability and liquidity. Instead of putting down a large sum of money to purchase property, an investor can buy units of a REIT and convert them to cash whenever necessary. In this sense REITs resemble "closed end" (having a fixed investment amount) mutual funds. REITs also offer a tax shelter, since they are taxed less heavily than interest income. Since the property holdings in a REIT are typically spread out in a number of areas, they are more diverse and therefore less risky than sinking all your money in one property. They also offer the bonus of being professionally managed, so you don't have to stay awake at night wondering when the best time is to sell. The volatility of the real estate market, however good the manager is at picking properties, makes any large investment in REITs a risky one, though.

Gold and Precious Metals

The allure of gold has, for as long as recorded history, been a representation of wealth at every level. As an investment, however, the numbers don't shine. The volatility of this once-stable investment has been an insane roller coaster over the last 20-odd years, with prices reaching staggering numbers in the early eighties (US$850 on January 21, 1980), and tanking to new lows in 1982 and 1985 (as low as US$296 by late June 1982). A volatile up-and-down history led to the four years from 1998 to 2001 when it couldn't even manage to break through the "floor" US$300 barrier. It was only in 2002 that it managed to do this.

FIGURE 3.2: Gold Prices 1968-2002 (Average)

Traditionally, gold has been seen as a safe investment—a "hedge" against market swings. When stocks and currencies start to slide, investors will get out and purchase gold as a "stable" commodity to sit on until the markets come back. The problem is that people still think that gold has some kind of direct relationship to *money*. It doesn't. True, the history of this unique metal is practically defined by its use as an exchangeable currency, but in fact, it has had no global connection to the value of currency since 1973, when the world's currencies were "floated"—that is, countries no longer valued their money by some set amount of actual, physical gold bullion (or promissory notes) hidden in a vault somewhere.

There are two primary sources of gold supply—mining and central bank vaults. Because of current market prices, most mines are wholly unprofitable; the supply is simply not enough to fill demand (Canada has one of the lowest per-ounce production costs at around US$225). The remaining gold is provided by the central banks, partly through sales and partly through leasing (estimates to as much as 20,000 tons of gold have been "borrowed" and sold into the market). It is estimated that in 2002, around 30,000 tons of gold are still held by central banks worldwide, despite a steady sell-off of these reserves. With estimates of annual world gold consumption at 4,000 tons, there is simply too much gold out there to push its price significantly higher.

The average price of gold in 1975 was US$161.02 per ounce. At the time of this book's writing, gold was trading at US$324.00 per ounce. This is less than a 50% gain in 27 years, and again, with inflation, you have actually realized a *42% loss*, hardly a good investment. Looking to the future, the viability of gold as an investment is bleak as well. During the recent and on-going bear market through 2002, the U.S. government (which once steadfastly held on to its reserves) began dumping large quantities of gold to shore up investment in stocks and bonds—an action that does not bode well for gold prices in the future.

Other precious metals have similar problems. Silver and platinum have mirrored the up-and-down swings of gold over the past few decades, and their current prices don't even come close to matching inflation. Platinum reached a whopping US$659 in 1987, and silver topped US$11.25 in the same year. In 2002, their prices had dropped to $588 and $4.30 respectively.

Fine Art

Another alternative investment strategy is investing in art. Collecting can be a highly enjoyable form of investment, but it comes with many potential pitfalls, not least of which is getting too attached to your investments and not wanting to sell them.

The main problems with investing in art come with the highly unpredictable whims of what society will see as *precious*. Vincent Van Gogh sold only *one painting* in his entire career. Rooting around in garage sales looking for the next Andy Warhol or Pablo Picasso can be fun, but it is hardly a secure form of investing.

Art prices also have demonstrated a historic correlation to stock prices—as commodities, their price fluctuates with the amount of available disposable income.

LIQUIDITY

The main problem with many of these alternative vehicles is liquidity. Liquidity is the ability of an investor to get out of—or liquidate—a given investment, and turn it back into cash. This is one of the most important features an investment should have, as even the most long-term plans can be derailed by any number of circumstances requiring actual *money*. Any immediate need for cash will require that you sell an investment. The amount of time and effort you have to put into that exercise represents the level of liquidity for that investment. As an example, stocks, bonds, and gold are extremely liquid. One phone call can immediately convert these vehicles to cash. Using the Internet, it's even simpler—you have the money, literally, in minutes.

Real estate is more complicated. Agents, advertising, open houses, market offers, lawyers, and all the details can take time, but the effort involved is never a guarantee of a sale. Even if you accept an offer, it takes an additional 30 to 60 days for the official close. Real estate is not a liquid investment by any means. You will remember the predicament Jim found himself in from the last chapter, when circumstances meant he needed to sell his property immediately.

THE IMPORTANCE OF CONSISTENT RETURNS

Every investor wants a consistent, reliable (and hopefully positive) return. Table 3.2 shows the returns of two funds for 12 months. For simplicity's sake, monthly numbers are not compounded, but totalled. Fund A returned 18% for the year, 2% more than Fund B. Is Fund A a better investment? It's a matter of how you handle risk and the stress that comes from seeing your investments losing money.

TABLE 3.2

	Jan	Feb	Mar	Apr	May	Jun	Jul	Aug	Sep	Oct	Nov	Dec	Total
Fund A	+5%	-7%	+4%	+8%	-7%	-1%	+11%	+2%	+1%	-5%	+9%	-2%	+18%
Fund B	+1%	+1%	+2%	+2%	+1%	+1%	+2%	+1%	+1%	+2%	+1%	+1%	+16%

Imagine you've invested in Fund A at the beginning of January and have just checked Saturday's paper at the end of February. Your total investment is down 2%, and suddenly you're asking questions, wondering if you should get out now, and frustrated because your broker doesn't work on the weekends. By the time you see the March numbers, you've had an entire month of uncertainty. April makes you feel better, but you do it all over again in May. This is *not* worry-free investing.

Now imagine that you've invested in Fund B. It only returned 16%, but did you ever question your judgment? The returns are consistent and reliable. To most people, the slight drop in potential profit is more than acceptable when it comes to your health and emotional state.

With the roller coaster effect predicted to continue for the next three to five years, investors are seeking a vehicle that will provide protection from volatility and still achieve better returns than GICs. Enter the hedge fund.

HEDGE FUND PERFORMANCE

As we understand from the previous chapter, hedge funds can utilize techniques such as short selling and leverage—techniques not available to mutual fund managers—to continue to achieve positive returns in a declining market. Table 3.3 on the next page shows the 12 negative quarters leading up to the first quarter of 2001.

The S&P 500 Index declined cumulatively 62.72%. During the same negative quarters, the average U.S. equity mutual fund declined 67.20%, while the average U.S. hedge fund had a cumulative negative return of only 0.40%. Furthermore, during this negative and highly volatile time, hedge funds had a much more consistent return rate—smoothing out the roller coaster.

TABLE 3.3

	S&P 500	VAN U.S. Hedge Fund Index	Morningstar Average Equity Mutual Fund
1Q90	-3%	2.20%	-2.80%
3Q90	-13.70%	-3.7%	-15.40%
2Q91	-0.20%	2.30%	-0.90%
1Q92	-2.50%	5.00%	-0.70%
1Q94	-3.80%	-0.80%	-3.20%
4Q94	-0.02%	-1.20%	-2.60%
3Q98	-93.90%	-6.10%	-15.00%
3Q99	-6.20%	2.10%	-3.20%
2Q00	-2.70%	0.30%	-3.60%
3Q00	-1.00%	3.00%	0.60%
4Q00	-7.80%	-2.40%	-7.80%
1Q01	-11.90%	-1.10%	-12.60%
Total	-62.72%	-0.40%	-67.20%

HEDGE FUNDS AND CONSISTENT RETURNS

Performance in the long run (during both bear and bull markets) shows the overall strength of hedge funds. Table 3.4 shows a 14-year history ending in 2001. Far from simply providing positive returns on a consistent, annual basis, hedge funds also, again, "smooth out the ride." The average U.S. hedge fund provided an 18.3% compounded return, as compared to the 10.9% of the average mutual fund. At the same time, the S&P 500 Index (the U.S. equity market) returned 14.4%, while the U.S. bond market only managed 8.5%.

Figure 3.3 clearly shows that hedge funds not only provide superior returns but give a much smoother ride. Even in the worst years, they still remained positive. Mutual funds, on the other hand, were negative 4 out of 14 years.

BLE 3.4

	1988	1989	1990	1991	1992	1993	1994	1995	1996	1997	1998	1999	2000	2001	Compounded Annual Return
n U.S. Hedge nds Index	24.7%	23.9%	7.7%	30.2%	17.3%	24.9%	20.9%	22.7%	20.9%	20.9%	11.7%	40.6%	11.0%	5.6%	18.3%
P 500	16.6%	31.7%	-3.1%	30.5%	7.6%	10.1%	1.3%	37.6%	23.0%	33.4%	28.6%	21.0%	-9.1%	-11.9%	14.4%
rningstar erage Equity itual Fund	14.9%	25.5%	-7.1%	31.9%	6.4%	19.3%	-2.3%	24.5%	14.7%	15.7%	10.7%	28.4%	-5.1%	-12.6%	10.9%
ıman Brothers gregate nd Fund	7.9%	14.5%	10.3%	14.6%	7.4%	9.8%	-2.9%	18.5%	3.6%	9.7%	8.7%	-0.8%	11.6%	8.4%	8.5%

FIGURE 3.3

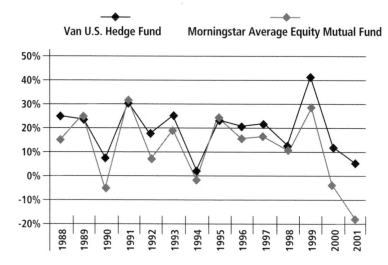

HEDGE FUND LIQUIDITY

Currently, some funds require a lock-up period of one year or more, meaning redemptions will not be honoured for that time period. However, more and more startup funds in Canada allow investors to make quarterly, monthly, or more commonly weekly withdrawals. Some even provide for daily redemptions, allowing for almost complete liquidity.

As the industry grows and more products are offered on the market, there will be choices between many different funds with alternative redemption rules. An investor can pick a fund that suits his or her needs the best, parcelling out a portfolio that balances superior returns and shorter lock-up periods. The key is flexibility.

THE FUTURE OF HEDGE FUNDS IN CANADA

Like any investment vehicle, some funds may invest in esoteric areas of the market or use strategies that are difficult to understand, but the majority will utilize securities that are familiar to the average investor and strategies that are relatively easy to understand. Chapter 4 discusses hedge fund styles in great detail.

It is not surprising that since the end of the bull market in 2000, there has been an exponential interest in hedge funds in Canada. At the beginning of 2000, there were approximately 20 hedge funds in the country managing around $1.5 billion; by May 2002 there were about 180 funds with a combined asset value of $5 billion. This huge growth is not likely to slow down.

Fuelling this growth is a change in regulations in the Canadian securities markets and more innovative financial instruments. In 2000, investment in a hedge fund required a minimum of $25,000 to $150,000 (depending on your province of residence), but today it is possible to invest as little as $500. As more and more investors realize that hedge funds (on average) are not only safer investments than mutual funds, but attempt to provide absolute returns that smooth out the roller coaster ride of market volatility, there will be an even larger influx of cash into these alternative vehicles. In turn, this will encourage the industry to come up with an even larger variety of funds providing choices currently only available in mutual funds.

Hedge Fund Styles

Looking back, we can see that since the days of Mr. Jones, the hedge fund industry has gone through considerable changes. Jones's first fund (his "long/short equity" style) held both long and short positions to make profits by taking advantage of increasing and decreasing markets. Since that time, however, managers have had to become more innovative and have developed different styles and methods to manage the money that is entrusted to them.

Today, we can classify hedge funds into six major categories, with different styles existing within these categories. These are the categories and their particular styles (in no particular order):

1. Directional Trading

a. Macro trading

b. Discretionary trading

c. Systems trading

2. Relative Value

a. Convergence arbitrage

b. Merger arbitrage

c. Fixed income arbitrage

3. Specialist Credit

a. Distressed securities

b. Private placements

4. Stock Selections

a. Long bias

b. Short bias

c. Variable bias

d. No bias, market neutral

5. Fund of Funds

6. "Hedge" Funds That Don't "Hedge"

This list may look daunting at first (hedge funds have a lingo all to themselves), but once the basic rules are laid out, they can be relatively easy to understand. First, we will define each category and then the separate styles within it.

DIRECTIONAL TRADING

Hedge fund managers in the directional trading category have travelled far from Jones's traditional method of "hedging" risks. These people are often considered to be the major risk takers in the business and make huge bets on the direction they believe the market will take. Their goal is to take advantage of major market moves and to use a lot of leverage to make the highest return possible. High risk is part of the package, and these types of funds *cannot* be recommended to the fainthearted.

Lately, directional trading has become more popular among CTAs, or commodity trading advisers. These managers can leverage their investments in certain directions (according to the market) by depositing only about 20% of their market exposure. This means that if a CTA has $100 million in assets, he or she can leverage these assets up to $500 million to take advantage of smaller spreads between securities. Or he or she can use $20 million to leverage up to $100 million and use the remaining $80 million to "hedge" his or her position. These traders can easily get in and out of positions, as they buy and sell *very liquid* investment vehicles, such as index futures.

Macro Trading

Macro events are changes in global economies, mostly the consequence of governmental policy changes, that affect interest rates. Interest rate changes affect all financial instruments, including currency, stock, and bond markets. Macro investors anticipate these changes and make investment decisions to take advantage of these new trends.

These hedge funds participate in all major markets of equities, bonds, currencies, and commodities (not necessarily at the same time) and often use high leverage and derivatives to heighten the impact of market moves. It is the use of leverage (which is not often hedged itself) that has had the greatest impact on the performance of these funds and creates high volatility (you win big or you lose big).

These are the most publicized hedge fund strategies, though only a relatively small number of funds follow this style. This is simply because making highly leveraged, high-stakes investments, often with huge gains (or in the case of Long-Term Capital Management's arbitrage strategy, as we saw in the first chapter, huge losses), is newsworthy material. This illustrious group of managers has no greater hero than George Soros with his Quantum Fund. Its many successes include shorting the British pound against the U.S. dollar in 1992. Soros speculated that the Bank of England would not be able to support the pound's unusually large exchange rate, and he guessed right.

The Quantum Fund had a base currency of U.S. dollars, meaning that investors put their money into that currency. Soros borrowed pounds and exchanged them for U.S. dollars, using the money in his fund as collateral for the loan. When the Bank of England finally threw in the towel and stopped supporting the pound, the currency lost 20% of its value virtually overnight. Soros immediately used his U.S. dollars to buy pounds at the now much lower price and gave back the pounds he had borrowed, pocketing the difference in the process. The "difference" was astounding; at the end of the transaction he had made a profit of $2 billion.

Though these kinds of funds can produce some unbelievable returns, they can also create unbelievable losses. Only money that is *not needed for anything else* should be invested in this kind of instrument. If you have money that you know is "disposable" (regardless of the financial situation you and your family are in) and you like wild rides (the financial types—not the ones you experience at your local amusement park), only then you should start even *thinking* about investing in a macro fund.

Discretionary Trading

Most funds in this discretionary style are based on the assumption that fashions change—what is hot this year may not be much in demand 12 months from now. How does this principle apply to the stock market? It is based on movements of shares in similar industries. The New York Stock Exchange has approximately 2,100 companies listed. These companies represent different industries, such as oil and gas or financial services. These are called sectors (you may have heard people refer to "financial services sector" or "oil and gas sector"). To make classification more precise, each sector has *sub-sectors*. The financial services sector, for instance, has the following sub-sectors:

Banking

Trust savings and loan

Investment companies and funds

Insurance

Finance and leasing

Investment house

Credit unions

Traditionally, share prices of companies in the same sub-sector tend to move together. For example, if there is a regulatory change that affects insurance companies positively, chances are that all the insurance company stocks will rise. Managers of discretionary funds take advantage of such changes. They find the sectors or sub-sectors that are hot or going to be hot and invest in them. As soon as the wave of fashion changes, they move on by liquidating their positions in the declining sector and going into the next "hot" one.

In 1999, for instance, Internet stocks were hot. Prices were not only going up, they were catapulted to levels that reason could no longer justify. Then in April 2000 the dot-coms came hurtling down. But in the summer of 2000, the fibre optic companies were still flying high. A successful manager of a discretionary fund would have been invested in Internet stocks in 1999 (and making triple-digit returns). At the first sign of trouble, however, the manager would have moved the fund's investments over to the fibre optic sector, until the end of 2000, when *that* sector started to decline.

Sound easy? It's not. There are two fundamental difficulties in applying this strategy. First, you need to be able to anticipate what is going to be hot. For most of us, by the time we read about a hot sector in the papers it is too late, and most of the potential profit has already been pulled out. A manager has to be able to anticipate the next hot sector and put the fund's money on the line before everybody else does. If your guess is right, the rewards are great, but if you're wrong (the sector is going nowhere or, even worse, going down), the potential losses are great as well.

The second challenge is to know when to get out. This can be even more difficult than guessing hot sectors. Again, by the time the public reads about problems in the papers it is too late—you have to anticipate it. Returning to our Internet stocks example, in March 1999 these stocks were making higher highs every day. However, the best managers were already selling. Based on their research, they knew the end was in sight. But think of the temptation. "Why should I sell? Prices just keep going up. I should stay in for a few more days. It may not collapse for months, and in that case I'll kick myself for selling too soon." Then the unavoidable happens, and most of the gains on the positions evaporate or, worse, the positions turn into losses.

The secrets of success in discretionary trading are to *sell too soon* rather than too late, and to have the skills to anticipate the next "fashion" sector.

Systems Trading

Since the invention of computers, the temptation to harness their data-crunching capabilities has been too hard to resist. Can computers find some kind of order in the chaos of stock price movements? Systems traders think so. In the early days of computers, major investment firms and banks were the only ones that could afford to buy the equipment and hire the talent needed to conduct research in this field. Today, however, for a few hundred dollars anyone can buy a powerful computer that packs the equivalent processing power of machines that as recently as 10 years ago would have cost a few million to acquire.

The Internet has made it possible to have access to real-time stock market data at relatively reasonable prices, and a number of Web sites deliver complex tools to analyze the data streams. Using the computer to find certain patterns in the price movements of stocks, futures, options, or bonds that can be exploited by the manager of the fund is only the beginning of systems trading, though. Most managers use much more sophisticated systems than the ones you can find on the Internet. They hire roomfuls of mathematicians, statisticians, and computer scientists to develop their own algorithms.

There are a number of pitfalls to this strategy, however. There is no good evidence to prove that the markets move in any kind of pattern whatsoever—rather, they are event driven. A computer could not predict the events of September 11, for instance (or, for that matter, any unpredictable events that affect the stock market). In a case where a systems trading fund is making profits on their investments by using patterns in an industry that is affected by a sudden event, the results can be catastrophic.

RELATIVE VALUE OR ARBITRAGE STRATEGIES

What is arbitrage? According to Investorwords.com, an online financial dictionary, arbitrage is defined as "attempting to profit by exploiting price differences of identical or similar financial instruments, on different markets or in different forms." Why is this so tempting? Because theoretically, you can make money without any risk.

A classic example would be an "interlisted" stock such as Nortel, which is listed on both the Toronto and the New York stock exchanges—trading on both exchanges at the same time. In New York it is quoted in U.S. dollars, and in Toronto in Canadian dollars. By knowing the exchange rate at any given time, one can calculate if there is a difference in price between the two quotes. If New York Nortel is US$0.86, for instance, and in Toronto it is CDN$1.16, and the exchange rate is CDN$1.52 for each U.S. dollar, buying Nortel in Toronto and simultaneously selling in New York makes CDN$0.147 for every share. The table below illustrates the technique.

TABLE 4.1

Buy 10,000 shares Nortel TSX	CDN$11,600
Sell 10,000 shares Nortel NYSE	US$8,600
Exchange Rate Adjusted Worth	CDN$13,072 (8,600 × 1.52)
Profit	CDN$1,470

The greatest danger for arbitrageurs is *other* arbitrageurs. The more people trying to perform the same arbitrage, the less likely opportunities will happen, or if they do, they will last for only a very short time before someone else grabs them. Once an opportunity is exploited, it becomes obsolete. The method in the above example is practised by so many individuals and institutions, that now it is very hard to make any reasonable profit at it.

There are, however, other arbitrage opportunities that hedge funds take advantage of. We will examine the most popular ones.

Convergence Arbitrage or Convertible Arbitrage

In order to understand the convergence arbitrage or convertible strategy, we have to define a number of financial terms:

Bond (not James): By definition, a bond is a debt instrument issued for a period of more than one year, with the purpose of raising capital by borrowing. The federal government, provinces, cities, corporations, and many other types of institutions sell bonds. A bond, then, is generally a promise to repay the principal along with interest on a specified date (maturity).

Corporate Bond: A corporate bond is any bond issued by a corporation (as opposed to a government).

Convertible Bond: This is a corporate bond that can be exchanged, at the option of the holder, for a specific number of shares of the company's stock on a certain date. This date is often referred to as the exercise date.

So why do corporations issue bonds? The answer is relatively simple: they need money to grow business.

Corporations can raise money in two fundamentally different ways: they can *sell equity* or *borrow money*. Selling equity is issuing stocks. The money received through selling these stocks becomes the company's and does not have to be paid back. The drawback is that a certain percentage of the company is given away in the process (stockholders "own a piece" of the company). By borrowing (through issuing bonds), the corporation does not give up any equity but must instead pay back the borrowed money with interest.

Market conditions will dictate which method companies will choose. When the stock markets are high, for instance, selling equity may seem the better alternative—the share prices are up. When interest rates are very low, however, issuing bonds would be a more economic alternative—the company pays less interest on borrowed money.

Why would a company issue convertible bonds? In order to attract more investors by sweetening the deal a little. Since there are a number of companies issuing bonds all the time, and they compete for the investors' money, a bond may be more attractive if investors can potentially participate in the appreciation of the underlying stock price.

A simple example can help to explain. Sunshine Yoga Incorporated is a fictitious company that runs yoga classes in the Vancouver area. Because of its huge success, it wants to expand to other parts of

British Columbia and into Ontario. In order to expand, it needs capital. Since the stock market has not caught up with the yoga craze (investors have not yet realized the growth potential of the industry), the company's stock trades only on the TSX at $0.57. The board of directors of Sunshine have realized that the company needs approximately $6 million for expansion. At the current stock price, they would have to issue over 10 million shares, which would considerably dilute the holdings—lessen the value of the existing shares—of the existing investors. The board could issue shares at $2 and only dilute the present holding by 3 million shares, but the market is only willing to pay $0.57. Their second alternative is to issue bonds for the $6 million. As we have seen earlier, a bond is a promise to repay the principal along with interest on a specified date. In this case, Sunshine issues the bonds for 10 years at 6.5% interest rate (a reasonable return of $3,250 on a $5,000 investment). However, to make the bonds more saleable, they attach a *convertible option* to it. The bonds can be *converted* to common stock, at the option of the bond holder (during set times in the 10-year period), for $2 per share.

Who would want to convert the bonds to shares at $2 when each of those shares is worth only $0.57? Nobody! But 10 years is a long time, and the aging baby boomers who prefer less strenuous types of exercise might just balloon the yoga market, driving up the stock price. As well, the expansion of Sunshine as a result of the bond issue (and the increased capital it creates) may be executed flawlessly, and the revenues and profits of the company could increase tenfold. Four years after you buy a bond, Sunshine stock is suddenly trading at $8.50. Wouldn't you exercise your option now? Sure you would. Had you invested $5,000 in the bonds at their time of issue, you would get 2,500 shares at conversion that you can turn around and sell immediately for $21,250, making a profit of $16,250 (a little better than the $3,250 after 10 years). That is in *addition* to the interest payments that you collected up until the time you exercised the option.

In this case, the company achieved what it set out to do. In essence, it issued the shares at $2. If the share price had *not* increased to over $2 in the 10-year time frame (or indeed had *lost* value), the investor would still receive his or her interest payments and, at expiry, the full amount of the principal.

A hedge fund can take advantage of this situation. The convertible bonds described above will trade in the markets after the issue. Their pricing will depend on a number of factors such as interest rates, time to maturity of the bonds, price of the underlying stock, growth rate of the company, the company's earning increases, and a number of other factors (if you knew that the yoga industry was on the way up, for instance, you would look to buy convertible bonds). A good hedge fund manager looks for convertible bonds that are priced such that by buying the bond, he or she will be able to acquire the company stock at a discount to current market value (Sunshine's $2 convertible price in our example). The manager will take a long position in the convertible bond (betting that it will go up in price because the underlying stock is undervalued) and sell the underlying stock short (betting that the bonds, because they represent a potential for profit, will be converted en masse and drive the stock price down).

A rising bond market and a falling stock market are ideal for this strategy. A manager can benefit from the increase in bond prices and from the decline of stock prices. He or she will also earn interest from the bonds in the long portfolio. We can illustrate this still using the example above. The Sunshine Yoga convertible bonds that I paid $5,000 for are now trading at $7,200, mostly due to the fact that interest rates declined. The company's stock is trading at $3. I have just met the love of my life, and I have decided to propose to her. In order to buy a huge diamond ring, I need to sell my bonds urgently. I call my broker, who makes the deal with a hedge fund manager.

But wait. Why do I not simply convert the bond myself and sell the shares? I could make a profit of $2,500! Because you can exercise the conversion *only on a specified future date*. In this case, that exercise date is four months from now. I need the money now. How does the hedge fund manager turn this transaction into a profit? He or she will buy my bond from me (at which point I go straight to the jewellery store) and then immediately short-sell 2,500 shares of Sunshine Yoga, making a profit of $300 in the process. How is this possible? Remember that the stock is currently trading at $3. If the manager borrows 2,500 shares and sells them short, he or she will receive $7,500 (2,500 × $3), or $300 more than was paid for the bond. This effectively locks in a profit, as four months from now, when the manager converts the bond, he or she simply returns the shares to the lender. The manager has not only locked in a $300 profit on the transaction immediately, but also receives interest payments on that profit. Should interest rates decline further and increase the value of the bonds to $7, and the share price of Sunshine falls to $2.50, the profit on the transaction would become $2,050.

As you can see, it is a pure arbitrage opportunity. The manager is making a profit by utilizing the price differences of similar financial instruments in different forms. These types of strategies have produced significantly higher returns, with only marginally higher volatility, than just investing in bonds. Because of the popularity of this strategy, a number of hedge fund managers have migrated to it. The major downside, though, is the lack of products. Only a limited number of convertible bonds are available, and too many managers are chasing after the same deals. As you saw earlier, the number one enemy of arbitrageurs is other arbitrageurs. Thus the margins are getting thinner and thinner, and it is getting harder and harder to make a decent return at it.

Merger Arbitrage

We already know what arbitrage is, but what is *merger* arbitrage? First, we need to define a merger and the opportunities it presents. The combining of two or more entities (companies) into one through a purchase acquisition is called a merger. In the most common form of merger, there are two separate companies: one that is doing the buying and one that is being bought. The number one reason that a company would want to buy another is growth. Combining the two companies' management can eliminate duplicate expenses, making the new entity more profitable.

In most cases, the buying company is willing to pay a higher price for the shares of the selling company than what the current market price is, because the result of the merger will create growth that is more valuable in the long run. After a merger is announced, the stock price of the target company will rise from its current price, getting closer to the new price of the merged entity's stock. The shares will usually not increase to the price it was acquired for, though, because there are risks of the deal not closing on time or at all. The difference can vary based on the public's perception of the associated risks.

A hedge fund manager involved in merger arbitrage will study that risk. He or she will look at all the possibilities of what could blow up the deal. There can be many reasons, such as shareholders not voting for it or a more lucrative competing offer coming in.

Once the manager believes the deal will close, and if it is a cash deal, all he or she has to do is buy shares in the selling company, wait until closing day of the merger, and surrender the shares at the higher price to the buying company, locking in a profit for the fund.

In most cases, however, companies acquire others not for cash but for shares in their own company. In this case, if you had shares in the target (selling) company, on the day of closing the merger you would receive shares in the buying company. How could a hedge fund manager profit from this situation? Another short example helps.

Company A is acquiring Company B. Company A's stock trades at $105, and it offers one share of its stock for each share of Company B stock, currently trading at $80. A fund manager, looking to create an arbitrage profit, would purchase Company B stock at $100 (the price to which it climbed immediately after the announcement) and sell short Company A stock at $105 in an amount equal to the exchange ratio—in this case 1 to 1. (In reality, particularly in megamergers, the acquirer's stock price usually drops as soon as the announcement is made, because of shorting pressure from fellow fund managers; but for this instance we'll keep it at $105.) As the merger date draws closer, this $5 spread will narrow as the prices of Company B and Company A stocks converge, because the risk of not closing the transaction starts to diminish. As the spread narrows, the fund's return grows. If Company B stock increases to $101 and Company A falls to $104, the fund earns $1 on the long side and $1 on the short side. Once the deal is closed, and Company B stock is converted to Company A shares, the fund locks in the $5 gain regardless of the current price of Company A stock.

As well, if during the interim the market has declined, sending Company A stock down to $80, the fund would make $25 on the short sale of Company A stock (at $105 minus the loss of $20 on the Company B shares for which the manager paid $100).

The following table illustrates this scenario:

TABLE 4.2

Buy 1 share of target Company B at $100; Sell short 1 share of acquirer Company A at $105			
Possible Outcomes of Merger	Gain or Loss on Long Position of $100	Gain or Loss on Short Position of $105	Net Gain or Loss
Rise in Company A stock price to $120	$20	($15)	$5
Fall in Company A stock price to $80	($20)	$25	$5

Another interesting example of a merger arbitrage opportunity can be demonstrated with the May 2002 merger of Hewlett-Packard and Compaq. This was a long, eight-month process that swayed back and forth a number of times. The merger was announced in early September 2001, and by the 18th of that month HP stocks were on the rise and had hit $16.15. Compaq, on the other hand, was standing at $8.85. HP had offered, as part of the merger, to give 0.6325 shares in HP for every Compaq share. With these numbers, it was easy to see where a profit could be made—if you could buy a share of Compaq and turn it into HP shares immediately, you would make a profit of about $1.36 per share!

How can this be done? A hedge fund manager begins by selling short 63.25 shares of HP (we know you can't sell a quarter of a share, but this makes the numbers easier) and buys 100 shares of Compaq. These amounts basically equal each other, should the deal go through—remember, HP is willing to give 0.6325 shares for every Compaq share. So the manager has now "locked in" a profit of $136.48 by capturing the difference between the two prices.

To be successful in this strategy the manager has to deal with three fundamental problems. The first problem is the risk of the transaction not closing. This could happen for many reasons, as we discussed earlier. In the case of Companies A and B above, where the deal does not go through, the price of the acquired company would fall back to where it started (to $80), causing a loss of $20 to the fund (that acquired the shares at $100). At the same time, Company A shares will rise, because all the other arbitrageurs want to get rid of their short positions and start feverishly buying, pushing the prices up. This creates the potential for the fund to lose on the short side as well.

The second problem is the lack of products. Since the beginning of the bear market in 2000, mergers have not been as popular as they were during the preceding bull market. Traditionally, though, this is a cyclical occurrence, and sooner or later we will get back to an environment that will be more positive for merger activities.

The third and final problem is, once again, the same for all arbitrage strategies. All the arbitrageurs are competing for the same stocks, narrowing the margins greatly and forcing managers to look at deals where the risk of not closing is higher or to go offshore to find opportunities.

Fixed Income Arbitrage

As you saw earlier, bonds pay a certain interest rate for the duration of their term, and thus provide a fixed income to their holders. How can a hedge fund manager make a profit here? The method is similar to the other arbitrage strategies. The hedge fund manager looks for bonds (corporate, government, municipal, or others) where the risk *characteristics* are the same but there is a difference in *price*.

The most popular of these strategies in Canada is to take advantage of the arbitrage opportunities that exist between federal government and provincial government bonds. Governments raise money by issuing bonds to invest in infrastructure or finance a deficit. In both cases, they hope that increased tax revenues will pay the interest (and eventually the principal as well).

The security for the bonds is the government's right and ability to collect taxes (and as Canadians, we all know how secure that can be). Generally, the larger the tax base (the number of people paying taxes), the lower the risk is for the bond holders (which is why U.S. government bonds are considered so secure). Since the federal government in Canada has a larger tax base than any one province, it can offer a lower interest rate to the buyers, since the perceived risk of default is lower. Provinces have a smaller tax base, so the perceived risk on the bonds is higher, meaning they have to pay a marginally higher interest on their issues. The emphasis here is on *perceived risk*. The chances of either the federal government or any of the provinces failing on their bonds is negligible (we are a fairly stable country). A hedge fund manager can thus buy the federal bond and sell the provincial one at the same time and profit from the arbitrage opportunity (provided that both bonds have the same term, or expiry date). Table 4.3 shows three separate opportunities.

TABLE 4.3

	Maturity	Offer Yield
Canada	1-Dec-05	3.607%
Alberta	1-Dec-05	3.682%
Canada	1-Dec-05	4.040%
British Columbia	1-Dec-05	4.180%
Canada	1-Jun-11	4.897%
Nova Scotia	1-Jun-11	5.262%

You will note that the differences in yields are fairly small, so fixed income arbitrage managers will leverage heavily to make money on these transactions. Because of the stability of these instruments, however, there is much less risk in leveraging.

SPECIALIST CREDIT

This strategy is based on lending to credit-sensitive issuers. Funds using this style conduct extensive research in order to identify relatively inexpensive securities.

Distressed Securities

To begin with, we should define what "distressed" securities are. Essentially, they are securities (stocks), bonds, and any bank loans or "trade claims" (claims held by suppliers owed for goods or services) outstanding from a company that is about to be subject to bankruptcy or financial distress. Distressed-securities fund managers attempt to capitalize on this situation. They are essentially the scavengers of the investment world. Sounds risky, doesn't it? In many cases it is, but there are exceptions.

When news of a company's financial trouble starts surfacing, investors will often react emotionally and start dumping the securities of the organization (the many cases of accounting scandals in 2002 demonstrate this well). The question is, are the investors all just focusing on the bad news and selling instinctively, or is there a real problem? Maybe they are haunted by the memory of a similar situation when they had huge losses. Or maybe they just believe they can put their money somewhere else and generate much better returns. Regardless, they sell and sell and sell. During this process, it is conceivable (and quite often true) that the price of that security will fall to below its true value. This is when hedge fund managers who specialize in this type of trading and understand the true risk of the situation start buying and potentially realizing value from the rubble.

An opportunity typically arises when a company, unable to meet all its debts, files for bankruptcy protection or liquidation. Liquidation involves shutting a company's doors and dividing its assets among its creditors. Bankruptcy *protection* gives the company court protection to continue operating while working out a repayment plan, known as a *plan for reorganization*, with a committee of its major creditors. These creditors can be banks that have made loans, utilities and other vendors owed for their goods and services, and investors who own bonds. Stockholders are compensated only with what is left over, and when it comes to dividing up the assets of the company, they are generally paid very little, if anything (in a bankruptcy, if a company does not have sufficient assets to repay all claims, the stockholders will get wiped out as they are last in line to receive any of the proceeds from the liquidation or reorganization). So, when looking for bargain-priced securities, a distressed-securities investor focuses mostly on the bank debt, the trade claims, and the bonds (which can vary in their place on the bankruptcy-claim totem pole, with senior bonds paid ahead of junior, for example).

The approach is essentially to be patient and to use strategies and instruments that are either unavailable to or not used by the creditors.

Most institutional investors, for instance (such as pension funds), are banned from buying or holding on to below-investment-grade securities (often called "junked" securities) even if the company is a potentially profitable one. Because of this constraint, they may sell these newly junked bonds at bargain basement prices, which has the net effect of lowering prices even further. Banks will usually prefer to sell their bad loans (ones no longer paying interest) in order to remove them from their books. As well, a bank is not in the business of trying to figure out how a reorganization process (which can last several years) will work and if there is any potential profit in waiting it out. Holders of trade claims are in the business of producing goods or providing services and have no interest in speculating on the outcome of the reorganization process. Creditors generally don't have the knowledge, interest, ability, or time to make decisions like this (such as how to keep the company alive) and will usually sell their claims at much lower prices than they would ultimately be worth, in which case the investor who buys the claims or securities can realize a profit—if all goes well.

Sorting out the value of these different claims is the specialty of the distressed-securities fund manager. Managers ask themselves how much a claim might be worth if the company's assets were divided among the creditors. If, for instance, a company has $50 million in assets and $100 million in debt, its assets would be divided at an average of 50 cents on the dollar to its creditors (minus related expenses, of course—we'll keep it simple). The manager's strategy is to buy the debt from the creditors at a lower cost than the actual debt is worth—in this case, say, 30 cents on the dollar. Because analyzing the reorganization is so complex (as mentioned above), most creditors are happy to sell their debt immediately and avoid the time, effort, and risks involved in waiting to see if they'll get their full 50 cents. The profit comes in being able to realize the 50-cent ceiling and keeping the "spread" of 20 cents.

How is this possible? The manager must undertake intensive research. Analyzing the different kinds of claims involved in reorganization or bankruptcy is a difficult job, as not all of them are paid back evenly and at the same time. Managers look at the debt structures to figure out where the priorities are. A mortgage backed by the collateral of a company's property, for instance, would be higher on the priority list than an uncollateralized loan or trade claim, which, in turn, would hold priority over publicly held bonds and shares.

The reason distressed-securities investing is considered "a hedge" is that it has little or no correlation to the overall performance of the stock market and bases its success on the manager's research and analysis of the variables and debt structures of a distressed company. It is, again, a daunting task, requiring in-depth knowledge of not only the distressed company itself, but all the involved creditor companies as well (the complexity of the claims, the creditor companies' regulations and patience, how long the reorganization will last, how the assets will be distributed, and much more). Some managers will go as far as buying up enough of the distressed company's debt to get a seat on the creditor committee and aid in making decisions on distribution of assets (now *there's* a good premise for a Wall Street movie).

Private Placements

Private placement is the sale of securities directly to institutional investors, such as banks, mutual funds, insurance companies, pension funds, and hedge funds, and does not require regulatory registration (provided the securities are bought for investment purposes only, rather than for resale). This means that the issuing company *does not have to go through the prospectus offering*. Offering a prospectus is a time-consuming and expensive—and legally required—process that a company has to go through if it wants to issue an IPO (initial public offering, or the first time a company sells shares publicly) or even a secondary offering of public shares. The cost of a prospectus offering can easily be in the millions of dollars, while a private placement offering can be done for a few thousand. When companies try to raise money through share offerings (selling equity), cost can be a major issue, especially if they do not need large sums of money. To raise $6 to $7 million, and then spend over a million on items such as a prospectus, is just not efficient.

So, if a corporation whose shares are publicly traded needs to raise, say, $7 million, the most efficient way to do it is through a private placement. The company will find an institution (in this case, a hedge fund) that is willing to buy the shares. The company draws up the private placement document (at a cost of a few thousand dollars in legal fees) and closes the deal.

Obviously, the question remains: how can the hedge fund make money on this transaction? After all, it could have simply bought the shares on the open market. The key is that because there is no prospectus issued, regulators put restrictions on what can be done with any shares acquired in this manner. Most often, there is a period during which they cannot be sold. This is why the definition states that they are for *investment purposes only*. In Ontario, for example, that period is currently four months—for four months, the hedge fund cannot sell those shares. After the four-month period, however, the shares become tradable. The trick is that to compensate the fund for that risk (which could be a serious drop in the liquidity of the investment), the issuing company will give a discount to the investor on the current market price. Depending on the price of the security, this discount can be up to 25% for TSX-traded stocks.

The job of the hedge fund manager is to find companies whose shares are *stable enough to last four months without a major fall*. If the share price is the same four months after the purchase, the manager will be able to realize a profit, depending on the discount he or she received from the issuing entity. In the case of a 25% discount, a share would have to lose more than a quarter of its underlying value in only four months for the manager to realize a loss.

There is another trick to this. If the hedge fund manager buys the shares at a discount by organizing a private placement, he or she can then borrow shares and short-sell them. This, as in the convertible bond strategy, locks in the profit for the manager, who will simply pocket the money from the sale of the borrowed shares, collect interest for four months, and then give the restricted shares back to the lender at the end of the four-month period. This guarantees the profit. However, most companies will put a clause in any private placement agreement to restrict this practice—for obvious reasons; short-selling a company's stock tends to drive the price down.

STOCK SELECTIONS

This category—selecting stocks—represents the most popular of the hedge fund strategies and is certainly the most romanticized investment strategy of them all. Movies, books, and television have all made real millions depicting fantasies of swashbuckling traders making virtual millions by picking the right stock at the right time. As is always the case with popular mythology, there is a grain of truth in it.

It was Alfred Winslow Jones's first hedge fund that created this strategy. As you will remember, Jones, by having long investments on stocks he felt were undervalued and short positions on stocks he felt were overvalued, was able to balance his investments and make money in both advancing and declining markets.

And to limit risk, Jones used the same strategy, by applying the formula you will remember from Chapter 1:

Market Exposure = (Long position − Short position) / Capital

This position is strengthened further by the fact that in an overall market decline, short positions will gain in value, offsetting losses on the long side.

When the markets were down, Jones could shift a larger portion of his portfolio to the short side and, when they went up, shift back to the long side. By applying leverage, he was able to greatly magnify his returns while minimizing risk. Far from the traditional buy and hold strategy, Jones actively managed his capital, getting in and out of short and long positions to guard against swings in the market and make profits in every market climate.

The stock selection strategy has come a long way since the days of Mr. Jones and has diversified into some interesting sub-categories.

Long Bias

Overall, the strategy in this category is to have both long and short positions in a portfolio, to minimize the effects of market fluctuations and to be able to provide an absolute return to the investors. In a long-bias portfolio, however, a larger percentage is invested in long positions than in short ones. For example, 60% of the portfolio can be long and 40% short. How does this work?

It is easy to understand that during a bull market, a long-bias portfolio will do very well, as the general market increases in value. But how about during a bear market? How can a hedge fund manager make money when the majority of the capital is invested on the long side, and most of the stocks are trending down? The answer can be found in the word "most" in the above sentence. Regardless of how strong the market decline is, there are always stocks that defy the trend—there are *always* companies that flourish in declining markets. These are generally companies whose stock price is contrary to general market trends. In 2002, a year of severe market decline, gold stocks did very well. "Gold stocks" does not refer to the precious metal itself, but rather companies involved in the mining and refining of gold bullion. This impressive performance was because of an increase in the price of gold (which traditionally represents a "flight to safety" during a bear market and subsequently sees gains in overall market declines). As gold prices go up, these companies can and will make more money, so it is logical that their share price should rise.

A good hedge fund manager of a long-bias portfolio has to find the sectors that "buck the trend" during declining markets and invest the long side of the portfolio in companies in those sectors. On the short side of the portfolio, the manager will place stocks that trend along with the market (i.e., that are going down in value), thus making money on both sides.

Short Bias

If you have just thought that the short-bias strategy is exactly the opposite to a long one, you are 100% right. In a bear market, the hedge fund manager goes with the flow (shorting the stocks that follow the downward trend of the markets), making money on overvalued securities and picking stocks on the long side that buck the trend as in the long-bias strategy, to earn profits on both sides.

The art of running a short-bias fund comes to the fore during a bull market, when the manager has to find companies on the short side that will decline even though the general market trend is going up (i.e., bucking the trend in the opposite direction). Interestingly, the gold sector did this in the latter stages of the 2002 bear market.

Variable Bias

If you thought that variable bias was a combination of the short- and long-bias strategies, you were right again. In this case, the manager goes with the flow, regardless of direction, and manages the fund in the traditional Jones style. When the market is going up, the manager will have a long-bias portfolio, where the stronger the bull market, the larger the percentage of the fund's investments will be on the long side. When the market turns down and the bears roar onto Wall Street, the manager will switch to a short bias. Sounds simple, doesn't it?

The challenge lies in *knowing when the market will turn*. Predicting or recognizing this change is much more difficult than it sounds. A bear market can have a temporary "pull-back" when prices inexplicably go up for a while (you may have heard of these moves as "hiccups"). A perfect example of this occurred in October and November of 2001. Figure 4.1 shows how the Dow Jones Industrial Average and the S&P 500 behaved during that time.

FIGURE 4.1

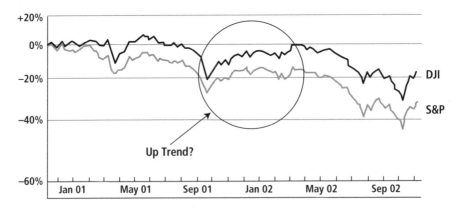

As we can see, there was a general down trend in the market that started back in June 2001 and really dived after September 11. But, by the end of September of that year, the markets started going up.

And they continued that up trend until March 2002, when the markets turned and the downward movement resumed.

What would our variable manager do at the beginning of October? The fund holds a *short-bias portfolio* (because of market trends), and now the market is going *against it*. The questions that have to be asked are the following:

Are we in an up trend now?

If this is a pull-back (a short period of growth in a bear market), how long will it last? Even if the manager realizes that this is a pull-back that could last for weeks or even months, the rebalancing of the portfolio could be prohibitively expensive. We must not forget that hedge fund managers pay commissions to their brokers just like any other investor. In fact, they pay more in commissions than most investors who have discount brokerage accounts. Since funds need to sell large blocks of shares when they try to get in and out of positions (to make the switch to a long or short bias), just dumping them into the market can seriously affect the price of their stocks (and thus the profit of the fund). So it is very important that the broker the fund utilizes "works" the order (to buy or sell the large amount of shares) and *slowly* trades it into the market or finds another institution to buy the large block of shares. This requires considerably more work than just executing a discount brokerage order for 500 shares, and it's why the cost of realigning a portfolio for a relatively short pull-back can be prohibitive.

The manager has to be certain that the market direction has changed before he or she attempts to realign. In our example in Figure 4.1, imagine what the manager would have thought on October 5 (or on November 5, for that matter). For over six weeks, the market was trending *against* the fund. Should the manager change?

If, in this case, the manager had made the move to realign, he or she would have regretted it, unless the execution cost was low enough to warrant a short switch. With today's technology, many of the managers in this category are switching over to *direct-access execution brokers*, a system in which they can perform their own executions at a fraction of the cost of the traditional brokerage houses. This practice has helped this strategy flourish by lowering costs and increasing the speed by which funds can realign their portfolios.

No Bias, Market Neutral

The no-bias, market neutral category is a very interesting one and, again, raises a lot of questions. The portfolio in these funds is divided exactly 50-50: half the money is in long positions, and the other half is in short ones. Theoretically, a portfolio such as this is not affected by market movements. If markets go up, the portfolio will lose on the short positions and gain on the long ones, and if markets go down the exact opposite will happen. So how can the manager make money at it?

The answer comes down, once again, to excellent stock-picking skills. As explained earlier, the market has different sectors, such as the gold sector. This sector includes companies that do exploration for, mine for, or refine gold. When gold prices go up, all the companies in the gold sector tend to move up. Some of them, however, move at a faster pace than others. They simply gain more than their peers. These are called the strong companies of the sector. Each sector also has weak companies, which tend to go down more than their peers when the sector trends down.

A good no-bias manager will go long on stocks that are strong in a particular sector and short on the ones that are weak. The logic is that when the market goes up, the portfolio will lose less money on the short side than it will gain on the long side. The opposite is true for a bear market, making more money on the short side than is lost on the long side. The greatest challenge for the manager is to know *when to rebalance*. A stock that was weak in a sector can become strong overnight in response to news on better than expected earnings, for example, or in the case of the gold sector, a large strike in mining exploration. Most of the time, however, the sign of a stock changing characteristics is much more subtle, and the manager has to realize this very quickly. No bias, market neutral is probably the most conservative of the hedge fund strategies, and as such, it generally offers a relatively low return.

FUND OF FUNDS

A fund of funds is, put simply, a hedge fund that invests in other hedge funds. At this point, you, the reader, know more about hedge funds than 90% of the population. So when you ask, "Why would anyone invest in something like that?" you are asking a very logical question.

So let's look at it again. A fund of funds collects investment capital from its customers and then puts the money into a number of different hedge funds. The investor receives a return that is the average return of the different hedge funds invested in, minus the management and performance fees charged by the fund of funds.

The question you likely have is this: why would I do that, when I could just as well invest in one or more funds and not pay a second layer of management and performance fees? Again, you are 100% correct to ask this. However, many very successful hedge funds have a *minimum investment* requirement that can be in the hundreds of thousands of dollars. If you have that kind of money to invest in a fund and you can do it a few times over, you can actually create your own fund of funds. Most of us, however, cannot invest such large sums into one place, and that is where a fund of funds fills a void, by consolidating investments from a number of individuals. This consolidation allows these individuals to easily invest in any of the successful funds that have huge minimum investment requirements, investments that would be otherwise out of the question.

The second reason you might want to invest in a fund of funds is *diversification*. Different funds of funds create different types of diversification options. As you saw in earlier chapters, hedge funds are not relative to market performance. And you have seen above that there are many different hedge fund styles that for all intents and purposes are completely unrelated to each other, with no correlation of their performances whatsoever. By investing in a number of different, unrelated hedge funds, you can achieve true diversification.

In understanding the strategies described above, it is easy to see that there is a normally low correlation among, for example, a long/short, a fixed-income arbitrage, and a distress-securities fund. Rather than investing all your money into only one of them, spreading it across all three will minimize risk and potentially provide a better return.

The third reason you would want to invest in a fund of funds is the *due diligence* the manager will have to apply. A prudent fund-of-funds manager will not just put his or her clients' money blindly into any hedge fund. Rather, he or she will go through a due diligence process, examining each of the potential funds in great detail, interviewing the managers, and making sure that these investments are the right ones for the clients. Not only will the manager do this at the beginning, he or she will maintain the process during the entire existence of the fund. Being close to the individual managers of these funds, the fund-of-funds manager can notice a potential "red flag" much sooner. A good fund-of-funds manager will notice a problem long before the general public and take the necessary steps to minimize exposure. As a result, the manager might reduce investment in the troubled fund in question or just eliminate it completely from the portfolio.

Undertaking this due diligence is extremely difficult for the average investor. Most of us have all kinds of other obligations in any given day that do not leave enough time to do serious research into investment vehicles. Doing that research is why a fund-of-funds manager can justify the second layer of fees.

TABLE 4.4

	Fund 1	Fund 2	Fund 3	Fund 4	Fund of Funds
1998	35%	22%	7%	(8%)	14%
1999	27%	(2%)	29%	19%	18%
2000	(10%)	39%	35%	45%	27%
2001	19%	25%	35%	35%	28%
2002	36%	20%	(1%)	16%	18%
5-year Compounded Return	20%	20%	20%	20%	21%

As you can see, it is possible that a fund of funds can provide a higher return than single-strategy funds and can also protect investors from an underperforming fund in its portfolio.

In summary, a fund of funds can be a very useful strategy. Its main advantages are that it

• Provides an investment portfolio with lower levels of risk and can deliver returns that are largely uncorrelated to the performance of the stock market.

- Delivers more stable returns under most market conditions because of the fund-of-funds manager's ability and his or her understanding of the various hedge strategies.

- Significantly reduces individual fund and manager risk.

- Eliminates the need for time-consuming due diligence otherwise required for making hedge fund investment decisions.

- Allows for easier administration of widely diversified investments across a large variety of hedge funds.

- Allows access to a broader spectrum of leading hedge funds that may otherwise be unavailable because of high minimum investment requirements.

- Is an ideal way to gain access to a wide variety of hedge fund strategies, managed by many of the world's premier investment professionals, for a relatively modest investment of second-tier fees.

There are disadvantages, however. Fund of funds are less risky and eliminate much of the research, but this does not come without a price. Fund of funds charge management and performance fees on top of the fees from the individual funds they invest in, significantly increasing costs. As well, their returns reflect their low volatility, being generally lower than many individual funds.

"HEDGE" FUNDS THAT DON'T "HEDGE"

As you will recall from the first chapter, "hedge funds" has become a kind of catchall term for any number of alternative investments. Many managers out there invest in a wide variety of exotic instruments, ranging from fine wine and antiques to stamps and baseball cards (just to mention a few).

Let's look at wine funds, which have become the talk of the town recently, as an example of these alternative investments. You have undoubtedly heard the expression "Wine gets better with age." Not only does it get better with age, but it gets more expensive as well. This is the basic premise of a wine "hedge" fund. Managers buy wines as soon as they are released from wineries and store them for a few years. They then often sell them at huge profits. How is this possible? There are four major fundamentals that affect wine prices:

1. The quality of the vintage,

2. Time value,

3. Rarity value,

4. General economic climate.

A little more detail will help. The quality of any wine from one year to another (the "vintage") depends, most importantly, on the weather. Was there enough rain? Did the rain come at the right time of the year? Was it warm enough? Did the grapes get the right amount of sunshine? When everything happens perfectly for specific wine regions, it produces outstanding vintages. Conversely, when the weather (among other factors) is not that great, the quality of the vintage declines. Given the same winery and the same grapes, the vintage that comes from the "perfect weather year" will demand a higher price.

Time value is related to the storing of the wine. Once the winery releases the bottles, they have to be stored somewhere in a perfect environment to achieve the benefits of aging. All kinds of chemical processes take place during aging that affect the flavour, texture, and body of the wine. Temperature and humidity have to be strictly controlled for the process not to fail. One also has to know when the optimum aging has occurred in the wine, at which point it should not be stored any further. So time value represents the cost of storing the wine, including the profit margin for providing the service.

Rarity value comes from the fact that wine is a perishable commodity. A winery produces a limited number of bottles each year. As time goes by, wine lovers open the bottles and drink the contents. With the consumption of each bottle, the remaining supply diminishes. Year after year, the supply gets smaller and smaller, and the wine becomes increasingly rare. That is what creates the rarity value.

We can all understand the general economic climate. When the economy is doing well and people are making more money, it is likely that they will want to splurge on luxuries, in this case creating a higher demand for expensive wines. The opposite is true for economic downturns.

Wine funds take advantage of these fundamentals. Due to their large buying power, the funds purchase directly from the wineries, store the wines, and sell them when the market (in the manager's estimation) is the best for a given vintage. One great advantage of investing in one of these funds is that you have the option to have your profit distributed in kind, meaning getting some great wines rather than cash.

Where's the hedge? There really isn't one. This strategy most closely resembles the stock-picking ones, in that a fund manager in wines, baseball cards, art, or antiques has to know the market extremely well. If you had recognized Wayne Gretzky's talent when he started his career and purchased as many Gretzky rookie cards as you could at that time, you'd have made a good investment. Much as managers of stock funds anticipate a stock's direction, these managers anticipate growth in the value of various commodities.

It's clear that the hedge fund market is a truly diverse one, with widely different strategies, some of which fall a long way outside the traditional Jones model. The underlying commonality, however, is that all these investments seek absolute returns and attempt to be uncorrelated to the general market trend. In the next chapters, we will be giving you some strategies to pick a hedge fund that is right for you.

Picking a Hedge Fund That's Right for You

So you want to buy a hedge fund. What should you look for? The Canadian hedge fund industry is still relatively small, but there are almost 200 funds to choose from nonetheless—where to begin?

First of all, we should review a couple of main points. If you think investing in hedge funds will be anything like investing in mutual funds, think again. You will remember from Chapter 2 that mutual funds are correlated to the broad markets and are homogeneous, meaning that they all have relatively similar performances and risk characteristics. This is because the mutual fund industry is based on a long-only strategy that prohibits them from holding short positions and restricts them to allocating no more than 10% of their assets to any one financial instrument.

These restrictions result in mutual funds delivering returns that are relative to the broad markets (when the markets go down, for the most part so do mutual funds). As well, mutual funds measure their returns relative to a benchmark, such as the S&P 500. The mutual fund culture is to outperform the benchmark. So if the benchmark loses 15% and the mutual fund loses only 10%, the fund managers rejoice. "We've outperformed the benchmark by 5 percentage points!"

they cry. Wait a minute. Your fund still *lost* 10%. What are you smiling about?

The other pitfall in mutual fund investing is the difficulty of assembling a diversified portfolio based solely on mutual funds. Because they are, by design, all widely diversified, long-only portfolios, they all move similarly to the markets and as a result end up being very similar to each other.

Because of the severely declining markets over the past few years, and because mutual funds move with the markets, over $6 billion was taken out of mutual funds in Canada from June 6, 2002 to January 3, 2003, as we saw at the beginning of Chapter 3.

So forget about looking at the S&P or other benchmarks. Stop watching the TSX wobbling unsteadily up and down. Grab a pencil, put on your slippers, and have a look at hedge funds.

HEDGE FUNDS AND MARKET CORRELATION

You will remember from Chapter 2 that hedge funds are heterogeneous, meaning that they all have widely different performances and risk characteristics. So when a number of them are put together in a portfolio, they can be very diversified. This is highly desirable, as it lowers the risk of being exposed to a particular market decline.

You also learned that hedge funds have a low correlation to the broad markets, because they are not restricted to long-only positions and are not subject to an asset allocation straitjacket. Again, this is a great advantage, as it protects the investor from overall declines in the market. This lack of correlation to the markets (and to each other) means that hedge funds can look for positive, absolute returns every year and can be highly diversified in a properly created portfolio.

So how do you choose a hedge fund? There are a number of important steps, beginning with a little research.

DUE DILIGENCE

First and foremost due diligence must be exercised. This fancy term has a simple definition. Due diligence is simply gaining a solid understanding of risk in an investment through research. Due to hedge

funds' diversity, proper due diligence for these funds is more complicated than for mutual funds. As well, mutual funds are relatively trans-
parent—strategies, risk factors, and histories are easily obtained. Most
information can be obtained merely by looking at the financial pages
of the Saturday paper or by visiting Web sites such as Globefund.com
or FundLibrary.com. By contrast, hedge fund managers are a fairly
secretive bunch and are not required to post their performances or
strategies publicly.

Fund managers often defend this lack of transparency among
hedge funds as one of their greatest advantages. The argument is that
if they had to openly report current portfolio holdings, other funds
could see the opportunity and jump in, destroying the delicate balance of a strategy. Regardless, obtaining information on hedge funds
can be a difficult but not impossible task.

By now we hope we've convinced you that investing in hedge
funds will provide you with superior returns and less risk. But we are
also telling you that there is a considerable amount of research and
work involved in investing wisely. You will need to find out the answers
to some very detailed questions regarding the funds, their managers,
their returns, and their risks. Maybe you are the type of person who
likes to do a lot of research. Some people enjoy looking at every possibility, lining up candidates, searching every nook and cranny, reading through every related document, and coming up with informed
decisions. In this case, looking for a hedge fund will be one of your
greatest and most enjoyable challenges.

What if you're not like that? What if you don't know where to
start?

Finding detailed information about anything is hard, so get someone else to do it for you. A financial adviser or broker is a good place
to start. Since these professionals earn money on your hedge fund
investment, you can get them to do the digging to answer your questions. It's their job! Again, the Canadian hedge fund market is still relatively small, so it may be difficult to find an adviser with experience
in this market. But don't let this be an excuse! An adviser or broker's
duty is to become educated on your behalf. If your adviser or broker
isn't doing what you ask or producing the results you want, simply tell
him or her that there are plenty of other people out there who will!
Remember that these people have a *client*-based business, and someone who has recently entered the field may want to work harder to

get your business than someone who already has an established clientele.

You should come up with a list of questions to get your adviser to answer. Some of the information you will need is listed below.

And remember: if the fund seems reluctant to answer your questions, you should ask yourself why!

THE MANAGER

By far the most important consideration in assessing any fund is the quality and reliability of its manager. As you have seen, hedge funds rely much more heavily on the talent of their managers than mutual funds do. They have a wide range of strategies and tools available to them, but they also need to be much more innovative, market savvy, and ahead of the game as they use these strategies and tools. Actively managing money in a hedge fund is a difficult and complicated task, so make sure you get the best. If you had a rare disease and needed a good medical specialist, wouldn't you research very carefully and ask a lot of questions? Wouldn't you want the best in the field? If you're not comfortable with a fund manager's background and experience, don't go any further.

Background

The background profile of the manager can tell you a lot about his or her style and help in assessing the potential risks of the fund. What is the manager's family situation? Single, married, 11 kids—it may seem funny, but a manager's family and lifestyle can have a large effect on his or her ability to actively manage a hedge fund. What is the manager's past credit history? This can certainly be an indicator of reliability and credibility.

Getting this information—even admitting you want these details —may seem a little "cloak-and-dagger" at first, but you *are* trusting the manager with *your* money, after all. And because of the lack of regulations in the hedge fund industry, managers tend to be more flamboyant (and talented), traits that can create risks. Many superstars (not only the ones in sports and pop music) have lost their edge because of personal or emotional problems!

Licensing

Intelligence, creativity, and wily money-management skills can come from a number of places. Some managers study widely, some gain experience through examining other managers, and some just have an inherent knack for the job. Regardless of where you think this kind of talent comes from, you at least need to find out if the manager is properly licensed. You may run across some funds that are private and that have found ways to get around the licensing rules. Be *very* careful here.

Since many provinces have different laws, it is important to make sure that the manager is licensed under the appropriate security legislation for the province it is operating in. Your adviser or broker can find this information for you, or you can contact your provincial securities commission to see which licences apply in your province.

Experience

Knowing about the manager's experience is very important information, and besides the obvious (you want someone with a good track record), it uncovers a number of concerns.

Did the manager ever manage more traditional investments (mutual funds or a similar investment)? This can tell you a lot about the potential risks. If a manager worked for a large mutual fund company for, say, 10 years, it is extremely important that you look carefully at the reasons he or she is now managing a hedge fund. The temptation to run a hedge fund because of the potential performance fees is a big one, and many mutual fund managers have left their salaried jobs in favour of making big bucks on profit sharing.

The question to ask is "How can a manager who has only held a long portfolio and never shorted stocks be an effective hedge fund manager?" The long-side (markets going up) mindset can be a very hard habit to kick, and in our opinion the relatively poor performance of some Canadian hedge funds can be traced to former mutual fund managers simply taking long positions and leveraging themselves to the neck. All those disciples of Alfred Winslow Jones in the late sixties and early seventies found out the hard way that no matter what the market climate, a short portfolio is *always* necessary. This is not to say that every mutual fund manager would make a bad hedge fund manager, but if *you* thought the only way to make money in the markets was to go long and wait it out, how would you handle the short side? Good hedge fund managers will have experience in managing prior hedge funds, in trading, or in managing discretionary accounts (building and managing an investment portfolio for individual investors).

THE FUND

Information on the fund itself (for the most part, anyway) should be a little easier to obtain, because funds are required by law to publish certain details in the offering memorandum for the fund. This is the creation document for the fund—its "bible"—and is invaluable to the investor.

The Offering Memorandum

The offering memorandum (OM) is designed to explain the details of the fund's structure. And be warned; it's *not* light reading. Rather, it is a very detailed, lengthy, "lawyerspeak" document that must be read *thoroughly*, as it is the investor's primary source of information. Understanding the offering memorandum completely will give you ammunition if the fund strays from its path, as it will also point out the potential risks of the investment and the legal rights of investors to sue the fund if the offering memorandum contains misrepresentations.

The OM is a confidential document that will often have its own identification number attached to it, so the fund can keep track of how many they have given out. It will include pricing, investment minimums, and legal and financial information on all parties involved. The Web sites of some funds may have the OM in a file you can download. Otherwise, call the fund and they will send you one.

An investor can usually get a good idea of the fund's general risks and returns by looking through the summary at the beginning—a lot of time and effort can be saved if you can just look at it quickly and say, "Nope." Therefore, it's a good idea to start with the summary, and if you find a section that is not clear or one that interests you, go to the relevant section of the OM to get information. If you don't get the information there, start asking questions!

You will also find the dealer compensation amounts in the OM. Read them so you don't feel so badly about making your broker or adviser work hard to get you the information you want.

And on the whole, the larger the document and the more fine print there is, the more likely the fund is to be above board. So if the offering memorandum is written in crayon on a napkin, run!

Strategy of the Fund

In the previous chapter, you read about a number of different strategies and styles in the hedge fund world. It is very important to have a basic understanding of the kind of strategy a hedge fund has. Under what conditions will the fund likely make money? More importantly, under what conditions will it likely *lose* money? What is the fund's risk-control mechanism? Not knowing this information is inviting disaster. Much like choosing a mutual fund, picking a hedge fund means considering your own risk tolerance—what are you willing to bet?

If someone asked you to give them a quarter and said they would bet you a dollar that the quarter would come up heads five times in a row, would you take the bet? Most people would; the odds are pretty good that the quarter will turn up tails at least *once*.

But what if the bet was $100? Or $1,000? Would you still be as confident? Assessing your risk tolerance is a very important step in choosing a style that's right for you. As we mentioned in the previous chapter, only someone with a large amount of disposable income would think about investing in a global macro fund, for instance.

So have a look at the different strategies and ask yourself how much risk you are willing to take for a certain return. This should give you a good idea of the kinds of styles that are right for you.

A Few Words About "Style Drift"

"Style drift" is a much-discussed topic in the funds-management world, and there are a variety of opinions about it. Style drift describes the situation when a fund manager moves away or drifts from a specific style that is described in the OM. For example, a hedge fund manager might drift from a merger arbitrage style to a long/short equity style. Why would this happen? There can be any number of reasons.

Maybe the manager realized that only a few mergers were available, and many other funds were competing for them, so it would be very hard to make any money. Then again, maybe the manager simply saw a great opportunity in the market and flipped the portfolio over to take advantage of it.

The question remains: is it a good or a bad thing? Should a manager be forced to remain in his or her OM-mandated style? Most experts would reply with a resounding "Yes!" This is because for mutual fund investment, the modern portfolio theory would say that style drift is *absolutely* unacceptable. Money managers in mutual funds are hired to handle capital in a particular asset class, with a particular style. The whole industry is founded on the diversification of capital over a wide range of asset classes, so if a single manager drifts from his or her style, it places that diversity in jeopardy by throwing everything off balance. For example, if a mutual fund manager is maintaining a growth fund and suddenly sells 40% of the fund's stocks and puts the capital into cash and bonds, the growth fund is changed to a balanced fund, and the risks, returns, and liquidity of the investment are changed too. Once again, the long-only, diversified portfolio mindset, based in prudent, fiduciary responsibility, comes into play.

But we must ask a few questions here. From an investor's perspective, if your fund manager saw that the current style he or she was in was going to result in losses, what would you like that manager to do? Would you prefer that he or she simply watch the losses accumulate and do nothing? Or maybe change style without telling you? Or would you rather that the manager inform you of his or her concerns regarding the possible change (in a monthly newsletter, for instance) and give you the choice of staying in or getting out?

And one more important question: is standing by, watching money go down the drain when one knows that there are alternatives, *really* a good example of fiduciary responsibility?

Size of the Fund (Asset Ceiling)

Once you have identified the strategy of the fund, it is also vital that you find out what limits it puts on the amount of assets under management (AUM), or its *asset ceiling*. This limit is generally put in place to allow flexibility for the manager's strategy. As you learned in Chapter 3, hedge funds, because of their unique strategies, have varying amounts of AUM they can manage at any one time, depending on a number of constraints. If a fund invests in a narrow market niche, it can be very hard to put loads of money into a tight space without affecting the markets. Smaller funds are able to make large returns mainly because it is easier to trade in and out of 5,000 shares than 500,000. Remember our discussion about variable-bias funds in Chapter 4? We explained that to sell large blocks of shares when a fund is trying to get in and out of positions, just dumping them into the market can seriously affect the price of the security (and thus the profit of the fund). So it is very important that the broker the fund utilizes "works" the order (to buy or sell the large amount of shares) and *slowly* trades it into the market. These larger orders make the fund much more cumbersome and less able to capitalize on profits.

Then there is the simple problem of market liquidity, or how much product is out there. Let's assume that there is about $500 million worth of mergers available in a given year. This means that an M/A (merger arbitrage) fund cannot, by definition, have a cumulative value of over $500 million. And there is certainly more than just one merger arbitrage fund out there competing for that money. So if in this situation an M/A fund has assets of $250 million, simple math tells you that the chances of that fund finding enough opportunities to supply that demand are slim to none!

So you need to look at the potential amount of product and ask a few questions. How much liquidity (product) is there to support the strategy?

You will also want to ask how far the fund is from its asset ceiling. If you think that the fund's ceiling is too high, getting in just as it starts to become too big to manoeuvre can be a mistake. A fund that works well at $10 million may not be effective at $100 million.

Past Performance

This is where the fun really starts—examining the actual numbers (when you get to start thinking about how much money you might make!). What returns did the fund produce, and what were the risks involved? First of all, you need a basic understanding of how to read some of the numbers you'll be looking at. We can all relate to a "15%

return," but how do you measure something like risk? How does a fund manage that risk?

MEASURING RISK

There are a number of ways to assess the potential risks in a hedge fund, and an outline of return and risks is almost always found in the offering memorandum. Managers are generally required to publicize their "numbers" in statistics such as the famous *Sharpe Ratio* (see below). It is necessary to understand this calculation, as it is a very useful tool in assessing "risk-adjusted performance," or the ratio of the *amount of return to the amount of risk involved in achieving it.*

Let's look at an example of how the Sharpe ratio can be useful for you. If Hedge Fund A returned 25%, and Hedge Fund B returned 15%, you would think that Hedge Fund A was a better choice. But if you were to examine the amount of *risk* that Hedge Fund A took, it might be much more extreme than B's. Therefore Hedge Fund A stands a better chance of losing money than B and will be a much more volatile investment.

The Sharpe ratio is a way of putting these two funds on a level playing field. The calculation of the ratio is complicated and really not necessary to spell out in great detail (unless you have an affection for complex calculations). Your adviser can tell you what the Sharpe ratio is—even if you don't figure it out yourself, it is worthwhile knowing what it is and what it means. One main component of the ratio is important to understand, however, as it is used to measure the volatility of a fund's returns. This measure is called *standard deviation*.

Standard deviation is a way to assess data, showing potential volatility. This calculation is achieved by measuring how far a fund's returns strayed from the average or "mean." For example, for the numbers 1, 2, and 3, the "mean" is 2. Let's look at another example.

Hedge Fund A has an annual return of 12%. This means that on average, it returned 1% per month (12 months × 1% each month = 12%). In a perfect world, the fund actually did this, that is, returned

FIGURE 5.1: Hedge Fund A – Monthly Returns

Jan	Feb	Mar	Apr	May	Jun	Jul	Aug	Sep	Oct	Nov	Dec
1%	1%	1%	1%	1%	1%	1%	1%	1%	1%	1%	1%

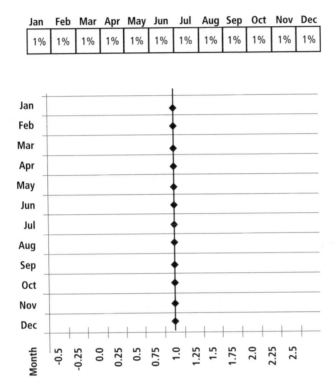

1% *consistently* every month. In this case, the fund would have *no standard deviation from the mean*. It returned 1% every month 100% of the time. Figure 5.1 illustrates this.

This, of course, is almost impossible in investment vehicles, but your savings account would look like this graph, as the bank guarantees you a steady, monthly interest rate (though unfortunately nothing *like* 12%).

Now let's look at Hedge Fund B. It returned 12% as well over the same year, but had a number of months in which it deviated from the mean of 1%. Figure 5.2 illustrates this.

FIGURE 5.2: Hedge Fund B – Monthly Returns

Jan	Feb	Mar	Apr	May	Jun	Jul	Aug	Sep	Oct	Nov	Dec
1%	1.1%	.9%	1%	1.3%	1%	.6%	1%	1.2%	.8%	1%	1.1%

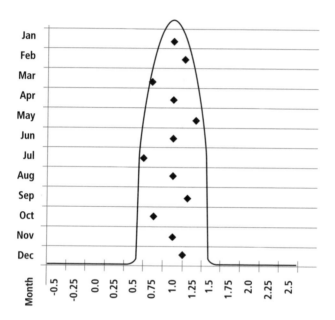

If you look at the numbers, this fund had a great success rate in returning the mean of 1%. As to the rest of the returns, they fell within either .6% on the low side or 1.3% on the high side. This is a more than acceptable deviation in most cases. If you are an investor in this fund, you can feel fairly confident in the manager's ability to provide consistent, reliable returns within the target range.

But now let's have a look at Hedge Fund C. This fund, while also returning 12% over the year, swung crazily back and forth, with returns as high as 2.5% and as low as -.5%.

FIGURE 5.3: Hedge Fund C – Monthly Returns

Jan	Feb	Mar	Apr	May	Jun	Jul	Aug	Sep	Oct	Nov	Dec
-.5%	1.8%	.8%	2.0%	2.5%	-2.5%	1.7%	1.4%	-.5%	2.1%	0%	.95%

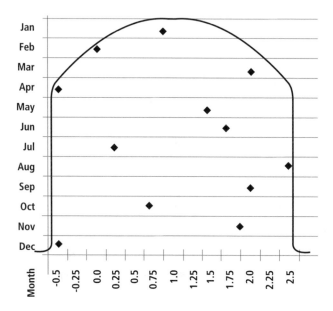

What a ride *this* fund was on. One month you're sitting at the breakfast table reading your monthly statement and thinking about buying a new house, and the next you're having a heart attack.

These are illustrations of the volatility of fund performance, and it is from these data that we calculate the standard deviation of a fund's returns. We won't bore you with the actual calculations—they're easy enough to find if you want to look for them. The bottom line is that standard deviation is the *average distance of the values from the mean.*

So, the lower the standard deviation, the less volatile a fund's returns will be.

FIGURE 5.4: Hedge Fund B – Standard Deviation

Jan	Feb	Mar	Apr	May	Jun	Jul	Aug	Sep	Oct	Nov	Dec
1%	1.1%	.9%	1%	1.3%	1%	.6%	1%	1.2%	.8%	1%	1.1%

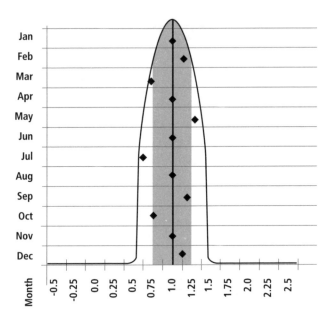

Table 5.1 illustrates how standard deviation can show the volatility of a particular fund. Five managers are represented, and their returns shown over a five-year period. The compounded return of each fund over these five years is the same—20%. But look at the standard deviations. Manager number 5 has a considerably lower standard deviation than the others. Why is this? The answer lies in the consistency of his or her returns. Look at Manager 5's returns: they varied between 14% and 27%. Manager 1, on the other hand, may have also returned 20%, but look at the huge swings between returns over the five-year period—from -10% all the way to 36%. So we can see that a higher standard deviation number indicates a higher volatility (or risk).

TABLE 5.1: Standard Deviation of a Fund Over Five Years

	Manager 1	Manager 2	Manager 3	Manager 4	Manager 5
1998	35%	22%	7%	(8%)	14%
1999	27%	(2%)	29%	19%	17%
2000	(10%)	39%	35%	.45%	25%
2001	19%	25%	35%	35%	27%
2002	36%	20%	(1%)	16%	18%
5-year Compounded Return	20%	20%	20%	20%	21%
Standard Deviation	16.86	13.20	15.07	18.12	5.50

THE SHARPE RATIO

As we have said, the Sharpe ratio is a measure of the risk-adjusted return of an investment, essentially allowing a calculation based not only on annualized (average) returns, but on the potential risk involved as well. The major advantage of using the Sharpe ratio over other models is that the Sharpe ratio uses the volatility of the fund's return instead of measuring the volatility against a benchmark (such as the S&P 500). This means that the calculations are not correlated to a benchmark—something that is very useful when assessing alternative investments.

The ratio was derived by Professor William Sharpe (one of three economists who received the Nobel prize for economics in 1990 for their contributions to what is now called modern portfolio theory—see Chapter 2). The ratio takes the excess return and divides it by something called the *annualized standard deviation of returns*. Don't panic; it's fairly simple.

The excess return is a measure of how much more return your investment provided than any risk-free return did. A risk-free return rate is usually calculated to be the return of a very stable investment such as Canadian treasury bills. It basically tells you how much better your investment performed relative to something that is a "safe bet."

The annualized standard deviation of returns is exactly what it says it is: the average amount of deviation the returns for the fund in question gave relative to the mean. This represents the risk, because if a fund's standard deviation is high, we know that its returns swing wildly above and below the mean.

Again, a lot of the calculations are mind-boggling, but when the dust clears, the Sharpe ratio provides us with a scale of sorts, where the lower the number, the less return you receive for the most risk, and the higher the number, the *more* return you receive for the *least* risk. So the higher the number the better!

The only real drawback to using Sharpe ratios to assess a single investment's risk-adjusted return rate is that it is expressed as just a number, meaning that it is very hard for an investor to evaluate the Sharpe ratio of an individual fund without seeing the ratio of funds in the same category. A Sharpe ratio of 1.5 is usually considered good (even great), but what if all the other funds in that category had ratios above 2.0?

So it is very important to compare Sharpe ratios among funds in the same category. This will give you a good understanding of how the funds are performing relative to each other.

BETA

You will come across a number of different ways in which people attempt to analyze risk in the hedge fund world. Because hedge funds are relatively uncorrelated to the markets, you would think that there would be no way (or reason) to measure their performance relative to the markets—it would be like comparing apples to oranges.

However, if you think of hedge funds as oranges and market indices such as the S&P 500 as apples, there is actually a lot of value in measuring how much less or more certain apples are like—or *not* like—oranges. This may seem confusing, but it makes sense. Using these statistics, a hedge fund can show how uncorrelated it actually is to the markets and their benchmarks. This is the role of *beta*.

Beta is the risks of a hedge fund relative to that of the S&P 500 (or other index). A stock with a beta of 1 is considered as volatile as the market. Less than 1 means it is less volatile, and more than 1 means it is more. So obviously you're looking for funds with betas less than 1. (If you're looking for less risky funds.)

JENSEN'S ALPHA

Jensen's Alpha, named for its creator, Michael Jensen, an influential Harvard Business School professor, is another complicated calculation to assess risk-adjusted performance. Alpha is basically a representation of a fund manager's ability to achieve a return that is above what would be expected, given the risk the fund takes or how much better the manager is doing than the numbers say he or she should. In this sense, it is similar to the Sharpe ratio in measuring performance.

By providing a basis of comparison for portfolios that have different risk exposures, this measurement is used to identify the part of the performance that can be attributed to the manager and not to blind luck. Calculated over a relatively extended period of time (most suggest no less than three years), positive alphas generally mean the fund manager is performing well, and negative ones mean he or she is not.

For example, if two hedge funds both have a 12% return, it stands to reason that an investor would want to buy the one with less risk. By analyzing the alpha, you can determine if a fund is earning the proper return for its level of risk. If the alpha is positive, then the portfolio is earning excess returns, or returns above and beyond what are expected. So a positive value for alpha means a fund manager has superior performance due to his or her strategy and experience.

CORRELATION TO A BENCHMARK

Correlating to a benchmark may seem like a strange concept. With all our talk of how hedge funds are uncorrelated to the markets and don't use benchmarks to measure their performance, why are we all of a sudden talking about correlation to a benchmark?

Essentially, it is because if you can see just *how* uncorrelated a hedge fund is to the markets, you can get a good idea of how to place it in your portfolio. In a diversified portfolio, you want each investment to be as uncorrelated to the others as possible. By using the correlation benchmark calculation, you can place hedge funds into the portfolio to give maximum diversity.

Using the S&P 500 as the benchmark, we can demonstrate how this information is useful. Correlation is measured between -1 and +1, where -1 means that a fund will be completely negatively correlated to the benchmark (when the S&P 500 goes down, the hedge fund will go up in an exact mirror reflection), and where +1 means that the fund is perfectly positively correlated to the benchmark (when the S&P 500 goes down, the fund will go down exactly parallel to it). A correlation of 0 means that there is absolutely no correlation between the hedge fund and its benchmark.

If we look at the correlation of a certain hedge fund to the S&P 500 in a declining market, we want to see numbers below 1, meaning that the hedge fund is going up as the market is going down.

RISK CONTROL MECHANISMS

Think of risk control mechanisms as being like the floodgates on a hydroelectric dam. When everything is running smoothly, water runs through the dam and power is generated. But when too much water is running through and the area below the dam is starting to flood, the engineers close the floodgates until the area dries up again. The floodgates help to minimize the risk of flooding.

With hedge funds, there can be any number of potential risks, and the manager has to put in place "floodgates" to help keep those risks to a minimum. These control mechanisms can include the following:

When to Cut Losses?

We all know the downfall of most gamblers. "Letting it ride" usually ends in disaster—anyone can tell you that there is no such thing as a lucky streak. With investing, the trick is to know when to get out of a bad situation. You will remember our discussions from Chapter 3 about the crash of tech stocks in 2002. Investors saw huge gains over a relatively short period of time and became greedy. When the stocks started falling, the investors held on, thinking that the downward movement would turn around. It never did, and in some cases investors lost literally everything.

A good hedge fund manager will know when to say "when" and will try to anticipate declines and get out before they happen. And when an unexpected decline does happen, they will know to sell even at a loss, to avoid further losses. It is important to ask questions about the fund's history and expectations of its risk control. What is the likely maximum drawdown (losses) a fund will endure before action?

Types of Investments Allowed

This is a simple question. Does the fund invest in any high-risk instruments? If so, what are the risks, and how much of the assets are dedicated to them? The more assets that are allocated to a high-risk venture, the greater the potential for loss. This information will be in the offering memorandum for the fund.

Net Market Exposure

You will remember Mr. Jones's formula from the first chapter. In a long/short equity hedge fund, he measured risk by calculating the amount of short positions versus long positions.

Market Exposure = (Long position − Short position) / Capital

This gave him a way to measure the minimum and maximum levels of market exposure, or how much of the assets were "exposed" to potential market fluctuations. By looking at how the assets are spread between long and short positions, you can get a good idea of what the potential risks are. By and large, the wider the range measured from 50%, the more risk the hedge fund has. Good long/short managers will usually report the current percentages of asset allocation, as they are constantly juggling positions to get the most out of the current market conditions.

There are other risk-assessing methods as well. In the hedge fund world, risks, as with many other aspects, are dependent on the manager and the correlation of strategy, style, and asset ceiling.

Again, it is important to match up your risk tolerance with the volatility level of a given fund's strategy and their methods of controlling that volatility, or risk.

Leverage—How Much?

You will recall from Chapter 1 that the collapse of Long-Term Capital Management in 1998 was due, for the most part, to extensive leveraging. Besides being wrong on both sides of its long/short strategy, it had borrowed huge amounts of money to amplify its returns. And as we saw, the company suffered extensive losses instead and had to be bailed out by the banks.

When leverage becomes high, we can see the potential risks expressed in raw numbers. This is rooted in the fact that losses tend to hurt more than gains help. If your investment loses, say, 10% in one month, it will take an 11% positive return the next month to get even again.

This is simple math. If you have $100 and lose 10% of that, you're left with $90. The question is, what percentage gain do you have to make to get back to having $100? The answer is a simple formula: 100/90 = 11.111. So you need an 11.1% gain to top up to your original $100.

Knowing this, we can see that with a leverage of 2 to 1, this investment would lose 20% in that same month. This requires a 25% gain to get back to where you started. And with a leverage of 5 to 1, you lose 50%, and you would need a 100% gain to get even.

And of course, with 10 to 1 leverage, this investment would lose 100% in that month, and you're broke!

You can assess the potential risk associated with investing in the hedge fund given the leverage range. Once again, the offering memorandum will have this information in it. You may want to ask questions about any reasons for increasing or decreasing leverage, however.

Return and Risk Characteristics

While past performance does not tell you the whole story, the past risk characteristics of a fund can tell you much more about its risk. The longer the past history (the longer the fund has been in existence), the better "feel" investors can get when analyzing the fund's risks. It is important to pay special attention to any losing months the fund may have had in periods of market upheaval (especially on the downside!). How well did the manager preserve the fund's assets in a down market? Also, it is a good idea to compare the fund's risk objectives to its risk record. If they are wildly different, you have more serious questions to ask before going any further.

Auditors

It is important to find out who the auditors of the fund are. Auditors add an extra layer of comfort for an investor. Obviously, a well-respected auditing firm lends credibility to the fund's offering. This information should be in the fund's OM.

Location of the Fund and Its Management

Many hedge funds operate offshore. This tactic is mostly undertaken for tax purposes and to add tools and strategies to the fund's arsenal by getting around onshore regulations. It is important to be extremely cautious with these operations. From where exactly is the fund operating? How accessible is information on the fund and its principals? It is much easier to conduct potentially fraudulent activities from outside the territory of regulatory watchdogs, so be careful!

Some people also have a moral dilemma in investing with firms who don't pay the same taxes as they do. We'll leave this decision up to you.

Management and Performance Fees

Remember, there are accepted standards in hedge fund fees, so if the fund's fees look a little wonky, make sure you find out why. The fee structure will be part of the offering (found in the OM), so it's important to see if the fees correlate with the standards and are relative to the other factors in the fund. Management fees are usually between 2 and 3% of your investment per year, and performance fees are generally around 20% of the fund's positive calendar year return.

Hurdle Rate

Most hedge funds will charge performance fees only on positive (any-thing over 0%) calendar-year performance. This means that unless the fund is net positive, you won't have to pay any performance fees. This feature is one of the best of hedge funds, as, unlike mutual fund managers who make their money regardless of performance, hedge fund managers get paid a performance fee only if the fund is positive. This incentive makes for good performance.

However, some hedge funds will charge a fee only when a certain performance level has been reached. This is called the *hurdle* rate. What this means is that the fund puts a *minimum* on calendar-year performance, say, 10%. It is only on returns *above* this hurdle rate in these funds that investors must pay a performance fee (as opposed to anything above 0%). Thus, the higher the hurdle rate, the better the fund is for the investor.

You may see hedge funds that use market indices, such as the S&P 500, as their hurdle rate. While this may seem a little odd, as we have been spending so much time talking about the lack of correlation between hedge funds and market indices, it actually makes sense, when you realize that it is another way to see how the fund is performing rel-ative to the markets.

Again, any hurdle rate will be outlined in the fund's OM. Be sure to ascertain if it seems reasonable by looking at historic returns for the fund.

High-Water Mark

The "high-water mark" is another unique twist in hedge fund invest-ing. Simply put, the high-water mark is the number that represents the highest net asset value the fund has attained in its history. Most hedge funds put this measure in place to ensure that investors don't have to pay performance fees more than once on the same return. This is how it works:

Let's say John bought 150 units of Hedge Fund A, at $1,000 per unit, in 1999. He has not added any units or redeemed any to date.

In Figure 5.5 (below), scenario one shows Hedge Fund A with a performance fee in place of 20%. In 1999 the fund made a return of 20%, meaning that John's units were worth $1,200 each—a $200 profit. But in 2000 it was negative 10%, decreasing the unit value to $1,080. It then made a return of plus 11% in 2001, bringing the unit price back up to its previous high of $1,200. Remember: performance fees apply only if the fund makes a profit. So John would have paid a performance fee in 1999 of 20% of his $200 gain. But in 2000 the fund was negative, so John didn't have to pay any performance fees at all. The insurance provided by the high-water mark is that John didn't have to pay any performance fees in 2001 either. This is because he had only regained his losses from 2000, and the fund had *not exceeded its high-water mark*. The fund would consider $1,200 per unit as the high-water mark, or the highest level of net asset value the fund attained. You can do the math: if John lost 10% in 2000 and gained 11% in 2001, he's only back where he started in 2000, with units that were worth $1,200 (you will remember that in order to regain a 10% loss, you need an 11.111% *gain*). So the high-water mark is the level the fund must attain in order for performance fees to kick in. If the fund had made a 15% return in 2001, as in scenario two, the fund would have exceeded its previous high-water mark and established a new one. John would have therefore paid a 20% fee on the amount over and above the previous high-water mark, or 20% of his $42 per-unit gain.

The high-water mark, and the stipulations surrounding it in a particular fund, are required to be in the OM.

FIGURE 5.5

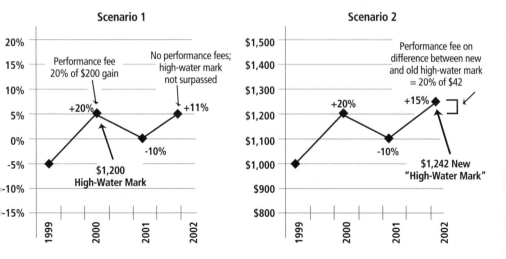

Liquidity

We have discussed liquidity thus far in great detail, with good reason. The liquidity of a hedge fund is a measure of how much notice the investor must give to the hedge fund manager before he or she can sell (redeem) units in the fund. Obviously, the longer this period is, the more careful you must be. Most hedge funds in Canada are redeemable on a weekly basis, but it is best to make sure.

And make sure you find out if the fund has a "lock-up" period. Some hedge funds will put in place a date, upon investment, before which you cannot redeem your units (even for a fee). This lock-up period can vary widely, and you need to examine the time frame to see if it seems too long.

As well, pay close attention to any "early redemption charge." Many hedge funds charge a 5% fee if redemption occurs within six months after the purchase of the fund. Again, this information will be in the OM.

PASSING THE DUE DILIGENCE BUCK: FUND OF FUNDS HEDGE FUNDS

There are some real advantages to fund of funds hedge funds, as they can take a lot of work out of the investor's hands.

As we saw in the last chapter, fund of funds managers, by definition, must perform on-going due diligence of hedge funds in their portfolio. This undertaking provides real benefits to the individual investor by conducting the due diligence on the investor's behalf. As well, these managers can diversify across a larger number of hedge funds than the average investor. And because of the high minimum investment levels in some high-performance funds, fund of funds managers can pool resources from a number of smaller investors to take advantage of better opportunities.

Using the same table as in our discussion about standard deviation, we can see the fictitious results of five years of performance with four single-strategy hedge funds and a fund of funds. The fund of funds outperformed the others (but with much less risk) due to its unique ability to exploit a number of hedge fund styles to widely diversify its portfolio.

TABLE 5.2: Single-Manager vs. Fund of Funds Returns Over Five Years

	Fund 1	Fund 2	Fund 3	Fund 4	Fund of Funds
1998	35%	22%	7%	(8%)	14%
1999	27%	(2%)	29%	19%	18%
2000	(10%)	39%	35%	45%	27%
2001	19%	25%	35%	35%	28%
2002	36%	20%	(1%)	16%	18%
5-year Compounded Return	20%	20%	20%	20%	21%

Investors in a fund of funds are advised, however, to still perform the due diligence process outlined in this chapter so far. In addition to these guidelines, though, the following points need to be considered in the case of a fund of funds investment.

How Many Hedge Funds Are in the Portfolio?

A number of research papers on hedge funds show that the optimal number of hedge funds for diversification is somewhere between 10 and 14. Fund of funds hedge funds having fewer funds in their portfolio than this are not true "fund of funds" hedge funds and therefore can be much more volatile because of their inability to effectively diversify.

Hands Off or On Approach?

Are the funds included in the fund of funds constant (or can they be changed only in remotely possible cases)? Does the fund swing within a wide basket of hedge funds? It is wise to seek a fund of funds with constant on-going management and that conducts its due diligence process on a daily basis. This means that the manager is constantly monitoring the performances of all the hedge funds in the portfolio and is quick to sense trouble, knowing when to get out or to cut losses in a particular fund.

Diversification Across Hedge Fund Styles

One of the biggest benefits of investing in a fund of funds hedge fund is the ease of diversification among other hedge funds. As stated earlier, hedge fund strategies allow for much wider and uncorrelated performances, so pay close attention to proper diversification. Funds included in the fund of funds must be as diverse as possible in order to achieve significant risk reduction in the fund of funds portfolio. The OM will include a list of all funds in the fund of funds portfolio and will usually tell you the percentage of assets that are allocated to each one.

What Are the Total Fees?

The ease of diversification, the risk reduction it creates, and entrusting a specialist to conduct a due diligence process come with a price tag. Fund of funds charge performance fees (usually 10%) and management fees (usually 1.5 to 2%) on top of the individual hedge funds' performance and management fees. It is important to evaluate the combined management and performance fees charged by the individual and fund of funds managers. Ask your adviser to give you a detailed calculation of the combined management and performance fees.

So in evaluating a fund of funds, you have to factor in the amount of fees with the return rates, and ask yourself just what you are willing to pay for. How much more are the returns for the fund of funds than for a single hedge fund, with how much less risk? Once again, knowing your own risk tolerances is key to making these decisions.

OTHER RESOURCES

Don't be dismayed. What we've outlined may seem like a lot of work, but most of it is a combination of a little understanding and common sense. There is a surprising amount of information available, if you just start looking around. The Internet is invaluable, and a number of sites are dedicated to hedge fund education and analysis. While most information you will come across will be for hedge fund investors in the United States, there are a few good Canadian sites to surf through.

We have included a list of resources at the back of this book and urge you to do a little digging of your own.

Remember, this should be fun! You are embarking on a financial journey that has potentially great rewards, so think of it as an adventure. With proper due diligence, you won't be disappointed!

CHAPTER SIX

Buying, Managing, and Selling Your Hedge Fund

Even after your short list has been completed and you are comfortable with the hedge funds you have selected, you may still run into a few obstacles. Maybe one hedge fund manager didn't return your calls, for instance, and you found yourself feeling uncomfortable, so you dropped that fund from the list, as one of the criteria for your "perfect" fund is decent customer service. Another fund turned out to have hit its asset ceiling while you were researching, so you had to shelve that one too. Finally, though, you have come to an informed, confident decision.

Once you have picked the fund (or funds) you want to invest in, there are still a few more important things to look at and consider. Owning a hedge fund is not like owning a piece of art; rather, it is an on-going process. This chapter will give you some tools for understanding this process by guiding you through the buying, managing, and selling of your hedge fund.

BUYING A HEDGE FUND

Due diligence complete, fund (or funds) chosen, and chequebook in hand, it's time to take the plunge. What's next? There are still a few aspects to consider.

How Is the Fund Priced?

It is important to know how the fund is priced, as it gives you a good idea of the relative value of the fund's units and some insight into performance. Unit pricing in hedge funds is based on *net asset value* or NAV. If you have already invested in mutual funds, you are probably familiar with this term.

Net asset value is pretty much exactly what it says it is: *the total value of the fund*. This number is calculated by adding up all the fund's assets, then subtracting all liabilities, such as any leverage the fund utilizes, and subtracting accrued expenses.

Based on what you already know about hedge funds, you won't be surprised to learn that it can be a difficult job to arrive at this final figure. Assets in hedge funds can vary from ones with a solid, identifiable value (such as cash) to ones that have value in theory only (like shares in a private company, for instance). So how do funds establish a value for their assets? Funds that trade highly liquid instruments (stock, futures, bonds) will simply use the closing price for the day as the basis to calculate the total assets. However, with less liquid instruments, such as thinly traded stocks or shares in private companies, the situation is much trickier. The manager will have to use *estimates* based on realistic criteria.

It is good to know at this point whether the fund is *internally* or *externally* priced, that is, is the NAV calculated by an outside source or does the fund handle it? An investor might be concerned about the potential for fraud in an *internally* priced fund, particularly a fund that deals in highly illiquid assets (ones with *theoretical* value), as the NAV requires *estimation* on the part of the manager. In this case, *external* pricing is much more credible as the pricing will be done by an outside, unbiased agency. You will most likely find this information in the offering memorandum.

Once the total value of the fund's assets are calculated, liabilities are deducted such as leverage, loans, etc. The next step is to deduct all accrued expenses, such as management fees, performance fees, audit fees, etc. What is left is the *net asset value*. This number is then *divided by the number of units the fund has outstanding* (the number that have been sold to date). The resulting number is the *NAV per unit*, which translates into the price you are being quoted for purchasing units. So, when you're investing in a fund, the fund will give you the price for a unit, based on the calculation described above. If you decide to invest $10,000 and the unit price is $11.56, you will receive 865.052 units (10,000/11.56). Why is this important to know?

Most (but not all) funds start selling their units at $10, $100, or $1,000 per unit. As the fund makes or loses money, the unit price goes up or down. This means you can see some hard evidence of performance. If, for instance, you are quoted the price of a fund's units at $11.56, you can be fairly sure that the units started out priced at $10, and that the fund has therefore made $1.56 profit for each unit since its inception. This, of course, is dependent on the history of the fund—if the fund in question started out 40 years ago at $1, then the returns are *much* better!

How Much Should You Invest?

How much you should invest really depends on the individual, but there are some good rules of thumb to consider. Let's say you have $1,000 to invest. If you find a hedge fund you like, there is really no good reason not to invest the whole $1,000. Why? Because you can't realistically diversify as little as $1,000. This relatively small amount of money will not perform well at all if it is spread out over 10 funds in $100 lots. However, if you have $5 million, you would most certainly be a fool to put the whole thing into a single fund, no matter how confident you were. Five million dollars is a lot of money to risk in one place even for extremely wealthy people, so you should seek to diversify that capital and spread out the risk of losing it.

So consider the amount of money you have to invest in hedge funds, and think carefully about how much risk you are willing to put on it. You should probably have a good idea of your goals by now, but you may want to have a quick self-examination!

Where Are You in Life?

This isn't a personal question! It's a way of assessing (again—we can't stress this enough) your risk level and what you have in mind for the future. What are your long- and short-term goals? Are you looking to strike it rich quick? Or are you hoping for long-term, better-than-a-bank-account performance that you can count on and still preserve your capital?

Once again, this is determined solely by the individual. If you are 25 years old, for instance, and have been working at a high-paying job, you have probably accumulated a reasonable amount of money. If you're not married and are healthy, you will more than likely have a fairly high risk tolerance. At only 25, there are many moneymaking years ahead, and you can afford to take a loss or two, betting on a big gain somewhere.

If, on the other hand, you are 75 and living on a fixed retirement, preserving that nest egg will probably be your main goal. In this case a guaranteed return will be what you are looking for. As you can imagine, though, there are virtually endless variations to the situations people find themselves in, and only you can assess your own.

If you are not sure about how to assess your situation, financial planners can be a great help. Their job is to look at such things as past investment history, your lifestyle, and your comfort level to give you a good basis from which to consider the appropriate strategies.

If you already have a number of investments, you may want to ask how much of your assets you should allocate to hedge funds in conjunction with other vehicles. The fact is, most decisions in hedge fund investment rely heavily on simple common sense and knowing your tolerances. The size of your portfolio, your income level, and the types of investments and assets contained in your portfolio besides hedge funds should help you (along with your adviser or broker) to make an informed decision.

Most experts agree that hedge fund allocation should be at least 15% to a maximum of 50% in an overall portfolio.

The Purchasing Process

The first part of the purchasing task is simple. Call the fund (or your adviser or broker) and ask for a copy of the *subscription agreement*. Most funds will include a subscription agreement with the offering memorandum in their promotional package, but if not, you will require one.

The Subscription Agreement

The subscription agreement is your application to be allowed to buy units in your chosen fund. It will require that you supply basic personal information. Some funds will require that you sign a certificate stating that you qualify as a "sophisticated investor." This rule was put into place to protect people from investing in instruments that are deemed too risky for their financial means (a kind of fiduciary responsibility). All Canadian provinces have different sophisticated investor rules, which are managed by their respective securities commissions. Your adviser or broker will be able to tell you what the rules are where you live, or you can check with your home province's department of finance.

Once you have filled out the subscription agreement and been accepted, all that's left is to pay your money. You are now the proud owner of a well-researched, properly placed high-performance investment!

MANAGING YOUR HEDGE FUND

So now you own units in a hedge fund. What next? As we have said, due diligence and purchasing are far from the only things to consider in hedge fund investment, as investing in these funds is a *process*, requiring on-going management and analysis. How does this work? To start with, you need to monitor the fund's performance.

Hedge funds calculate their net asset value either daily, weekly, or monthly, depending on the fund, its manager, and its strategy. Some hedge funds print returns in the business section of the newspaper, but not all do. You, as an investor, should receive at least a monthly statement of the value of your "piece of the pie." This information should also be available to you on demand, either by calling the fund or accessing the fund's Web site, if it has one, via a password. Some funds even post daily returns on their Web sites. Tracking the fund in this way can be fun for investors, as they can watch the progress of the fund on a daily basis!

Better managers will issue monthly or quarterly newsletters that explain their on-going strategy and views on the economy and the markets. Your job as an investor is to decide whether you agree and assess why. Just because you disagree with the manager doesn't mean that he or she is wrong. After all, he or she has much more experience than you do—that's why you invested with that fund in the first place! Think of yourself as a voting member on the fund's board of directors—if the manager believes that buggy whips are poised to be the next hot thing, what kind of questions are you going to ask and how are you going to vote if he or she decides to put all the fund's assets into Acme Buggy Whips Inc.? You can "vote" against this move by pulling out of this hedge fund.

Remember, you need to be comfortable with your investment. It's your money, and regardless of how smart or experienced you believe the manager to be, do not, under any circumstances, let yourself be convinced of a strategy or idea that you are not comfortable with.

And also remember, all of this on-going management is not to monitor the fund's success (although that can be a source of great enjoyment if it is doing well), but to safeguard you against possible losses. Selling a hedge fund, like stepping away from a perceived "winning streak," can be a *very* difficult thing to do. So if a manager starts losing after four years of consistent profits, you need to have in place your own criteria for getting out.

SELLING YOUR HEDGE FUND

As stated above, selling a hedge fund can be a big decision and needs to be a quick, decisive, and well-thought-out move. We hinted above at the potential for losses, but there may be other reasons for selling.

Need Some Money Immediately?

One of the bonuses of owning investments is the flexibility it potentially gives you in case you need immediate cash. Reasons for needing
cash vary widely, from buying a home, starting a business, or even
attending to a family emergency to whimsical purchases such as
engagement rings, cars, and much-needed vacations (you will recall
our numerous discussions throughout the book about liquidity).

If you are likely to need cash for any of these reasons, you will
have factored this expectation in to the liquidity of your hedge fund
units and purchased a fund that has no "lock-up" period and little or
no penalty or time restrictions on redemption of units. Selling these
funds is a relatively simple transaction. Call the fund (or your adviser
or broker) and declare that you wish to sell all or a certain number of
your units, depending on the amount of cash you require. Remember,
you are not required to tell anyone why you are selling, so don't let
them make you feel guilty!

Found a Better Investment Vehicle?

Perhaps you have been smart and have continued to look around for
investments that are even better than the ones you currently own.
Then again, maybe your lifestyle or financial situation has changed,
and with it, your risk tolerances and long-term goals. Either way, these
can be compelling reasons to sell your units in a hedge fund.

But beware: hedge fund units are not something you can just convert into a different investment without potential tax liabilities from
your profits. It is a very good idea to not only perform due diligence
on the new investment, but to factor in the value of that investment
against potential gains in the existing fund and potential tax liabilities.

Is the Fund Performing Badly?

Here is where the hard decisions come in, and they need to be assessed
very carefully, as they go right to the heart of some of your fundamental beliefs and behaviours that may or may not need some modi-
fications. If a fund is not living up to your expectations, what
mechanisms should you have in place to handle the situation? How

stringently should you abide by your expectations, no matter what your gut feeling is? A number of issues can come into play here, and they need to be addressed.

Greed

We have spoken extensively about greed. In Chapter 3, we talked about the reasons that so many people lost huge amounts of money during the crash of tech stocks through 2000. We have also talked about the need for prudent hedge fund managers to be proactive in getting out while the "getting's good" and cutting losses when necessary. Selling your hedge fund because it is performing badly is a very similar situation, but the responsibility for the decision whether to sell lies solely on your shoulders.

Staying in too long and losing is almost human nature, and it takes almost a Herculean effort to resist the temptation to hang on, yet resisting it is the key to prudent investment and financial success. Don't let us make you think that greed is necessarily bad, as it is greed that has made you decide to invest so you can improve your material and social well-being. Rather, greed has the ability to take over and cloud your judgment.

Hope

Another uniquely human trait, hope, can be as disastrous as greed, and they often go hand in hand. When things go wrong, the tendency is to hope they will get better. While this is a nice sentiment, hoping will do nothing to change the situation either way. It takes courage and discipline to jump from a sinking ship early, but it's something that every investor must learn to do.

Setting Your Own Risk Control

It is vital, in your on-going diligence, that you create and strictly adhere to rules about the level of loss below which you will not hold on to your units. This is your own version of a risk-control mechanism. Let's illustrate with Figure 6.1 showing performances of a hedge fund over a period of time.

FIGURE 6.1

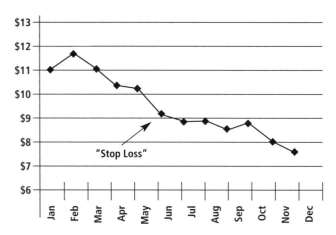

The figure assumes you bought units in this fund on January 1 with a net asset value of $11. Obviously this was not a wise choice, as the fund went up by 50 cents and then started a solid downward slide. What should your risk-control mechanism be here? You should put in place loss restrictions and abide by them no matter what.

Stop Loss

What you should have done was to have a *stop loss* in place. A stop loss is just what it sounds like: when to *stop* your *losses*. In this case, you bought in at $11. Let's say you decide, based on your risk tolerance, that the most you can afford to lose on this investment is $2 per unit. This means that when the price hits $9, you *sell no matter what*. This is where the discipline comes in—selling at a loss is one of the hardest things to do in life. As we can see in the above example, however, if you sold at $9, you would have avoided much more *extensive* losses.

The Rolling Stop

Look at Figure 6.2 below, and think about why you invested in the first place: to make money and improve your financial stability, right? So when you look at your investment four months after you bought it, it has gained $3. Excellent!

FIGURE 6.2

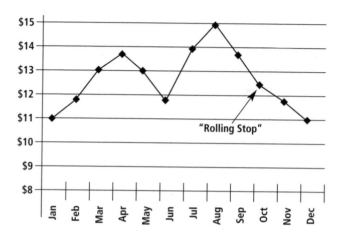

In May, however, it comes down to $13. Still $2 more than you paid for it. But the next month, it's down to just below $12. Should you sell? You have lost $1, but you're still up $1. Thankfully, while you are contemplating this, it goes back up to $14. Relax.

Suddenly the unit value jumps to over $14, and you're "on a roll" again (we're sure you can see where this is going by now). By August, your $11 investment is now worth $15, and life is grand. Over the next few months, sadly, the price begins to drop steadily. When do you sell? Probably, you would sell when the price hits $11 (you wouldn't have sold it at $12, because the last time it was there it went right back up); you'd end up actually *losing* money because you were hoping it would eventually come back.

Sometimes a fund will go up and down in small fits and starts, like the one depicted in Figure 6.2. This can be a hair-raising ride (and hopefully the fund you have chosen is more even than this!), but you can smooth it out by putting in place a *rolling stop*. This is a mechanism stating that there is a certain amount *below the most recent high* at which point you will sell. It is vital that your adviser or broker know where your "rolling stop" is.

In the above case, let's say you set a rolling stop at $2.50 (rolling stop levels are usually higher than stop losses, as you are in a *winning* situation). This means that at any point if the fund is $2.50 below its most recent high, you will sell your units—again, *no matter what*. So here, you would have sold it in October, when it dipped to $12.50 from its previous August high of $15.00, eight months into the investment. You would have made a little money and could sit back and begin looking for a new venture.

Discipline, Discipline, Discipline

We've given you an example where your rolling stop was absolutely the right decision: you sold while you still had a profit and before you started losing. The thing to remember is that *no matter what*, you must stick to your rules. Even if the above fund had continued to rise through the *roof* after your rolling stop happened and you sold, you made the best decision and lived to invest another day.

And believe us, this will happen. You will set your risk management, stick rigidly to it, and get out when your own rules tell you to, only to sadly watch the fund start to gain, and gain, and gain. These are the stories you hear about—*not* the ones where it continued to lose. The "one that got away" is a major fear of investors. How many times have you heard someone whining about how they could have bought Microsoft in 1985 or IBM in 1960?

But know this: if you choose to ignore your risk control, over the long run, you will lose. If, however, you stick to your guns, the payoff will be great.

PART 2

50 Hedge Funds in
Canada Today

Introduction to the Selection and Rating of 50 Canadian Hedge Funds

As of the end of 2002, there are about 200 hedge funds available in Canada. Many of these funds are "duplicates," though. In most cases, the reason for this is that the fund company offers investors a US-dollar or 100% RSP eligible version of the same hedge fund. New funds are also created simply to change the fee structure on them. One of the oldest hedge funds in Canada, BPI Global Opportunities, actually operates under six slightly different names. Since each of these "twins" (and there are many of them) is essentially the same, we will feature only one of them in our list—usually the one with the longest track record (we will mention all their "twins" however, because they are also available, and will generally perform the same as their "family members").

We do not show all the funds available in Canada; rather, our selection process was designed to give investors a good cross-section of what is available, based on the size of the fund, its length of operation, minimum investment level, and return and risk records.

The Nagy-Beck Hedgehog Rating System (NBHRS)

In the interest of simplifying the following 50 hedge fund analyses, we have devised our own rating system (patent pending), called the "Nagy-Beck Hedgehog Rating System." And in the interest of keeping the whole exercise lighthearted, we've decided that one "hedgehog" will represent our *worst* rating, and 5 "hedgehogs" will be the *best* (we're financial analysts, not movie critics).

Our rating system starts with an evaluation of each fund based on the following criteria:

Manager	1 (worst) – 10 (best)
Offering hedge fund company	1 (worst) – 5 (best)
Fees and their structure	1 (worst) – 5 (best)
Risk control mechanism	1 (worst) – 5 (best)
Liquidity	1 (worst) – 3 (best)
Historical returns	1 (worst) – 10 (best)
Historical risks	1 (worst) – 12 (best)
Size (asset ceiling)	1 (worst) – 5 (best)
Transparency	1 (worst) – 5 (best)

You will notice that we have "weighted" these numbers to reflect what we believe are more or less important aspects of hedge funds. Obviously, the manager will be given more weight than liquidity, for instance, and historical risks, which are hard facts, will be given even more weight than the manager. The end result is a number out of 60 to work with. The total points are tallied, and ratings are given according to the following formula:

1 – 12	1 hedgehog
13 – 24	2 hedgehogs
25 – 36	3 hedgehogs
37 – 48	4 hedgehogs
49 – 60	5 hedgehogs

So there you have it. Hopefully we have given you a good insight into the rapidly growing world of hedge funds in Canada, and have demonstrated the value of including them in your portfolio. Hedge funds are not the playground of the super rich any more, and with their continued growth, we can only hope that these nimble, absolute return oriented investments will become more and more available to all investors so that everyone can benefit from these unique, fascinating, and potentially profitable vehicles.

Happy Hedgehogging!

ABRIA DIVERSIFIED ARBITRAGE TRUST

Abria Financial Group
20 Adelaide Street East, Suite 200
Toronto, ON
M5C 2T6

Telephone Number: (416) 367-4777
Fax Number: (416) 367-4555
Toll-Free: 1-877-512-2742
Web Site: www.abriafunds.com

Similar funds: Abria Diversified Arbitrage Trust Class B

PORTFOLIO MANAGER(S)

Henry Kneis, Manager   **Abria Financial Group Ltd.**

Henry Kneis is the president and chief investment officer of Abria. He has 15 years of specialized experience in the field of market-neutral investing as a senior partner of one of Canada's most successful proprietary arbitrage trading organizations, and then as founder of Abria. Prior to launching Abria in 1999, he was the CEO of Maple Partners Financial Products. At Maple, he managed proprietary trading portfolios for the firm and its affiliates with aggregate balance sheet assets of $3 billion. He began his career with First Marathon Securities and became a senior partner of FM Financial Products in 1989. He has served on various derivative and index committees of the Toronto Stock Exchange and has developed capital margin rules for derivative securities that currently exist as industry regulations. He is a past chairman of the Board of Governors of the Toronto Futures Exchange. Kneis holds an MBA and a degree in Engineering Science.

FUND DESCRIPTION

The investment objectives of the Abria Diversified Arbitrage Trust are

- To achieve annual net asset value growth at the U.S. treasury-bill rate + 5 to 7% (net of fees and expenses)
- To generate these returns at low levels of volatility, similar to the volatility of mid-term bond indices
- To minimize the frequency and extent of losses under hostile market conditions
- To have a low correlation with the major equity and fixed-income markets
- To offer a tax deferral until disposition for unit holders
- To limit and restrict the use of leverage by the Abria Trust to cash management and portfolio rebalancing purposes

The performance objectives of the Abria Diversified Arbitrage Trust can be summarized by the following targets:

	Target
Net Pre-tax Annual Return	US 90-day T-Bills + 5 to 7%
Annual Standard Deviation	3 to 4%
Sharpe Ratio	2.0
Positive Monthly Returns	> 80%
Correlations to Stocks and Bonds	< 0.40

TERMS AND CONDITIONS

Fund style: Fund of Funds
Sub-style: Market Neutral Arbitrage Funds
Inception date: March 2000
Management fee: 1.95%
Performance fee: 10%
Hurdle rate: 0%
Liquidity: Monthly
subject to provincial statutory minimums

* Min. investment: $150,000
Benchmark: TSX
RRSP eligibility: Yes (100% Canadian content)
Asset size: $41 million
NAV: $103.88

Early red'n period: 90 days
Early red'n fee: 2%
High-water mark: Yes, perpetual
Redemption notice: 3 months
Max. leverage: None at Abria Trust level

PERFORMANCE (AS OF DECEMBER 31, 2002)

	1 month	3 month	6 month	YTD	1 year	2 year	3 year	5 year	10 year	Since Inception
Fund:	1.45%	1.66%	3.93%	6.81%	6.81%	8.02%				9.82%
TSX	0.67%	7.03%	-7.43%	-13.97%	-13.97%	-13.96%				-10.75%

Year:		Jan	Feb	Mar	Apr	May	Jun	Jul	Aug	Sep	Oct	Nov	Dec
Fund: 2002	6.81%	0.86%	0.16%	0.72%	0.62%	0.24%	0.16%	0.56%	0.83%	0.83%	0.13%	0.07%	1.45%
TSX 2002	-13.97%	-0.52%	-0.14%	2.80%	-2.40%	-0.10%	-6.67%	-7.56%	0.10%	-6.53%	1.11%	5.15%	1.45%
Fund: 2001	9.23%	0.62%	0.74%	0.32%	0.82%	0.26%	1.60%	0.19%	0.80%	0.79%	1.11%	0.77%	0.85%
TSX 2001	-13.94%	4.35%	-13.34%	-5.83%	4.45%	2.71%	-5.21%	-0.60%	-3.78%	-7.58%	0.69%	7.84%	3.54%
Fund: 2000	11.97%			0.67%	1.94%	0.67%	1.94%	1.56%	1.22%	0.03%	0.73%	1.71%	0.38%
TSX 2000	-2.14%			3.65%	-1.21%	-1.02%	10.20%	2.07%	8.09%	-7.74%	-7.12%	-8.50%	1.29%

PERFORMANCE COMPARISON

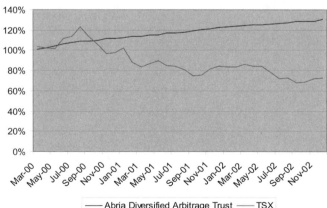

—— Abria Diversified Arbitrage Trust   —— TSX

RISK DATA (AS OF DECEMBER 31, 2002)

Alpha: 9.93%   Benchmark: TSX

Beta: 0.01   Correlation to benchmark: 0.11

St. deviation (annualized): 1.83%   Maximum drawdown: N/A

St. deviation (1 year): 1.31%   Largest monthly drop: none

St. deviation (2 year): 1.34%   Percentage of negative months: 0.00%

Sharpe Ratio: 3.44   Percentage of positive months: 100.00%

Sortino Ratio:

NAGY-BECK HEDGE RATING:

@RGENTUM CANADIAN L/S EQUITY PORTFOLIO

@rgentum Management and
Research Corporation
1555 Peel Street, Suite 1201
Montreal, PQ • H3A 3L8

Telephone Number: (514) 288-1262
Fax Number: (514) 288-1265
Toll-Free: 1-877-274-3688
Web Site: www.@rgentum.com

PORTFOLIO MANAGER(S)

ChabotPage Investment Counsel Inc.

Andre Chabot, president of ChabotPage Investments Counsel of Montreal, is managing the fund's investments. He produced solid positive results in several funds in 2001, and was one of Canada's top hedge fund managers in that year. Chabot has been the subject of numerous national reports for successful fund management.

FUND DESCRIPTION

The Canadian L/S Equity Portfolio seeks to provide consistent long-term growth through capital appreciation while maintaining minimal portfolio exposure to general equity market risk by holding security positions in both a long and a short portfolio. This investment objective will be met regardless of the general direction of the stock market by taking both long positions (anticipating an increase in the price of the stock) and short positions (anticipating a decrease in the price of the stock). The objective of the Canadian L/S Equity Portfolio is to maintain a short portfolio that will range from 20% to 50% of the value of the long portfolio and over any three-year period, to maintain a short portfolio of approximately 38% and long portfolio of approximately 62% (approximately 37.5% of the portfolio exposed to the market). It will take positions in mainly selected large-and medium-market-capitalization Canadian corporations trading on recognized Canadian markets with a medium-market float of CAN$250 million.

TERMS AND CONDITIONS

Fund style: Stock Selection

Sub-style: Long Bias

Inception date: May 2000

Management fee: 2.00%

Performance fee: 20% over benchmark

Hurdle rate:

Liquidity: Daily

Min. investment: $500

Benchmark: TSX

RRSP eligibility: Yes

Asset size: $1 million

NAV: $10.72

Early red'n period:

Early red'n fee:

High-water mark:

Redemption notice:

Max. leverage:

(Not available in YK, NWT, NUV)

PERFORMANCE (AS OF DECEMBER 31, 2002)

	1 month	3 month	6 month	YTD	1 year	2 year	3 year	5 year	10 year	Since Inception
Fund:	3.46%	-11.98%	-13.97%	-2.71%	-2.71%	5.23%				2.84%
TSX	0.67%	7.03%	-7.43%	-13.97%	-13.97%	-13.96%				12.21%

	Year:		Jan	Feb	Mar	Apr	May	Jun	Jul	Aug	Sep	Oct	Nov	Dec
Fund:	2002	-2.71%	0.09%	0.41%	1.95%	0.30%	11.40%	-1.21%	-2.88%	1.35%	-0.71%	-6.58%	-8.93%	3.46%
TSX	2002	-13.97%	-0.52%	-0.14%	2.80%	-2.40%	-0.10%	-6.67%	-7.56%	0.10%	-6.53%	1.11%	5.15%	0.67%
Fund:	2001	13.82%	-3.38%	6.79%	6.06%	-1.95%	-0.10%	-0.90%	5.14%	7.86%	3.66%	-2.71%	-0.75%	-5.60%
TSX	2001	-13.94%	4.35%	-13.34%	-5.83%	4.45%	2.71%	-5.21%	-0.60%	-3.78%	-7.58%	0.69%	7.84%	3.54%
Fund:	2000	-3.25%				0.00%	2.10%	-10.93%	0.31%	-1.03%	-4.04%	2.05%	4.43%	4.79%
TSX	2000	-5.58%				-1.21%	-1.02%	10.20%	2.07%	8.09%	-7.74%	-7.12%	-8.50%	1.29%

PERFORMANCE COMPARISON

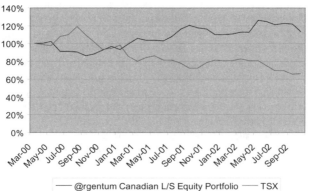

—— @rgentum Canadian L/S Equity Portfolio —— TSX

RISK DATA (AS OF DECEMBER 31, 2002)

Alpha: 0.00%	Benchmark: TSX
Beta: -0.39	Correlation to benchmark: -45.56
St. deviation (annualized): 16.76%	Maximum drawdown: 21.29%
St. deviation (1 year): 17.50%	Largest monthly drop: 10.93%
Sharpe Ratio: 15.81	Percentage of negative months: 45.45%
Sortino Ratio:	Percentage of positive months: 54.55%

NAGY-BECK HEDGE RATING:

@RGENTUM MARKET NEUTRAL PORTFOLIO (POOLED)

@rgentum Management
and Research Corp.
1555 Peel Street, Suite 1201
Montreal, PQ • H3A 3L8

Telephone Number: (514) 288-1262
Fax Number: (514) 288-1265
Toll-Free: 1-877-274-3688
Web Site: www.argentum.com

PORTFOLIO MANAGER(S)

Andre Chabot, Manager

Andre Chabot, president of ChabotPage Investments Counsel of Montreal, is managing the fund's investments. He produced solid positive results in several funds in 2001, and was one of Canada's top hedge fund managers in that year. Chabot has been the subject of numerous national reports for successful fund management.

FUND DESCRIPTION

The investment objective of the fund is to provide consistent and above-average long-term growth regardless of the general direction of the stock market by taking both long positions (anticipating an increase in the price of the stock) and short positions (anticipating a decrease in the price of the stock) in selected large and medium capitalization US corporations having market capitalization averaging US $5 billion and trading on recognized markets and international large-cap companies. These investments may include certain derivative instruments upon the manager or portfolio manager complying with applicable regulatory requirements.

TERMS AND CONDITIONS

Fund style: Stock Selection

Sub-style: No Bias	**RRSP eligibility:** Yes (Foreign Content)
Inception date: May 1998	**Asset size:** $2 million
Management fee: 2.00%	**NAV:** $7.06
Performance fee: 20% over cumulative benchmark	**Early red'n period:**
Hurdle rate:	**Early red'n fee:**
Liquidity: Daily	**High-water mark:**
* Min. investment: $150,000	**Redemption notice:**
Benchmark: S&P 500	**Max. leverage:**

* or less based on provincial legislation (not available in YK, NWT, NUV)

PERFORMANCE (AS OF DECEMBER 31, 2002)

	1 month	3 month	6 month	YTD	1 year	2 year	3 year	5 year	10 year	Since Inception
Fund:	-0.78%	-12.67%	-9.20%	-15.15%	-15.15%	-10.60%	-7.13%			-6.03%
S&P 500	-5.48%	7.42%	-7.07%	-23.14%	-23.14%	-15.15%	-12.23%			-1.62%

	Year:	Jan	Feb	Mar	Apr	May	Jun	Jul	Aug	Sep	Oct	Nov	Dec
Fund:	2002	-15.15%	1.54%	-2.69%	-0.48%	0.45%	-4.02%	-1.43%	1.01%	-0.68%	3.64%	-9.32%	-2.94%	0.78%
S&P 500	2002	-23.14%	-1.70%	-1.16%	3.33%	-7.67%	-3.25%	-7.77%	-3.73%	0.98%	-9.25%	6.85%	6.36%	-5.48%
Fund:	2001	-5.81%	1.34%	6.65%	8.67%	-7.61%	-3.59%	-0.48%	1.15%	0.26%	-3.50%	-4.03%	-3.67%	-0.01%
S&P 500	2001	-6.33%	3.51%	-6.78%	-3.95%	4.99%	0.87%	-3.94%	0.27%	-5.18%	-6.42%	2.50%	6.63%	2.16%
Fund:	2000	0.22%	-0.63%	0.92%	1.83%	-1.53%	2.13%	-1.67%	0.64%	-0.83%	0.26%	3.34%	1.46%	-5.41%
S&P 500	2000	-6.07%	-5.31%	-1.70%	9.80%	-0.87%	-1.01%	1.34%	-1.17%	5.20%	-3.27%	0.85%	0.93%	-9.72%
Fund:	1999	-26.25%	3.38%	-0.84%	-3.37%	-5.47%	-3.86%	-5.76%	7.22%	-0.01%	-8.96%	-0.63%	-4.31%	-6.33%
S&P 500	1999	14.73%	2.85%	-3.27%	4.00%	0.32%	-1.19%	4.73%	-0.18%	-1.47%	-4.37%	6.56%	2.29%	4.19%
Fund:	1998	27.30%				0.40%	-0.20%	1.00%	8.20%	3.56%	0.18%	0.62%	11.37%
S&P 500	1998	19.45%				0.05%	4.78%	2.05%	-11.44%	3.91%	9.00%	5.39%	5.56%

PERFORMANCE COMPARISON

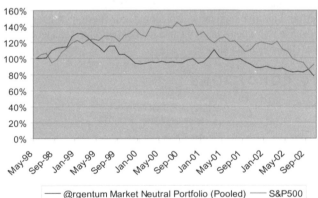

— @rgentum Market Neutral Portfolio (Pooled) —— S&P500

RISK DATA (AS OF DECEMBER 31, 2002)

Alpha:	Benchmark: S&P 500
Beta: -0.20	Correlation to benchmark: -22.98
St. deviation (annualized): 14.34%	Maximum drawdown: 19.43%
St. deviation (1 year):	Largest monthly drop: 9.32%
St. deviation (2 year):	Percentage of negative months: 56.36%
Sharpe Ratio: 0.42	Percentage of positive months: 43.64%
Sortino Ratio:	

NAGY-BECK HEDGE RATING:

@RGENTUM US MARKET NEUTRAL PORTFOLIO

@rgentum Management
and Research Corp.
1555 Peel Street, Suite 1201
Montreal, PQ • H3A 3L8

Telephone Number: (514) 288-1262
Fax Number: (514) 288-1265
Toll-Free: 1-877-274-3688
Web Site: www.argentum.com

PORTFOLIO MANAGER(S)

Andre Chabot, Manager

Andre Chabot, president of ChabotPage Investments Counsel of Montreal, is managing the fund's investments. He produced solid positive results in several funds in 2001, and was one of Canada's top hedge fund managers in that year. Chabot has been the subject of numerous national reports for successful fund management.

FUND DESCRIPTION

The US Market Neutral Portfolio seeks to provide consistent long-term growth through capital appreciation while maintaining minimal portfolio exposure to general equity market risk by holding equivalent positions in both a long and a short portfolio of securities. This investment objective will be met regardless of the general direction of the stock market by taking equivalent long positions (anticipating an increase in the price of the stock) and short positions (anticipating a decrease in the price of the stock). The objective of the US Market Neutral Portfolio is to maintain the long portfolio and short portfolio on a 50/50 basis. It will take positions in mainly selected large- and medium-market-capitalization US corporations (over US$1 billion dollars) trading on recognized U.S. markets.

TERMS AND CONDITIONS

Fund Style: Stock Selection

Sub-style: No Bias	**Min. investment:** $500	**Early red'n period:**
Inception date: May 2000	**Benchmark:** S&P 500	**Early red'n fee:**
Management fee: 2.00%	**RRSP eligibility:** Yes (Foreign content)	**High-water mark:**
Performance fee:	**Asset size:** $0.1 million	**Redemption notice:**
Hurdle rate:	**NAV:** $4.47	**Max. leverage:**
Liquidity: Daily		

(Not available in YK, NWT, NUV)

PERFORMANCE (AS OF DECEMBER 31, 2002)

	1 month	3 month	6 month	YTD	1 year	2 year	3 year	5 year	10 year	Since Inception
Fund:	0.75%	-15.97%	-13.07%	-24.65%	-24.65%	-25.38%				-21.71%
S&P500	-5.48%	7.42%	-7.07%	-23.14%	-23.14%	-15.15%				-14.07%

Year:	Jan	Feb	Mar	Apr	May	Jun	Jul	Aug	Sep	Oct	Nov	Dec
Fund: 2002	-24.65%	0.20%	-7.22%	-4.06%	0.28%	-5.93%	3.02%	2.11%	-0.76%	2.09%	-10.70%	-6.60%	0.75%
S&P500 2002	-23.14%	-1.70%	-1.16%	3.33%	-7.67%	-3.25%	-7.77%	-3.73%	-0.98%	-9.25%	6.85%	6.36%	-5.48%
Fund: 2001	-26.10%	-4.03%	4.97%	8.78%	-12.75%	-1.92%	0.19%	-0.03%	-1.37%	-3.97%	-5.13%	-7.30%	-5.54%
S&P500 2001	-6.33%	3.51%	-6.78%	-3.95%	4.99%	0.87%	-3.94%	0.27%	-5.18%	-6.42%	2.50%	6.63%	2.16%
Fund: 2000	-6.51%				1.30%	0.66%	0.32%	-0.59%	2.93%	4.12%	0.22%	-14.40%
S&P500 2000	-7.29%				-1.01%	1.34%	-1.17%	5.20%	-3.27%	0.85%	0.93%	-9.72%

PERFORMANCE COMPARISON

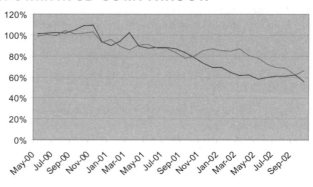

——— Argentum US Market Neutral Portfolio ——— S&P500

RISK DATA (AS OF DECEMBER 31, 2002):

Alpha: -0.02%

Beta: -0.49

St. Deviation (annualized): 31.45%

St. Deviation (1 year):

St. Deviation (2 year):

Sharpe Ratio: -0.70

Sortino Ratio:

Benchmark: S&P 500

Correlation to benchmark: -25.20

Maximum drawdown: 43.26%

Largest monthly drop: 14.40%

Percentage of negative months: 53.13%

Percentage of positive months: 46.88%

NAGY-BECK HEDGE RATING:

ARROW ASCENDANT ARBITRAGE FUND

Arrow Hedge Partners Inc.　　　Telephone Number: (416) 323-0477
111 Queen Street East, Suite 502　Fax Number: (416) 323-3199
Toronto, ON • M5C 1S1　　　　Toll-Free: 1-877-327-6048
　　　　　　　　　　　　　　Web Site: www.arrowhedge.com
Similar funds: Ascendant Limited Partnership

PORTFOLIO MANAGER(S)

David Jarvis and Rick Kung, Advisers

The fund is advised by David Jarvis, CFA, and Rick Kung, CFA, of Ascendant Capital Management Inc., which is an asset management company based in Toronto. The fund is a market-neutral arbitrage fund designed to generate absolute returns independent of market direction. Specifically, the fund will participate in merger arbitrage, volatility arbitrage, and special situation arbitrage in Canada and the United States.

David Jarvis began his investment career at Capital Group Securities Limited, eventually being promoted to vice president and director, secretary-treasurer. Prior to establishing Ascendant Capital Management, Jarvis was founder and senior vice president and director of the Equity Derivatives Group at Midland Walwyn Capital Inc. (now Merrill Lynch Canada Inc.).

Rick Kung began his investment career as a senior treasury analyst at Nesbitt Burns. Kung was vice president, equities markets, with Merrill Lynch International/Midland Walwyn (U.K.) Limited. Previously, he was vice president of the Capital Markets Risk Management Group at Midland Walwyn Capital Inc.

FUND DESCRIPTION

The Arrow Ascendant Arbitrage Fund is a market-neutral arbitrage fund that focuses on strategies that are independent of stock market movements. Combined with Ascendant's risk management programs, the fund should generate consistent positive absolute returns uncorrelated to major market indices. The fund also has the following characteristics:

- Fund participates in merger arbitrage
- Fund participates in special situation arbitrage
- Leverage portfolio assets to a maximum of 3:1
- Options strategies are employed primarily from a risk management perspective within the merger arbitrage strategy. Option strategies are also used in volatility arbitrage transactions by definition.

TERMS AND CONDITIONS

Fund style: Relative Value

Sub-style: Merger Arbitrage

Inception date: January 2002

Management fee: 2.25%

Performance fee: 20%

Hurdle rate: 0%

Liquidity: Weekly

*Min. investment: $150,000

Benchmark: S&P 500

* or less based on provincial legislation

RRSP eligibility: Yes (Foreign Content)

Asset size: $6 million

NAV: $9.97

Early red'n period: 6 months

Early red'n fee: 5%

High-water mark: Yes

Redemption notice:

Max. leverage: 300%

PERFORMANCE (AS OF DECEMBER 31, 2002)

(From November 1999 through December 2001, performance is for the Ascendant Capital LP net of performance fees. Returns from January 2002 are gross of performance fees for the Arrow Ascendant Fund, a fund advised by Ascendant Capital Management Inc.)

	1 month	3 month	6 month	YTD	1 year	2 year	3 year	5 year	10 year	Since Inception
Fund:	2.10%	-2.51%	-1.44%	-0.26%	-0.26%	5.14%	9.76%			10.52%
S&P500	-5.48%	7.42%	-7.07%	-23.14%	-23.14%	-15.15%	-12.23%			-9.83%

	Year:	Jan	Feb	Mar	Apr	May	Jun	Jul	Aug	Sep	Oct	Nov	Dec
Fund:	2002	-0.26%	0.40%	-0.70%	0.90%	0.10%	0.70%	-0.20%	0.00%	0.30%	0.80%	0.40%	-4.90%	2.10%
S&P500	2002	-23.14%	-1.70%	-1.16%	3.33%	-7.67%	-3.25%	-7.77%	-3.73%	-0.98%	-9.25%	6.85%	6.36%	-5.48%
Fund:	2001	10.83%	2.00%	1.80%	1.50%	0.40%	2.10%	0.60%	1.70%	0.80%	-1.70%	0.90%	-0.60%	0.90%
S&P500	2001	-6.33%	3.51%	-6.78%	-3.95%	4.99%	0.87%	-3.94%	0.27%	-5.18%	-6.42%	2.50%	6.63%	2.16%
Fund:	2000	19.62%	6.20%	-2.10%	5.80%	5.00%	1.10%	1.90%	-2.60%	0.10%	-0.90%	0.60%	2.00%	1.40%
S&P500	2000	-6.07%	-5.31%	-1.70%	9.80%	-0.87%	-1.01%	1.34%	-1.17%	5.20%	-3.27%	0.85%	0.93%	-9.72%
Fund:	1999	3.82%											0.50%	3.30%
S&P500	1999	6.58%											2.29%	4.19%

PERFORMANCE COMPARISON

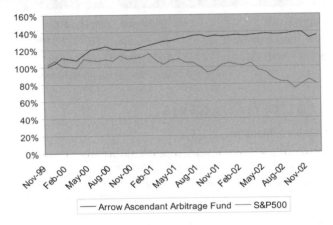

——— Arrow Ascendant Arbitrage Fund ——— S&P500

RISK DATA (AS OF DECEMBER 31, 2002)

Alpha:

Beta:

St. deviation (annualized): 7.10%

St. deviation (1 year):

St. deviation (2 year):

Sharpe Ratio: 0.96

Sortino Ratio:

Benchmark: S&P 500

Correlation to benchmark: 0.03

Maximum drawdown: 4.90%

Largest monthly drop: 4.90%

Percentage of negative months: 20.51%

Percentage of positive months: 79.49%

NAGY-BECK HEDGE RATING:

ARROW ELKHORN US LONG-SHORT FUND

Arrow Hedge Funds
111 Queen Street East, Suite 502
Toronto, ON • M5C 1S1

Telephone Number: (416) 323-0477
Fax Number: (416) 323-3199
Toll-Free: 1-877-327-6048
Web Site: www.arrowhedge.com

PORTFOLIO MANAGER(S)

Robert Sanborn, Manager

Mr. Robert Sanborn has over 20 years' experience in portfolio management and investment analysis and has been a strong and consistent proponent of value investing. Before co-founding Sanborn Kilkollin Partners in June 2001, Sanborn was the portfolio manager of the Oakmark Fund, the flagship mutual fund of Harris Associates from its launch in August 1991 through March 2000. In 1998, Lipper Inc. ranked Oakmark in the top 10% of value mutual funds, and *Barron's* named Sanborn the 1997 Fund Manager of the Year. Sanborn holds a BA from Dartmouth College and an MBA from the University of Chicago.

FUND DESCRIPTION

The Arrow Elkhorn US Long/Short Fund is an investment fund offered only to sophisticated investors, managed by Arrow Hedge Partners Inc. This U.S. long/short equity fund is advised by Sanborn Kilcollin Partners LLC based in Chicago, Illinois. The objective of the fund is to achieve superior capital appreciation with volatility below that of the S&P 500. The manager invests primarily in U.S.-listed highly liquid large and mid-capitalization stocks. The manager follows a "bottom-up" value investing strategy and selects both long and short securities using fundamental analysis.

TERMS AND CONDITIONS

Fund style: Stock Selection

Sub-style: Long Bias

Inception date: July 2002

Management fee: 2.50%

Performance fee: 20%

Hurdle rate: 0%

Liquidity: Weekly

*Min. investment: $150,000

Benchmark: S&P 500

* or less based on provincial legislation

RRSP eligibility: No

Asset size: $3.5 million

NAV:

Early red'n period: 6 months

Early red'n fee: 5%

High-water mark:

Redemption notice:

Max. leverage: 160%

PERFORMANCE (AS OF DECEMBER 31, 2002)

	1 month	3 month	6 month	YTD	1 year	2 year	3 year	5 year	10 year	Since Inception
Fund:	-2.00%	4.62%	-3.15%	14.87%	14.87%					13.16%
S&P500	-5.48%	7.42%	-7.07%	-23.14%	-23.14%					-16.46%

Year:		Jan	Feb	Mar	Apr	May	Jun	Jul	Aug	Sep	Oct	Nov	Dec
Fund:	2002	14.87%	2.80%	6.70%	2.60%	2.50%	1.60%	1.20%	-2.70%	3.30%	-7.90%	1.00%	5.70%	-2.00%
S&P500	2002	-23.14%	-1.70%	-1.16%	3.33%	-7.67%	-3.25%	-7.77%	-3.73%	-0.98%	-9.25%	6.85%	6.36%	-5.48%
Fund:	2001	4.80%							2.10%	6.70%	-5.30%	2.40%	-0.50%	-0.30%
S&P500	2001	-0.66%							0.27%	-5.18%	-6.42%	2.50%	6.63%	2.16%

PERFORMANCE COMPARISON

(Performance is in USD for the units of the Elkhorn Fund, LLC net of all fees since July 2, 2001 through August 31, 2002. The returns from September 1, 2002 are gross of performance fees for the Arrow Elkhorn U.S. Fund.)

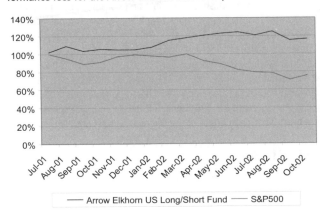

—— Arrow Elkhorn US Long/Short Fund —— S&P500

RISK DATA (AS OF DECEMBER 31, 2002)

Alpha:	Benchmark: S&P 500
Beta:	Correlation to benchmark: 0.43
St. deviation (annualized): 13.30%	Maximum drawdown: 7.90%
St. deviation (1 year):	Largest monthly drop: 7.90%
St. deviation (2 year):	Percentage of negative months: 33.33%
Sharpe Ratio: 0.73	Percentage of positive months: 66.67%
Sortino Ratio:	

NAGY-BECK HEDGE RATING:

ARROW MILFORD CAPITAL FUND

Arrow Hedge Partners Inc.   Telephone Number: (416) 323-0477
111 Queen Street East, Suite 502   Fax Number: (416) 323-3199
Toronto, ON • M5C 1S1   Toll-Free: 1-877-327-6048
                                      Web Site: www.arrowhedge.com

PORTFOLIO MANAGER(S)

Christopher D.J. Currie, CFA President and Portfolio Manager

Milford Capital Management Inc. (Milford Capital) is a Canadian-based investment adviser specializing in the management of high-yield bonds. Milford Capital was incorporated in June 2001 and is a portfolio manager, investment counsellor, and a limited market dealer. Milford Capital maintains its office in Toronto.

Christopher Currie began specializing in the high-yield bond market in 1986 with the Ontario Municipal Employees Retirement Board (O.M.E.R.S.), where he was a portfolio manager for private equity and high-yield bonds. He joined investment dealer CIBC World Markets in 1992 where he established Canada's first corporate bond research group. This group was awarded subsequent number 1 rankings by institutional investors and managers as surveyed by Greenwich Associates. Prior to forming Milford Capital Management Inc., Currie was a vice president at TAL Global Asset Management Inc. At TAL he was responsible for strategy and management of several high-yield bond portfolios which totalled over $450 million. His extensive experience includes over 15 years of specializing in high-yield and corporate bond research and portfolio management.

As Milford Capital Management Inc. president, Currie is primarily responsible for research, trading, and portfolio management of the Milford Capital Fund, LP.

FUND DESCRIPTION

Milford Capital Management Inc. (Milford Capital) will actively manage a portfolio of both long and short security holdings, adjusting this long/short ratio to the current or anticipated investment environment. Individual security selection is based on bottom-up, fundamental research and analysis which will ultimately determine the long/short ratio of the portfolio.

Milford Capital will not attempt to forecast future changes in the economic environment; rather, the strategy is to focus on individual industry groups and specific companies within these groups. Security selection is ratio based with qualitative additions such as quality and consistency of management, acquisition strategy, quality of assets, and rating agency views.

The fund's primary source of hedging will be accomplished through the construction of a diverse portfolio of 25 to 30 positions. In addition, individual shorts will be initiated as a result of intensive research with the expectation of reducing volatility and adding potential capital gains.

The fund's average holding period is expected to range between one and three years.

The fund will seek opportunities in all areas of the U.S. bond market with a particular emphasis on corporate high-yield issues.

TERMS AND CONDITIONS

Fund style: Specialist Credit
Sub-style: Distressed Securities
Inception date: January 2002
Management fee: 2.25%
Performance fee: 20%
Hurdle rate: 0%
Liquidity: Weekly
* or less based on provincial legislation

* Min. investment: $150,000
Benchmark: ML High Yield Index
RRSP eligibility: Yes (Foreign content)
Asset size: $4 million
NAV:

Early red'n period: 6 months
Early red'n fee: 5%
High-water mark: Yes
Redemption notice:
Max. leverage: 300%

PERFORMANCE (AS OF DECEMBER 31, 2002)

(From January 2002, performance is for the Arrow Milford Capital Class "A" Fund before performance fees.)

	1 month	3 month	6 month	YTD	1 year	2 year	3 year	5 year	10 year	Since Inception
Fund:	2.00%	1.58%	-1.07%	4.15%	4.15%					4.15%
ML High Yld Idx	n/a	n/a	n/a	-2.70%						-2.70%

Year:		Jan	Feb	Mar	Apr	May	Jun	Jul	Aug	Sep	Oct	Nov	Dec
Fund:	2002	4.15%	0.30%	-0.80%	4.30%	3.30%	-0.70%	-1.10%	-2.20%	1.00%	-1.40%	-1.40%	1.00%	2.00%
ML High Yld Idx	2002	0.00%											

PERFORMANCE COMPARISON

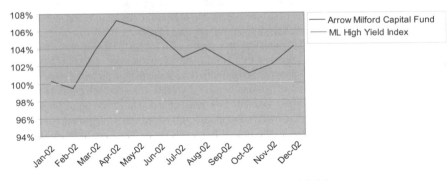

RISK DATA (AS OF DECEMBER 31, 2002)

Alpha:
Beta:
St. deviation (annualized): 7.00%
St. deviation (1 year): 7.00%
St. deviation (2 year):

Sharpe Ratio: 0.12
Sortino Ratio:
Benchmark: ML High Yield Index
Correlation to S&P 500: 0.13

Maximum drawdown: 5.70%
Largest monthly drop: 2.20%
Percentage of negative months: 50.00%
Percentage of positive months: 50.00%

NAGY-BECK HEDGE RATING:

ARROW GLOBAL LONG/SHORT FUND

Arrow Hedge Partners Inc.
111 Queen Street East, Suite 502
Toronto, ON • M5C 1S1

Telephone Number: (416) 323-0477
Fax Number: (416) 323-3199
Toll-Free: 1-877-327-6048
Web Site: www.arrowhedge.com

Similar funds:
Arrow Global Long/Short Fund, RSP
Arrow Global Long/Short Fund, US$

PORTFOLIO MANAGER(S)

Multi-manager Fund of Hedge Funds

ARROW WF ASIA FUND:
Asian long/short equity fund

ARROW CLOCKTOWER PLANTINUM FUND:
Global Market Neutral long/short

GlOBAL ENSO CAPITAL FUND:
Global long/short equity

ARROW ELKHORN U.S. FUND:
U.S. long/short equity

ARROW GOODWOOD FUND:
Canadian long/short equity

ARROW EPIC CAPITAL FUND:
Canadian long/short equity

FUND DESCRIPTION

The Arrow Global Long/Short Fund currently includes six Arrow single-manager funds where the allocation to each fund is generally in line with the MSCI World Index weightings to create a truly global portfolio with regional specialists. The Arrow Multi-Manager Funds are committed to providing their clients with access to broadly diversified equity hedge or long/short portfolios that are diversified by manager, investment style, and regional focus. Multi-manager hedge funds are considered the preferred entry route for institutional investors and high-net-worth individuals. The approach offers an effective way for an investor to gain exposure to a range of hedge funds through a single investment without having to commit substantial assets or resources to individual hedge fund selection. The objective of the fund is to exceed the performance of the MSCI World Index with less volatility. Additional benefits are as follows:

• Greater diversification than investing in an individual hedge fund

• Accessing multiple hedge fund managers through a single investment allows for lower capital.

TERMS AND CONDITIONS

Fund style: Multi-Manager Fund of Long/Short Equity Funds

Sub-style:	*** Min. investment:** $150,000	**Early red'n period:** 6 months
Inception date: July 2001	**Benchmark:** MSCI World Index	**Early red'n fee:** 5%
Management fee: 2.50%	**RRSP eligibility:** No	**High-water mark:** Yes

Performance fee: 20%
Hurdle rate: 0%
Liquidity: Weekly
* or less based on provincial legislation

Asset size: $16 million
NAV: $8.89

Redemption notice:
Max. leverage:

PERFORMANCE (AS OF DECEMBER 31, 2002)

	1 month	3 month	6 month	YTD	1 year	2 year	3 year	5 year	10 year	Since Inception
Fund:	-0.60%	-1.01%	-8.18%	-11.81%	-11.81%					-7.59%
MSCI World Idx	-4.83%	7.74%	-11.97%	-19.55%	-19.55%					-17.42%

Year:		Jan	Feb	Mar	Apr	May	Jun	Jul	Aug	Sep	Oct	Nov	Dec
Fund:	2002	-11.81%	-0.10%	-1.00%	0.90%	-0.30%	-1.60%	-1.90%	-3.30%	-3.20%	-0.90%	-1.50%	1.10%	-0.60%
MSCI	2002	-19.55%	-3.02%	-0.85%	4.44%	-3.36%	0.23%	-6.05%	-8.42%	0.21%	-10.97%	7.40%	5.41%	-4.83%
Fund:	2001	0.74%							-2.60%	1.30%	-0.80%	1.00%	0.20%	1.70%
MSCI	2001	-6.72%							-1.26%	-4.67%	-8.80%	1.93%	5.93%	0.64%

PERFORMANCE COMPARISON

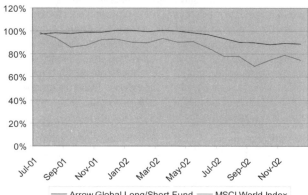

—— Arrow Global Long/Short Fund —— MSCI World Index

RISK DATA (AS OF DECEMBER 31, 2002):

Alpha:	**Sharpe Ratio:**	**Maximum drawdown:** 12.20%
Beta:	**Sortino Ratio:**	**Largest monthly drop:** 3.30%
St. deviation (annualized): 5.30%	**Benchmark:** MSCI World Index	**Percentage of negative months:** 55.56%
St. deviation (1 year):	**Correlation to benchmark:** 0.37	**Percentage of positive months:** 44.44%
St. deviation (2 year):		

NAGY-BECK HEDGE RATING:

ARROW MULTI-STRATEGY FUND

Arrow Hedge Partners Inc.   Telephone Number: (416) 323-0477
111 Queen Street East, Suite 502   Fax Number: (416) 323-3199
Toronto, ON • M5C 1S1   Toll-Free: 1-877-327-6048
                                        Web site: www.arrowhedge.com
Similar funds:
Arrow Multi-Strategy, US$
Arrow RSP Multi-Strategy

PORTFOLIO MANAGER(S)

The Arrow Multi-Strategy Fund allocates assets to all single-manager hedge funds managed by Arrow Hedge Partners. The fund is managed by Arrow Hedge Partners.

FUND DESCRIPTION

Arrow Multi-Strategy Fund currently allocates to 13 Arrow funds, including long/short, merger arbitrage, risk arbitrage, volatility arbitrage, high yield bonds, and global macro. The Arrow Multi-Manager Funds are committed to providing our clients with access to funds that are broadly diversified by manager, investment strategy, investment style, and regional focus. Multi-manager hedge funds are considered the preferred entry route for institutional investors and high-net-worth individuals. The approach offers an effective way for an investor to gain exposure to a range of hedge funds through a single investment without having to commit substantial assets or resources to individual hedge fund selection. The objective of the fund is to achieve absolute returns with low volatility and low correlation to major market indices.

• Greater diversification than investing in an individual hedge fund
• Accessing multiple hedge fund managers through a single investment allows for lower capital outlay and simple administration.

TERMS AND CONDITIONS

Fund style: Fund of Funds
Sub-style: Well diversified across styles   **RRSP eligibility:** Foreign Content
Inception date: January 2002   **Asset size:** $8 million
Management fee: 2.50%   **NAV:** $8.90
Performance fee: 20%   **Early red'n period:** 6 months
Hurdle rate: 0%   **Early red'n fee:** 5%
Liquidity: Weekly   **High-water mark:** Yes
*Min. investment: $150,000   **Redemption notice:**
Benchmark: MSCI   **Max. leverage:**

* or less based on provincial legislation

PERFORMANCE (AS OF DECEMBER 31, 2002)

(Performance is net of all fees in CAD for the historical performance of the fund since July 2001 and for each of the underlying managers from January 2001 to June 2001.)

	1 month	3 month	6 month	YTD	1 year	2 year	3 year	5 year	10 year	Since Inception
Fund:	0.30%	0.20%	-2.29%	-2.70%	-2.70%					-2.70%
MSCI	-4.83%	7.74%	-11.97%	-19.55%	-19.55%					-19.55%

	Year:	Jan	Feb	Mar	Apr	May	Jun	Jul	Aug	Sep	Oct	Nov	Dec
Fund:	2002	-2.70%	0.10%	-0.80%	1.30%	0.60%	-0.50%	-1.10%	-1.70%	-0.60%	-0.20%	0.50%	-0.60%	0.30%
MSCI	2002	-19.55%	-3.02%	-0.85%	4.44%	-3.36%	0.23%	-6.05%	-8.42%	0.21%	-10.97%	7.40%	5.41%	-4.83%

PERFORMANCE COMPARISON

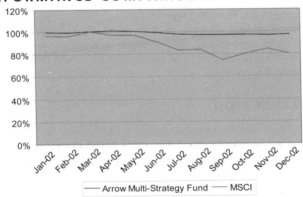

— Arrow Multi-Strategy Fund — MSCI

RISK DATA (AS OF DECEMBER 31, 2002)

Alpha:	Benchmark: MSCI
Beta:	Correlation to benchmark: 0.32
St. deviation (annualized): 2.90%	Maximum drawdown: 4.20%
St. deviation (1 year): 2.90%	Largest monthly drop: 1.70%
St. deviation (2 year):	Percentage of negative months: 58.33%
Sharpe Ratio:	Percentage of positive months: 41.67%
Sortino Ratio:	

NAGY-BECK HEDGE RATING:

ARROW WF ASIA FUND

Arrow Hedge Partners Inc.   Telephone Number: (416) 323-0477
111 Queen Street East, Suite 502   Fax Number: (416) 323-3199
Toronto, ON   Toll-Free: 1-877-327-6048
M5C 1S1   Web Site: www.arrowhedge.com

PORTFOLIO MANAGER(S)

Peter Ferry, Lead Manager
Prior to the establishment of Ward Ferry, Peter Ferry was fixed-income investment specialist and chief marketing officer at Lloyd George Management. Ferry has over 22 years of investment banking experience in equity research, institutional sales, and securities trading. He has spent the last 15 years in Asia.

Scobie Ward, Lead Hedge Fund Manager
Prior to establishing Ward Ferry, Ward was chief investment officer of Lloyd George Management. He was a founding director and responsible for managing several of Lloyd George Management's major accounts, including the LG Asian Smaller Companies Fund and the LG Asian PLUS Hedge Fund.

FUND DESCRIPTION

The manager invests in Asian companies that have strong fundamentals and superior management and are reasonably valued. The fund's objective is to achieve strong absolute returns with volatility below that of the MSCI Asia Pacific Free index.

The fund also has the following characteristics:

- Portfolio of 35 to 40 equities when fully invested
- Leverage portfolio assets to a maximum of 2:1
- Maintain short positions that are event driven and opportunistic
- On average, the fund is net invested between 60% and 70%.

TERMS AND CONDITIONS

Fund style: Stock Selection
Sub-style: Long Bias   **RRSP eligibility:** No
Inception date: February 2001   **Asset size:** $8 million
Management fee: 2.25%   **NAV:** $11.02
Performance fee: 20%   **Early red'n period:** 6 months
Hurdle rate: 0%   **Early red'n fee:** 5%
Liquidity: Weekly   **High-water mark:** Yes
*Min. investment: $150,000   **Redemption notice:**
Benchmark: MSCI Asia-Pacific   **Max. leverage:** 200%

* or less based on provincial legislation

PERFORMANCE (AS OF DECEMBER 31, 2002)

(From August 2001, performance is for the Arrow WF Asia Fund before performance fees. Prior returns are net of all fees and converted to CAD for the Ward Ferry Asia Fund Ltd., a fund advised by Ward Ferry domiciled in the Cayman Islands.)

	1 month	3 month	6 month	YTD	1 year	2 year	3 year	5 year	10 year	Since Inception
Fund:	-2.00%	-2.84%	-7.74%	-2.71%	-2.71%					
MSCI Asia-Pacific				-10.10%						

Year:		Jan	Feb	Mar	Apr	May	Jun	Jul	Aug	Sep	Oct	Nov	Dec
Fund:	2002	-2.71%	3.60%	1.50%	1.70%	3.20%	-2.00%	-2.50%	-0.10%	-3.70%	-1.30%	-2.80%	2.00%	-2.00%
MSCI Asia Pacific	2002	-10.10%											
Fund:	2001	26.19%		3.10%	1.40%	-0.30%	3.50%	0.40%	0.30%	4.70%	-2.30%	3.40%	5.60%	4.00%
MSCI Asia Pacific	2001	-20.60%											

PERFORMANCE COMPARISON

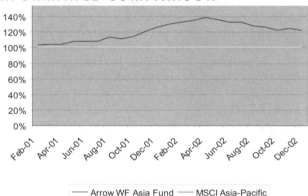

—— Arrow WF Asia Fund —— MSCI Asia-Pacific

RISK DATA (AS OF DECEMBER 31, 2002)

Alpha:	Sharpe Ratio: 0.83	Maximum drawdown: 11.80%
Beta:	Sortino Ratio:	Largest monthly drop: 3.70%
St. deviation (annualized): 9.40%	Benchmark: MSCI Asia-Pacific	Percentage of negative months: 39.13%
St. deviation (1 year):	Correlation to benchmark: 0.37	Percentage of positive months: 60.87%
St. deviation (2 year):		

NAGY-BECK HEDGE RATING:

ARROW CLOCKTOWER PLATINUM FUND

Arrow Hedge Partners Inc.
111 Queen Street East, Suite 502
Toronto, ON
M5C 1S1

Telephone Number: (416) 323-0477
Fax Number: (416) 323-3199
Toll-Free: 1-877-327-6048
Web Site: www.arrowhedge.com

PORTFOLIO MANAGER(S)

David M. Benwell, ClocktowerCapital, Managing Member

David Benwell has long-standing experience in the hedge fund business. He was one of four investment principals at Strome-Sunskind & Co. (a top performing hedge fund in 1993) with assets under management of $1 billion. More recently, Benwell was a principal at Rader Reinfrank & Co., a Los Angeles-based private equity fund (a predecessor of Clarity Partners). He formed the investment adviser in July 2001. Benwell has a Bachelor of Commerce (Honours) from Queen's University and an MBA from Stanford University.

Kerr Neilson, Managing Director

Kerr Neilson has some 30 years of experience in financial markets both in broking and funds management. This has involved a stint in London, followed by managing the research department for a stockbroker in South Africa. Upon migrating to Australia he joined Bankers Trust, where he made important contributions to the development of that company's highly successful retail funds management division. Kerr left Bankers Trust as an executive vice president to form Platinum Asset Management in February 1994, where he is the principal shareholder and the chief investment officer.

FUND DESCRIPTION

The Arrow Clocktower Platinum Global Fund is an investment fund offered only to sophisticated investors, managed by Arrow Hedge Partners Inc. This global long/short fund is advised by Clocktower Capital, LLC, based in Los Angeles and a North American affiliate of Platinum Asset Management of Sydney, Australia. The managing director of Clocktower Capital is David M. Benwell.

Platinum Asset Management is an Australia-based global equity fund manager, controlled by Kerr Neilson. A minority stake in Platinum is owned by the Soros Fund Management organization. Platinum was founded in February 1994 by a group of professionals who had established strong performance records with Bankers Trust Australia. Platinum Asset Management currently manages approximately US$3 billion of global equity products with a quarter of this amount from investors outside Australia.

Platinum Asset Management applies its unique stock selection methodology to the objective of achieving above-average returns for its clients. The emphasis of the organization is on managing clients' money rather than gathering funds under management.

The adviser's approach is to identify overlooked or out-of-favour situations in which

1. there is a significant difference between inherent business value and current market price and
2. there is a catalyst that will close the gap.

The fund also has the following characteristics:
- Portfolio of 60 to 80 equities when fully invested
- Leverage portfolio assets to a maximum of 2:1
- Maintain short positions that are fundamental but with a shorter time horizon
- On average, the fund is typically net long invested between 50% and 60%.

TERMS AND CONDITIONS

Fund style: Stock Selection
Sub-style: No Bias   * **Min. investment:** $150,000   **Early red'n period:** 6 months
Inception date: December 2002 **Benchmark:** MSCI   **Early red'n fee:** 5%
Management fee: 2.25%   **RRSP eligibility:** No   **High-water mark:** Yes
Performance fee: 20%   **Asset size (program):** US$325 million   **Redemption notice:**
Hurdle rate: 0%   **NAV:**   **Max. leverage:** 200%
Liquidity: Weekly
* or less based on provincial legislation

PERFORMANCE (AS OF DECEMBER 31, 2002)

(From June 1994 to November 2002, returns are net of all fees for the Platinum Fund Ltd., a fund advised by Platinum Asset Management.)

	1 month	3 month	6 month	YTD	1 year	2 year	3 year	5 year	10 year	Since Inception
Fund:	-0.80%	7.38%	-3.03%	10.09%	10.09%	11.10%	11.33%	17.89%		14.77%
MSCI	-4.83%	7.74%	-11.97%	-19.55%	-19.55%	-18.04%	-16.37%	-7.49%		4.75%

Year:	Year	Jan	Feb	Mar	Apr	May	Jun	Jul	Aug	Sep	Oct	Nov	Dec
Fund:	2002	10.09%	0.10%	3.60%	3.30%	2.80%	3.50%	-0.40%	-3.90%	0.50%	-6.50%	2.90%	5.20%	-0.80%
MSCI	2002	-19.55%	-3.02%	-0.85%	4.44%	-3.36%	0.23%	-6.05%	-8.42%	0.21%	-10.97%| 7.40%	5.41%	-4.83%
Fund:	2001	12.13%	6.50%	-1.00%	-3.40%	3.80%	-1.60%	-0.10%	-2.20%	4.40%	-3.70%	5.60%	3.50%	0.40%
MSCI	2001	-16.51%	2.00%	-8.43%	-6.61%	7.37%	-1.37%	-3.11%	-1.26%	-4.67%	-8.80%	1.93%	5.93%	0.64%
Fund	2000	11.79%	-2.70%	2.80%	-1.70%	-3.20%	1.40%	3.60%	-2.00%	2.40%	-1.50%	2.60%	4.70%	5.30%
MSCI	2000	-12.93%	-5.72%	0.28%	6.92%	-4.22%	-2.52%	3.38%	-2.80%	3.27%	-5.31%	-1.66%	-6.06%	1.63%
Fund:	1999	51.06%	-2.00%	-0.60%	4.30%	4.00%	-0.50%	9.00%	5.20%	0.00%	2.00%	1.90%	9.00%	10.60%
MSCI	1999	25.23%	2.19%	-2.65%	4.16%	3.97%	-3.67%	4.66%	-0.29%	-0.17%	-0.96%	5.21%	2.82%	8.11%
Fund:	1998	9.24%	4.50%	1.80%	5.00%	1.90%	1.60%	-3.50%	1.40%	-5.10%	-3.00%	1.80%	1.90%	1.10%
MSCI	1998	24.83%	2.82%	6.78%	4.23%	0.99%	-1.25%	2.38%	-0.14%	-13.32%	1.80%	9.07%	5.97%	4.90%
Fund:	1997	5.12%	2.00%	2.80%	0.60%	0.40%	3.20%	3.40%	3.30%	-5.40%	2.80%	-6.00%	-0.90%	-0.60%
MSCI	1997	16.10%	1.24%	1.15%	-1.99%	3.29%	6.19%	5.01%	4.63%	-6.76%	5.45%	-5.24%	1.77%	1.23%

	Year													
Fund:	1996	4.71%	3.50%	0.70%	0.40%	4.20%	-0.40%	-0.10%	-4.40%	-0.40%	0.70%	-1.70%	2.30%	0.10%
MSCI	1996	14.04%	1.88%	0.62%	1.67%	2.36%	0.09%	0.54%	-3.53%	1.19%	3.93%	0.69%	5.64%	-1.57%
Fund:	1995	15.40%	-2.10%	1.00%	0.60%	4.00%	1.50%	2.60%	5.50%	1.40%	-0.80%	-2.50%	1.00%	2.50%
MSCI	1995	21.37%	-1.50%	1.50%	4.84%	3.51%	0.91%	-0.02%	5.02%	-2.22%	2.95%	-1.55%	3.49%	2.94%
Fund:	1994	12.79%						1.40%	1.04%	1.53%	1.67%	2.37%	1.74%	2.40%
MSCI	1994	1.39%						-0.27%	1.93%	3.04%	-2.61%	2.88%	-4.32%	0.97%

PERFORMANCE COMPARISON

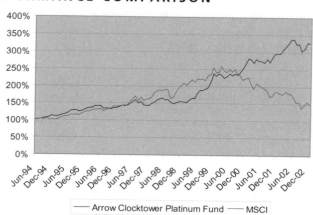

Arrow Clocktower Platinum Fund ——— MSCI

RISK DATA (AS OF DECEMBER 31, 2002)

Alpha:

Beta:

St. deviation (annualized): 10.90%

St. deviation (1 year):

St. deviation (2 year):

Sharpe Ratio: 0.94

Sortino Ratio:

Benchmark: MSCI

Correlation to S&P 500: 0.61

Maximum drawdown: 10.10%

Largest monthly drop: 6.50%

Percentage of negative months: 33.01%

Percentage of positive months: 66.99%

NAGY-BECK HEDGE RATING:

BDC MANAGED FUTURES NOTE SERIES N-2

Tricycle Asset Management Corp.
2345 Yonge Street, Suite 601
Toronto, ON • M4P 2E5

Telephone Number: (416) 440-7990
Fax Number: (416) 440-7989
Toll-Free: 1-800-315-5298
Web Site: www.3-wheeler.com

Similar funds:
BDC Managed Futures Note Series N-3   BDC Managed Futures Note Series N-4
BDC Managed Futures Note Series N-5   BDC Managed Futures Note Series N-6
BDC Managed Futures Note Series N-7

PORTFOLIO MANAGER(S)

John Hock, Altrinsic Global Advisers

Fred Hirshfeld, Manager

Fred Hirshfeld is responsible for marketing, implementation, and overall risk evaluation. For two decades he has held senior positions in commodities, futures, and money management, and is a frequent guest lecturer on managed futures and derivatives in various North American venues. He also served on the Derivative Committee of the Investment Dealers Association, where he helped draft policies. Hirshfeld was vice president and director of Nesbitt Burns Managed Futures Corp., a related company of Nesbitt Burns Inc.

Jan Holland, CA, Manager

Jan Holland is responsible for research, structuring, marketing, and implementation. His experience in tax, accounting, financial consultation, and research and development of proprietary trading programs is invaluable to NB MANFU. He is a frequent speaker on the subjects of managed futures and derivatives, and has also helped draft policies for the Derivative Committee of the Investment Dealers Association. Holland was vice president and director of Nesbitt Burns Managed Futures Corp., a related company of Nesbitt Burns Inc.

Robert Bourgeois, Manager

Rob Bourgeois is responsible for overall operations and product development. He has held senior management positions for Nesbitt Burns Inc. in domestic and non-North American fixed income, as well as debt capital markets. Bourgeois, a member of the Nesbitt Burns Advisory Board, brings to his leadership position extensive capital markets experience including trading, sales, origination, underwriting, and structuring. Bourgeois was president and CEO of Nesbitt Burns Managed Futures Corp., a related company of Nesbitt Burns Inc.

FUND DESCRIPTION

Managed futures is the use of professional futures traders who specialize in trading in the commodities and futures markets. Institutional investors, such as pension funds, have been investing in managed futures for more than 10 years to help balance and diversify their portfolios. Managed futures notes provide a way for individual investors to take advantage of the potential returns of the futures market without risking loss of their capital investment. Managed futures can be defined as the investing in futures contracts by professional futures traders who trade in global futures markets, as either buyers or sellers of real assets such as gold, silver, wheat, corn, crude oil, and natural gas—as well as financial assets such as government bonds and currencies.

Tricycle Assest Management's current series N-7A guarantees the initial principal plus 8% in 7 years and 10 months. Investors are also provided by any upside of the managed futures program.

TERMS AND CONDITIONS

Fund style: CTA

Sub-style:	Min. investment: $2,000	Early red'n period:
Inception date: August 2000	Benchmark: TSX	Early red'n fee: 4% (In the first year after two years.)
Management fee: 4.50%	RRSP eligibility: Yes	High-water mark: Yes
Performance fee: 22.5%	Asset size: $20 million	Redemption notice:
Hurdle rate: 0%	NAV: $133.83	Max. leverage:
Liquidity: Semi-annual after a two-year hold		

PERFORMANCE (AS OF DECEMBER 31, 2002)

	1 month	3 month	6 month	YTD	1 year	2 year	3 year	5 year	10 year	Since Inception
Fund:	3.14%	-1.20%	10.00%	15.11%	15.11%	5.72%				13.83%
TSX	0.67%	7.03%	-7.43%	-13.97%	-13.97%	-13.96%				-18.15%

	Year:		Jan	Feb	Mar	Apr	May	Jun	Jul	Aug	Sep	Oct	Nov	Dec
Fund:	2002	15.11%	0.06%	-2.52%	-4.00%	-1.00%	4.57%	7.95%	5.66%	3.05%	2.26%	-2.85%	-1.40%	3.14%
TSX	2002	-13.97%	-0.52%	-0.14%	2.80%	-2.40%	-0.10%	-6.67%	-7.56%	0.10%	-6.53%	1.11%	5.15%	0.67%
Fund:	2001	-2.91%	0.74%	-4.06%	4.93%	-3.69%	-1.39%	-4.08%	-1.66%	2.57%	6.11%	2.70%	-2.16%	-2.28%
TSX	2001	-13.94%	4.35%	-13.34%	-5.83%	4.45%	2.71%	-5.21%	-0.60%	-3.78%	-7.58%	0.69%	7.84%	3.54%
Fund:	2000	19.75%										2.45%	8.37%	7.86%
TSX	2000	-13.92%										-7.12%	-8.50%	1.29%

PERFORMANCE COMPARISON

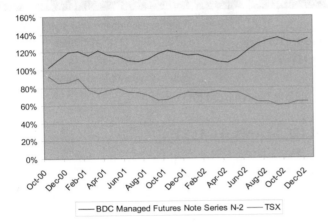

 BDC Managed Futures Note Series N-2 ——— TSX

RISK DATA (AS OF DECEMBER 31, 2002)

Alpha: Benchmark: TSX

Beta: Correlation to benchmark:

St. deviation (annualized):   Maximum drawdown: 11.37%

St. deviation (1 year):   Largest monthly drop: 0.08%

St. deviation (2 year):   Percentage of negative months: 44.44%

Sharpe Ratio: Percentage of positive months: 55.56%

Sortino Ratio:

NAGY-BECK HEDGE RATING:

CI ALTRINSIC OPPORTUNITIES FUND

CI Funds
151 Yonge Street, 11th Floor
Toronto, ON • M5C 2W7

Telephone Number: (416) 364-1145
Fax Number: (416) 364-2969
Toll-Free: 1-800-268-9374
Web Site: www.cifunds.com

Similar funds: Altrinsic Opportunities (US$)

PORTFOLIO MANAGER(S)

John Hock
Altrinsic Global Advisors

FUND DESCRIPTION

The objective of the fund is to earn superior, absolute, risk-adjusted returns over the long term with a low correlation to, and lower volatility than, broad market indices such as the MSCI World Index and the S&P 500 Total Return Index. In order to maintain flexibility and to capitalize on investment opportunities as they arise, the fund is not required to invest any particular percentage of its portfolio in any type of investment or region, and the amount of the fund's portfolio invested in any type of investment (whether long or short) or weighted in different countries or different sectors can change at any time based on the availability of attractive market opportunities.

TERMS AND CONDITIONS

Fund style: Stock Selection

Sub-style: Long Bias

Inception date: April 2002

Management fee: 2.25%

Performance fee: 20%

Hurdle rate: 0%

Liquidity: Weekly

*Min. investment: $150,000

Benchmark: MSCI World Index

RRSP eligibility: Yes (Foreign Content)

Asset size: $2 million

NAV: $101.92

Early red'n period: 6 months

Early red'n fee: 5%

High-water mark: No

Redemption notice:

Max. leverage: 100%

* or less based on provincial legislation

PERFORMANCE (AS OF DECEMBER 31, 2002)

	1 month	3 month	6 month	YTD	1 year	2 year	3 year	5 year	10 year	Since Inception
Fund:	-3.15%	10.57%	5.44%							2.69%
MSCI World Idx	-4.83%	7.74%	-11.97%						-19.89%	

Year:		Jan	Feb	Mar	Apr	May	Jun	Jul	Aug	Sep	Oct	Nov	Dec
Fund:	2002	2.69%			-0.08%	-0.97%	-1.57%	-1.61%	2.17%	-5.14%	8.72%	5.01%	-3.15%
MSCI World Idx	2002	-19.89%			-3.36%	0.23%	-6.05%	-8.42%	0.21%	-10.97%	7.40%	5.41%	-4.83%

PERFORMANCE COMPARISON

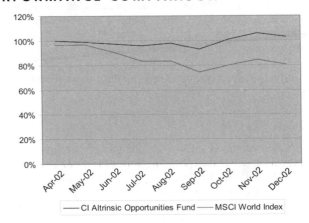

—— CI Altrinsic Opportunities Fund ——— MSCI World Index

RISK DATA (AS OF DECEMBER 31, 2002)

Alpha:	Benchmark: MSCI World Index
Beta:	Correlation to benchmark:
St. deviation (annualized):	Maximum drawdown: 7.12%
St. deviation (1 year):	Largest monthly drop: 5.14%
St. deviation (2 year):	Percentage of negative months: 66.67%
Sharpe Ratio:	Percentage of positive months: 33.33%

NAGY-BECK HEDGE RATING:

BPI AMERICAN OPPORTUNITIES FUND

CI Funds   Telephone Number: (416) 364-1145
151 Yonge Street, 11th Floor   Fax Number: (416) 364-2969
Toronto, ON• M5C 2W7   Toll-Free: 1-800-268-9374
                                      Web Site: www.cifunds.com

Similar funds:
BPI American Opportunities (US$)
BPI American Opportunities RSP

PORTFOLIO MANAGER(S)

Paul Holland, BPI Global Asset Management LLP, Lead Manager

Paul Holland is managing director and portfolio manager at BPI Global Asset Management LLP. Holland, who specializes in U.S. equity selection, has more than 13 years of experience in the investment industry. Before co-founding BPI Global in March 1997, he was vice president, investments, at A.G. Edwards and Sons, Inc., a major U.S. investment dealer.

Holland earned his bachelor of economics degree from Concordia College in Moorhead, Minnesota.

FUND DESCRIPTION

The objective of BPI American Opportunities RSP Fund is to achieve long-term capital appreciation by investing in a diversified portfolio consisting primarily of stocks, bonds, and other securities of United States issuers likely to benefit in the near term from structural change affecting specific companies and industries. It invests directly in units of BPI American Opportunities Fund and in forward contracts that link the returns of BPI American Opportunities RSP Fund to the returns of BPI American Opportunities Fund while maintaining 100% eligibility for tax-deferred plans.

In selecting investments, the fund will, among other things,

1. focus on companies with a dominance in their industry;

2. focus on companies in sectors that demonstrate value because of increasing margins, for example, companies in a sector with significant pricing power;

3. seek out companies that are trading at a discount to earnings, assets, or cash flow compared to their peers;

4. look for short-term trading opportunities in companies with impaired valuations caused by temporary events, for example, lower-than-anticipated quarterly financial results or market overreaction to negative corporate news; and

5. look for strategic short-sale opportunities in overvalued companies, for example, companies whose fundamentals are deteriorating and such deterioration is not reflected in the stock price.

TERMS AND CONDITIONS

Fund style: Stock Selection
Sub-style: Long Bias
Inception date: November 1999
Management fee: 2.77%
Performance fee: 20%
Hurdle rate: 0%
Liquidity: Weekly
* or less based on provincial legislation

* Min. investment: $150,000
Benchmark: S&P 500
RRSP eligibility: Yes (Foreign Content)
Asset size: $90 million
NAV: $105.81

Early red'n period: 6 months
Early red'n fee: 20%
High-water mark: Yes
Redemption notice:
Max. leverage: 100%

PERFORMANCE (AS OF DECEMBER 31, 2002)

	1 month	3 month	6 month	YTD	1 year	2 year	3 year	5 year	10 year	Since Inception
Fund:	5.32%	13.69%	2.47%	-2.75%	-2.75%	-6.04%	1.67%			2.74%
S&P500	-5.48%	7.42%	-7.07%	-23.14%	-23.14%	-15.15%	-12.23%			-10.74%

Year:		Jan	Feb	Mar	Apr	May	Jun	Jul	Aug	Sep	Oct	Nov	Dec
Fund:	2002	-2.75%	-1.25%	0.44%	-0.43%	1.06%	-2.89%	-2.08%	-1.69%	-1.80%	-6.65%	2.51%	5.31%	5.32%
S&P500	2002	-23.14%	-1.70%	-1.16%	3.33%	-7.67%	-3.25%	-7.77%	-3.73%	-0.98%	-9.25%	6.85%	6.36%	-5.48%
Fund:	2001	-9.21%	-1.01%	-4.98%	0.43%	0.32%	-1.42%	-3.11%	-0.32%	0.17%	0.55%	-0.01%	0.25%	-0.34%
S&P500	2001	-6.33%	3.51%	-6.78%	-3.95%	4.99%	0.87%	-3.94%	0.27%	-5.18%	-6.42%	2.50%	6.63%	2.16%
Fund:	2000	19.02%	19.00%	15.12%	3.20%	-0.65%	-5.95%	1.24%	-3.34%	8.93%	-4.32%	-0.68%	-6.51%	-4.86%
S&P500	2000	-6.07%	-5.31%	-1.70%	9.80%	-0.87%	-1.01%	1.34%	-1.17%	5.20%	-3.27%	0.85%	0.93%	-9.72%
Fund:	1999	3.43%												3.43%
S&P500	1999	4.19%												4.19%

PERFORMANCE COMPARISON

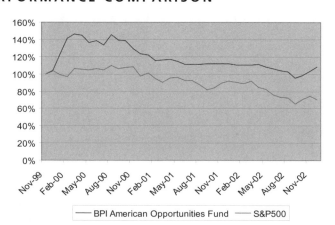

—— BPI American Opportunities Fund   —— S&P500

RISK DATA (AS OF DECEMBER 31, 2002)

Alpha (3 year): 22.22%

Beta (3 year): 0.37

St. deviation (annualized):

St. deviation (1 year): 10.96%

St. deviation (2 year):

Sharpe Ratio (3 year): -0.26

Sortino Ratio:

Benchmark: S&P 500

Correlation to benchmark:

Maximum drawdown: 14.30%

Largest monthly drop: 6.65%

Percentage of negative months: 56.00%

Percentage of positive months: 44.00%

NAGY-BECK HEDGE RATING:

BPI GLOBAL EQUITY HEDGE FUND INC., CLASS "A"

Arrow Hedge Partners International Inc.
Lauriston House, Suite 101
Lower Collymore Rock, St. Michael
Barbados, B.W.I.

Telephone Number: (416) 323-0477
Fax Number: (246) 429-2380
Toll-Free: 1-877-327-6048
Web Site: www.arrowhedge.com

Similar funds: BPI Global Equity
Hedge Fund Inc., Class "I"

PORTFOLIO MANAGER(S)

Paul Holland, Senior Portfolio Manager

Paul Holland has been a managing director and portfolio manager at BPI Global Asset Management since March 31, 1997. Holland specializes in U.S. equities and has over 14 years of experience in the investment industry. From December 1987 until he joined BPI, he held the position of vice president of investments with A.G. Edwards & Sons, a major US investment dealer. He was the subject of an article in *Barron's* (August 2, 1999). Holland earned his bachelor of economics degree from Concordia College in Moorhead, Minnesota. He is married with two children and his interests include fishing and basketball.

Matt Miller, CFA

Matt Miller has been the head trader at BPI Global Asset Management since April 1997. He is responsible for the bulk of hedge fund trading at BPI. He joined BPI from ZPR Investment Management where he specialized in trading U.S. small-cap equities and fixed-income securities from December 1995 through March, 1997. He earned his bachelor of arts degree from Stetson University in 1995, specializing in corporate finance. His hobbies include fishing and baseball.

FUND DESCRIPTION

The investment objective of the fund is to maximize absolute return by investing in a globally diversified portfolio of equity and fixed-income securities. To achieve this objective, the fund uses a long/short investment strategy and generally maintains net exposures of 50% short to 50% long of the net assets of the fund. The fund focuses on large-, mid-, and small-capitalization companies and uses a bottom-up, relative-value investment approach. From time to time, the fund also may invest in "hot issues."

BPI believes the gradual trend toward trade liberalization is permanently altering the competitive make-up of the global economy, requiring a fundamental change in the way one approaches global equity research. Specifically, the firm sees three key implications:

- Security analysis must shift from a geographic to an industry focus as companies globalize.
- Companies with strong competitive positions leverage them on a global scale.
- Valuation screens based on industry-specific criteria best uncover appreciation potential.

The investment process for selecting long candidates for the fund involves three key steps.

The first step is to segment over 10,000 companies by industry or sector (e.g., automotive, pharmaceuticals, capital equipment etc.) using the MSCI industry segments. For the long portion of the fund, BPI concentrates on those industries experiencing a "tailwind," i.e., where there is sustainable future growth in corporate profits.

The second step is to identify companies within those industries that are the leaders. Leading companies have sustainable competitive advantages that lead to strong operating leverage, i.e., they are the "category killers" with superior profitability, improving business outlook and pricing power. Databases such as Baseline estimates and Factset are used extensively at this stage. This step produces approximately 1,000 U.S. securities upon which further due diligence is conducted.

The third step involves fundamental analysis and company visits. Once a company is verified as a long candidate it is put on a watch list and monitored daily. Standard technical analysis is used as the principal guide.

TERMS AND CONDITIONS

Fund style: Stock Selection
Sub-style: Variable Bias
Inception date: February 2002
Management fee: 2%
Performance fee: 20%
Hurdle rate: n/a
Liquidity: Monthly

* Min. investment: US$100,000
Benchmark: MSCI World Index
RRSP eligibility: No
Asset size: $5 million
NAV: US$1,005.04

Early red'n period: 6 month lock up
Early red'n fee: Up to 5%
High-water mark: Yes
Redemption notice: 30 days
Max. leverage: US$100%

* or less based on provincial legislation

PERFORMANCE (AS OF DECEMBER 31, 2002)

	1 month	3 month	6 month	YTD	1 year	2 year	3 year	5 year	10 year	Since Inception
Fund:	-1.72%	0.26%	-2.25%							
MSCI:	-4.83%	7.74%	-11.97%							

	Year:	Jan	Feb	Mar	Apr	May	Jun	Jul	Aug	Sep	Oct	Nov	Dec
Fund:	2002	-0.52%	0.34%	0.49%	2.04%	-1.43%	0.35%	-0.20%	0.05%	-2.36%	-0.04%	2.06%	-1.72%
MSCI:	2002	-17.04%	-0.85%	4.44%	-3.36%	0.23%	-6.05%	-8.42%	0.21%	-10.97%	7.40%	5.41%	-4.83%

PERFORMANCE COMPARISON

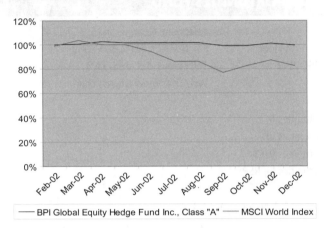

─── BPI Global Equity Hedge Fund Inc., Class "A" ─── MSCI World Index

RISK DATA (AS OF DECEMBER 31, 2002)

Alpha: 1.87%

Benchmark: MSCI World Index

Beta: 0.09

Correlation to benchmark: 0.227

St. deviation (annualized): 4.84%

Maximum drawdown: -2.36%

St. deviation (1 year):

Largest monthly drop: -2.36%

St. deviation (2 year):

Percentage of negative months: 7.50%

Sharpe Ratio (annualized): -1.15

Percentage of positive months: 62.50%

Sortino Ratio:

NAGY-BECK HEDGE RATING:

BPI GLOBAL OPPORTUNITIES FUND

CI Funds
151 Yonge Street, 11th Floor
Toronto, ON • M5C 2W7

Telephone Number: (416) 364-1145
Fax Number: (416) 364-2969
Toll-Free: 1-800-268-9374
Web Site: www.cifunds.com

Similar funds:
BPI Global Opportunities II
BPI Global Opportunities III
BPI Global Opportunities (US$)
BPI Global Opportunities III, RSP

PORTFOLIO MANAGER(S)

Daniel R. Jaworski, BPI Global Asset Management LLP, Lead Manager

Dan Jaworski is chief investment officer, managing director, and portfolio manager at BPI Global Asset Management LLP. He oversees BPI Global's portfolio management and stock selection process, and is lead manager for several funds.

Jaworski has 13 years of experience in managing international equity portfolios. Before co-founding BPI Global in 1997, he was managing director of International Portfolio Management and Research, and senior portfolio manager at STI Capital Management/Sun Trust Inc. Prior to joining STI, he held positions as an international equity portfolio manager at Lazard Frères Asset Management and at Principal Financial Group/Invista Capital Management. He holds the chartered financial analyst designation, an MBA from the University of Minnesota, and a BA in economics and computer science from Concordia College.

FUND DESCRIPTION

The fund's objective is to achieve long-term capital appreciation by investing in a globally diversified portfolio of stocks, bonds, and other securities that are likely to benefit in the near term from structural change affecting specific companies, industries, and national economies.

The fund focuses on

* companies with a global presence that are dominant in their industry
* companies in sectors with increasing profit margins
* companies trading at a discount to earnings, assets, or cash flow, compared to their global peers
* short-term trading opportunities in companies with impaired valuations, thanks to temporary events such as lower quarterly results or market overreaction to negative corporate news
* strategic short-sale opportunities in overvalued companies, such as companies whose fundamentals are deteriorating

TERMS AND CONDITIONS

Fund style: Stock Selection
Sub-style: Long Bias
Inception date: May 1995
Management fee: 2.66%
Performance fee: 20%
Hurdle rate: 10% (BPI Global Opportunities I and II)
Liquidity: Weekly
* Min. investment: None
Benchmark: MSCI

RRSP eligibility: Yes (Foreign Content)
Asset size: $195 million
NAV: $17.20
Early red'n period: 6 months
Early red'n fee: 20%
High-water mark: No
Redemption notice:
Max. leverage: 100%

* BPI Global Opportunities II is a closed end fund traded on the TSX

PERFORMANCE (AS OF DECEMBER 31, 2002)

	1 month	3 month	6 month	YTD	1 year	2 year	3 year	5 year	10 year	Since Inception
Fund:	-5.65%	2.14%	-8.26%	-15.44%	-15.44%	-13.27%	-9.76%	17.06%		23.59%
MSCI	-4.83%	7.74%	-11.97%	-19.55%	-19.55%	-18.04%	-16.37%	-1.78%		4.03%

Year:		Jan	Feb	Mar	Apr	May	Jun	Jul	Aug	Sep	Oct	Nov	Dec
Fund:	2002	-15.44%	-2.85%	0.05%	-0.51%	0.71%	-3.03%	-2.40%	-1.60%	-1.84%	-7.01%	2.67%	5.44%	-5.65%
MSCI	2002	-19.55%	-3.02%	-0.85%	4.44%	-3.36%	0.23%	-6.05%	-8.42%	0.21%	-10.97%	7.40%	5.41%	-4.83%
Fund:	2001	-11.04%	-0.88%	-5.52%	0.00%	0.19%	-1.31%	-2.69%	-0.15%	0.10%	0.63%	-0.15%	0.19%	-1.88%
MSCI	2001	-16.51%	2.00%	-8.43%	-6.61%	7.37%	-1.37%	-3.11%	-1.26%	-4.67%	-8.80%	1.93%	5.93%	0.64%
Fund:	2000	-2.31%	-2.42%	21.02%	0.34%	-3.23%	-4.30%	0.15%	-5.13%	8.16%	-6.10%	-1.13%	-6.98%	0.31%
MSCI	2000	-12.93%	-5.72%	0.28%	6.92%	-4.22%	-2.52%	3.38%	-2.80%	3.27%	-5.31%	-1.66%	-6.06%	1.63%
Fund:	1999	75.61%	10.67%	-10.83%	7.10%	8.71%	-2.10%	8.62%	7.39%	1.76%	1.11%	6.12%	13.85%	7.67%
MSCI	1999	25.23%	2.19%	-2.65%	4.16%	3.97%	-3.67%	4.66%	-0.29%	-0.17%	-0.96%	5.21%	2.82%	8.11%
Fund:	1998	70.33%	-0.52%	8.03%	8.86%	2.78%	1.18%	2.53%	10.05%	-1.22%	-2.48%	4.52%	14.81%	7.34%
MSCI	1998	24.83%	2.82%	6.78%	4.23%	0.99%	-1.25%	2.38%	-0.14%	-13.32%	1.80%	9.07%	5.97%	4.90%
Fund:	1997	45.32%	1.67%	6.33%	0.38%	-4.49%	8.82%	7.75%	10.42%	1.16%	8.58%	0.78%	-0.91%	-1.27%
MSCI	1997	16.10%	1.24%	1.15%	-1.99%	3.29%	6.19%	5.01%	4.63%	-6.76%	5.45%	-5.24%	1.77%	1.23%
Fund:	1996	31.92%	5.00%	5.36%	-5.25%	8.44%	3.62%	-0.91%	-6.36%	3.35%	1.42%	-0.39%	12.45%	2.81%
MSCI	1996	14.04%	1.88%	0.62%	1.67%	2.36%	0.09%	0.54%	-3.53%	1.19%	3.93%	0.69%	5.64%	-1.57%
Fund:	1995	20.37%					7.30%	12.77%	-0.50%	0.33%	0.58%	-2.06%	1.09%	0.07%
MSCI	1995	11.86%					0.91%	-0.02%	5.02%	-2.22%	2.95%	-1.55%	3.49%	2.94%

PERFORMANCE COMPARISON

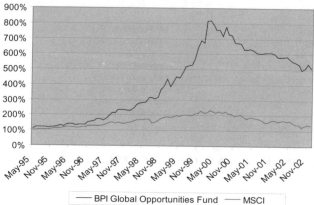

——— BPI Global Opportunities Fund ——— MSCI

RISK DATA (AS OF DECEMBER 31, 2002)

Alpha (5 year): 15.61%

Beta (5 year): 0.75

St. deviation (annualized):

St. deviation (1 year): 11.48%

St. deviation (2 year):

Sharpe Ratio (5 year): 0.60

Sortino Ratio:

Benchmark: MSCI

Correlation to benchmark:

Maximum drawdown: 14.99%

Largest monthly drop: 10.83%

Percentage of negative months: 39.13%

Percentage of positive months: 60.87%

NAGY-BECK HEDGE RATING:

CI MULTI-MANAGER OPPORTUNITIES FUND

CI Funds
151 Yonge Street, 11th Floor
Toronto, ON • M5C 2W7

Telephone Number: (416) 364-1145
Fax Number: (416) 364-2969
Toll-Free: 1-800-268-9374
Web Site: www.cifunds.com

Similar funds: CI Multi-Manager Opportunities (US$)

PORTFOLIO MANAGER(S)

Derek H. Webb, CFA, MBA, Manager   **Webb Capital Management LLP**

Derek Webb, president and CEO of Webb Capital Management LLP, has 17 years of investment industry experience. Prior to managing CI funds, he managed Canadian and international equity portfolios for AIM Funds. He began his career on Wall Street in 1983 as an associate at Brown Brothers Harriman & Co., a privately owned commercial and investment bank. He later worked as a bond trader at Trust Company of the West and at Salomon Brothers before moving to Citicorp. In 1992 he joined INVESCO, a sister company to AIM, as a Canadian and U.S. investment analyst. Webb holds the chartered financial analyst designation, an MBA from the Wharton School of Business at the University of Pennsylvania, and a BA from Dartmouth College.

Daniel R. Jaworski, Manager   **BPI Global Asset Management LLP**

Dan Jaworski is chief investment officer, managing director, and portfolio manager at BPI Global Asset Management LLP. He oversees BPI Global's portfolio management and stock selection process, and is lead manager for several funds.

He has 13 years of experience in managing international equity portfolios. Before co-founding BPI Global in 1997, he was managing director of International Portfolio Management and Research, and senior portfolio manager at STI Capital Management/Sun Trust Inc. Prior to joining STI, he held positions as an international equity portfolio manager at Lazard Frères Asset Management and at Principal Financial Group/Invista Capital Management. Jaworski holds the chartered financial analyst designation, an MBA from the University of Minnesota, and a BA in economics and computer science from Concordia College.

Nandu Narayanan, Manager   **Trident Asset Management**

Nandu Narayanan, founder and chief investment officer of Trident Investment Management, LLC, has 12 years of investment industry experience. Prior to founding Trident, he worked as an independent consultant on emerging markets to Credit Suisse Asset Management, as well as managing CI's Asian and emerging markets funds. He also worked as chief equity and emerging market strategist at hedge fund manager Caxton Corporation, and as an investment analyst at Tiger Management, another hedge fund firm. He holds a PhD in finance and international economics and a master's degree in management, both from the Massachusetts Institute of Technology, as well as a bachelor's degree with a double major in economics and computer science from Yale University (summa cum laude).

FUND DESCRIPTION

The fundamental investment objective of the fund is to achieve long-term capital appreciation.

TERMS AND CONDITIONS

Fund style: Fund of Funds
Sub-style: Stock Selection
Inception date: April 2002
Management fee: 2.25%
Performance fee: 20%
Hurdle rate: 0%
Liquidity: Weekly
* or less based on provincial legislation

* Min. investment: $150,000
Benchmark: MSCI
RRSP eligibility: Yes (Foreign Content)
Asset size: $0.3 million
NAV:

Early red'n period: 6 months
Early red'n fee: 5%
High-water mark: Yes
Redemption notice:
Max. leverage: 100%

PERFORMANCE (AS OF DECEMBER 31, 2002)

	1 month	3 month	6 month	YTD	1 year	2 year	3 year	5 year	10 year	Since Inception
Fund:	-2.19%	1.64%	-3.88%							-7.07%
MSCI	-4.83%	7.74%	-11.97%							-19.89%

Year:		Jan	Feb	Mar	Apr	May	Jun	Jul	Aug	Sep	Oct	Nov	Dec
Fund:	2002	-7.07%			0.02%	-1.16%	-2.20%	-1.59%	-0.11%	-3.80%	2.42%	1.46%	-2.19%
MSCI	2002	-19.89%			-3.36%	0.23%	-6.05%	-8.42%	0.21%	-10.97%	7.40%	5.41%	-4.83%

PERFORMANCE COMPARISON

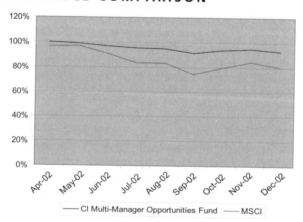

CI Multi-Manager Opportunities Fund ——— MSCI

RISK DATA (AS OF DECEMBER 30, 2002)

Alpha:

Beta:

St. deviation (annualized):

St. deviation (1 year):

St. deviation (2 year):

Sharpe Ratio:

Sortino Ratio:

Benchmark: MSCI

Correlation to benchmark:

Maximum drawdown: 8.59%

Largest monthly drop: 3.80%

Percentage of negative months: 66.67%

Percentage of positive months: 33.33%

NAGY-BECK HEDGE RATING:

CI LANDMARK GLOBAL OPPORTUNITIES FUND

CI Funds
151 Yonge Street, 11th Floor
Toronto, ON • M5C 2W7

Telephone Number: (416) 364-1145
Fax Number: (416) 364-2969
Toll-Free: 1-800-268-9374
Web Site: www.cifunds.com

Similar funds:
CI Landmark Global Opportunities, US$
CI Landmark Global Opportunities, RSP

PORTFOLIO MANAGER(S)

Derek H. Webb, CFA, MBA, Manager   **Webb Capital Management LLP**

Derek Webb, president and CEO of Webb Capital Management LLP, has 17 years of investment industry experience. Prior to managing CI funds, he managed Canadian and international equity portfolios for AIM Funds. He began his career on Wall Street in 1983 as an associate at Brown Brothers Harriman & Co., a privately owned commercial and investment bank. He later worked as a bond trader at Trust Company of the West and at Salomon Brothers before moving to Citicorp. In 1992 he joined INVESCO, a sister company to AIM, as a Canadian and U.S. investment analyst. Webb holds the chartered financial analyst designation, an MBA from the Wharton School of Business at the University of Pennsylvania, and a BA from Dartmouth College.

FUND DESCRIPTION

To achieve absolute returns that have a low correlation with the broader indices while protecting clients at all times.

TERMS AND CONDITIONS

Fund style: Stock Selection
Sub-style: Market Neutral
Inception date: August 2001
Management fee: 2.67%
Performance fee: 20%
Hurdle rate: 0%
Liquidity: Weekly
* or less based on provincial legislation

* Min. investment: $150,000
Benchmark: S&P 500
RRSP eligibility: Yes (Foreign Content)
Asset size: $53 million
NAV: $11.17

Early red'n period: 6 months
Early red'n fee: 5%
High water mark: Yes
Redemption notice:
Max. leverage: 100.00%

PERFORMANCE (AS OF DECEMBER 31, 2002)

	1 month	3 month	6 month	YTD	1 year	2 year	3 year	5 year	10 year	Since Inception
Fund:	1.79%	-4.51%	-6.26%	-1.07%	-1.07%					
S&P500	-5.48%	7.42%	-7.07%	-23.14%	-23.14%					

Year:		Jan	Feb	Mar	Apr	May	Jun	Jul	Aug	Sep	Oct	Nov	Dec
Fund:	2002	-1.07%	1.32%	0.63%	-0.76%	5.24%	-1.21%	0.32%	-1.90%	-1.50%	1.59%	-1.52%	-4.74%	1.79%
S&P500	2002	-23.14%	-1.70%	-1.16%	3.33%	-7.67%	-3.25%	-7.77%	-3.73%	-0.98%	-9.25%	6.85%	6.36%	-5.48%
Fund:	2001	11.87%							0.00%	-0.03%	3.21%	2.58%	5.70%
S&P500	2001	-0.92%							-5.18%	-6.42%	2.50%	6.63%	2.16%

PERFORMANCE COMPARISON

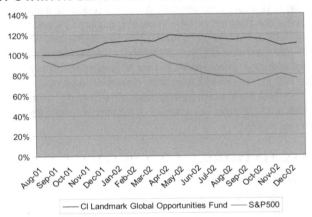

—— CI Landmark Global Opportunities Fund —— S&P500

RISK DATA (AS OF DECEMBER 31, 2002)

Alpha (1 year): -6.70%

Beta (1 year): -0.21

St. deviation (annualized):

St. deviation (1 year): 8.51%

St. deviation (2 year):

Sharpe Ratio: -0.41

Sortino Ratio:

Benchmark: S&P 500

Correlation to benchmark:

Maximum drawdown: 6.18%

Largest monthly drop: 4.74%

Percentage of negative months: 41.18%

Percentage of positive months: 58.82%

NAGY-BECK HEDGE RATING:

TRIDENT GLOBAL OPPORTUNITIES FUND

CI Funds   Telephone Number: (416) 364-1145
151 Yonge Street, 11th Floor   Fax Number: (416) 364-2969
Toronto, ON • M5C 2W7   Toll-Free: 1-800-268-9374
                                      Web Site: www.cifunds.com

Similar funds:
Trident Global Opportunities RSP
Trident Global Opportunities (US$)

PORTFOLIO MANAGER(S)

Nandu Narayanan, Manager   Trident Asset Management

Nandu Narayanan, founder and chief investment officer of Trident Investment Management, LLC, has 12 years of investment industry experience. Prior to founding Trident, he worked as an independent consultant on emerging markets to Credit Suisse Asset Management, as well as managing CI's Asian and emerging markets funds. He also worked as chief equity and emerging market strategist at hedge fund manager Caxton Corporation, and as an investment analyst at Tiger Management, another hedge fund firm. He holds a PhD in finance and international economics and a master's degree in management, both from the Massachusetts Institute of Technology, as well as a bachelor's degree with a double major in economics and computer science from Yale University (summa cum laude).

FUND DESCRIPTION

The investment objective of the fund is to generate superior risk-adjusted long-term rates of return through investments in global securities. The fund invests principally in publicly traded equity and equity-related instruments in the developed and, to a lesser degree, emerging markets, and may also take positions in the currency and fixed-income markets either to hedge or to express its views. The investment approach is primarily geared to investing in large-capitalization industry sectors and stocks in developed markets, which generally provide the best liquidity in the market, with a secondary focus on the developing countries. Trident uses a top-down analysis of macroeconomic, political, and industry-sector information to determine which global equity markets or sectors are likely to exhibit sustained trend moves. Then it applies traditional, bottom-up valuation measures to select stocks within the identified markets or sectors.

TERMS AND CONDITIONS

Fund style: Stock Selection
Sub-style: Variable Bias   * **Min. investment:** $150,000   **Early red'n period:** 6 months
Inception date: February 2001   **Benchmark:** MSCI   **Early red'n fee:** 5%
Management fee: 2.20%   **RRSP eligibility:** Yes (Foreign Content)   **High-water mark:** No

Performance fee: 20%
Hurdle rate: 0%
Liquidity: Weekly
* or less based on provincial legislation

Asset size: $26 million
NAV:

Redemption notice:
Max. leverage: 100%

PERFORMANCE (AS OF DECEMBER 31, 2002)

	1 month	3 month	6 month	YTD	1 year	2 year	3 year	5 year	10 year	Since Inception
Fund:	-1.27%	-1.27%	-1.66%	-1.68%	-1.68%					2.11%
MSCI	-4.83%	7.74%	-11.97%	-19.55%	-19.55%					-19.59%

Year:		Jan	Feb	Mar	Apr	May	Jun	Jul	Aug	Sep	Oct	Nov	Dec
Fund:	2002	-1.68%	-0.39%	0.72%	0.37%	0.47%	0.18%	-1.35%	0.48%	-0.14%	-0.74%	0.73%	-0.72%	-1.27%
MSCI	2002	-19.55%	-3.02%	-0.85%	4.44%	-3.36%	0.23%	-6.05%	-8.42%	0.21%	-10.97%	7.40%	5.41%	-4.83%
Fund:	2001	5.86%		0.00%	7.74%	-2.01%	1.33%	-0.78%	0.05%	0.32%	0.93%	-0.45%	-0.64%	-0.47%
MSCI	2001	-18.15%		-8.43%	-6.61%	7.37%	-1.37%	-3.11%	-1.26%	-4.67%	-8.80%	1.93%	5.93%	0.64%

PERFORMANCE COMPARISON

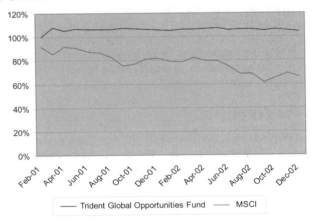

—— Trident Global Opportunities Fund   —— MSCI

RISK DATA (AS OF DECEMBER 31, 2002)

Alpha (1 year): -2.71%
Beta: (1 year): 0.06
St. deviation (annualized):
St. deviation (1 year): 2.38%
St. deviation (2 year):

Sharpe Ratio: 1.72
Sortino Ratio:
Benchmark: MSCI
Correlation to benchmark:

Maximum drawdown: 2.01%
Largest monthly drop: 2.01%
Percentage of negative months: 47.83%
Percentage of positive months: 52.17%

NAGY-BECK HEDGE RATING:

CASURINA PERFORMANCE FUND

Front Street Capital   Telephone Number: (416) 597-9595
87 Front Street East, Suite 400   Fax Number: (416) 364-8893
Toronto, ON • M5E 1B8   Toll-Free: 1-800-513-2832
                                        Web Site: www.frontstreetcapital.com

PORTFOLIO MANAGER(S)

Frank L. Mersch, Manager

Frank Mersch has over 22 years of experience in the investment industry, including 11 years as an investment manager with Altamira Management LTD. Prior to joining Altamira in 1987, he was president of special investments and vice president of Guardian Capital Group and vice president of investments at Morgan Trust Company of Canada. From 1987 to 1998 Mersch was a shareholder, director, and vice president of Altamira. During that period he was instrumental in building an organization that had over 300 employees and approximately $17 billion of assets under management. At Altamira, Mersch managed and marketed private wealth, mutual funds, and pension funds and earned a reputation as one of the most highly regarded investment managers in Canada, frequently making appearances on "Wall Street Week" and other investment programs. From May 1998 to June 1999, Mersch was active in providing angel financing to fledgling technology companies. Since June 1999, he has been an officer of the investment adviser and in that capacity has managed the portfolio of Casurina Limited Partnership. Mersch intends to purchase personally, or through parties related to him, not less than $2.5 million of units pursuant to the offering.

FUND DESCRIPTION

The objective of the fund is to outperform major North American equity indexes through active management. The fund will have a long bias and will employ sophisticated investment strategies involving taking long and short positions on equity and debt securities.

TERMS AND CONDITIONS

Fund Style: Stock Selection

Sub-style: Variable Bias	**Min. investment:** None	**Early red'n period:**
Inception date: April 2002	**Benchmark:** TSX	**Early red'n fee:**
Management fee: 1.10%	**RRSP eligibility:** Yes	**High-water mark:** Yes
Performance fee: 20%	**Asset size:** $40.1 million	**Redemption notice:**
Hurdle rate: 6%	**Nav:**	**Max. leverage:** 100%
Liquidity: Daily		

PERFORMANCE (AS OF DECEMBER 31, 2002)

	1 month	3 month	6 month	YTD	1 year	2 year	3 year	5 year	10 year	Since Inception
Fund:	5.17%	9.97%	-11.57%	-9.41%						-9.41%
TSX	0.67%	7.03%	-7.43%	-13.69%						-13.69%

Year:		Jan	Feb	Mar	Apr	May	Jun	Jul	Aug	Sep	Oct	Nov	Dec
und:	2002 -9.41%					2.74%	-0.29%	-6.63%	-6.77%	-7.63%	-0.46%	5.05%	5.17%
5X	2002 -13.69%					-0.10%	-6.67%	-7.56%	0.10%	-6.53%	1.11%	5.15%	0.67%

PERFORMANCE COMPARISON

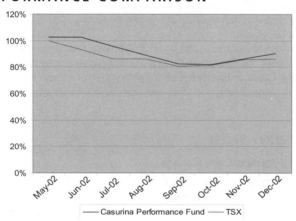

—— Casurina Performance Fund —— TSX

RISK DATA (AS OF DECEMBER 31, 2002)

Alpha:	Sharpe Ratio:	Maximum drawdown: 20.19%
Beta:	Sortino Ratio:	Largest monthly drop: 7.66%
St. deviation (annualized):	Benchmark: TSX	Percentage of negative months: 62.50%
St. deviation (1 year):	Correlation to benchmark:	Percentage of positive months: 7.50%
St. deviation (2 year):		

NAGY-BECK HEDGE RATING:

DELTAONE ENERGY FUND LP

DeltaOne Capital Partners Corp.   Telephone Number: (416) 815-1692
Citibank Tower, 123 Front Street West Fax Number: (416) 862-0576
Suite 1601, Toronto, ON   Web Site: www.deltaonecapital.com
M5C 1S1

PORTFOLIO MANAGER(S)

Peter Linder

Peter Linder has over eight years' experience in the securities industry as an oil and gas analyst. Prior to joining DeltaOne Capital Partners Corp. as an energy specialist, he spent two years as an analyst with Research Capital, and previously spent four years with Wood Gundy.

Linder is a widely recognized expert on North American natural gas markets, having worked as a natural gas consultant with a prominent gas consulting firm and as VP Natural Gas at the Canadian Energy Research Institute (CERI). He also worked for 15 years with various major oil firms, including nine years with Amoco Canada as a senior energy economist.

FUND DESCRIPTION

DeltaOne Capital Partners Corp. (Canada)

DeltaOne Capital Partners Corp. (Canada) specializes in derivative-based hedge funds for sophisticated individual and institutional investors. Their goal is to provide their clients with superior absolute performance and lower levels of risk. Their Energy fund adds value through superior security selection while concurrently hedging varying amounts of market exposure. Hedge funds can be an attractive alternative to long-only investments for sophisticated investors seeking capital appreciation with reduced portfolio volatility and lower market correlation. Their management team consists of recognized experts with decades of experience in the field of oil and gas, equities, derivatives, and futures trading.

This investment fund is offered only to sophisticated investors in Canada. The fund is a long/short sector fund designed to generate absolute returns independent of market direction. The investment objective of the fund is to provide returns through the purchase and sale of listed equities and other securities related to the North American energy sector. The fund will seek a low correlation to the S&P/TSX Canadian Energy Index.

TERMS AND CONDITIONS

Fund Style: Long/Short

Sub-style: Energy Sector	**Benchmark:** TSX/S&P Energy Index	**Redemption notice:** 30 days
Inception date: October 2002	**RRSP eligibility:** No	**Max. leverage:** 70%
Management fee: 2.00%	**Asset size:** $11 million	
Performance fee: 20%	**NAV:** $16.31	
Hurdle rate: 8%	**Early red'n period:** 180 days	
Liquidity: Monthly	**Early red'n fee:** 3%	
***Min. investment:** $150,000	**High-water mark:** Yes	

* or less based on provincial legislation

PERFORMANCE (AS OF DECEMBER 31, 2002)

	1 month	3 month	6 month	YTD	1 year	2 year	3 year	5 year	10 year	Since Inception
Fund:	23.09%	63.08%								63.08%
Benchmark:	6.45%	-1.99%								-1.99%

Year:		Jan	Feb	Mar	Apr	May	Jun	Jul	Aug	Sep	Oct	Nov	Dec
und:	2002	63.08%										12.66%	17.60%	23.09%
'SX/S&P 2002 nergy Idx		-1.99%										-6.90%	-1.10%	6.45%

PERFORMANCE COMPARISON

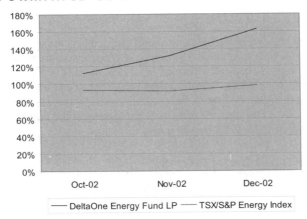

—— DeltaOne Energy Fund LP —— TSX/S&P Energy Index

RISK DATA (AS OF SEPTEMBER 30, 2002)

Alpha:	Sharpe Ratio:	Largest monthly drop:
Beta:	Sortino Ratio:	Largest monthly drop:
St. deviation (annualized):	Benchmark: TSX/S&P Energy Index	Percentage of negative months: 0.00%
St. deviation (1 year):	Correlation to benchmark:	Percentage of positive months: 100.00%
St. deviation (2 year):	Maximum drawdown:	

NAGY-BECK HEDGE RATING:

DYNAMIC EQUITY HEDGE

Dynamic
Scotia Plaza, 55th Floor
40 King Street West
Toronto, ON • M5H 4A9

Telephone Number: (514) 908-3212
Fax Number: 1-800-419-5119
Toll-Free: 1-800-268-8186
Web Site: www.dynamic.ca

PORTFOLIO MANAGER(S)

Brian Chait, B.Compt, CA, RFA, Manager
Orbital Capital Management LLC

Morton Cohen, MBA, CFA, Manager
Orbital Capital Management LLC

FUND DESCRIPTION

The investment objective of the fund is to protect capital during a wide range of economic and market environments while earning superior equity or equity-related returns that are not co-related to major stock market indices. The objective is to reduce risk and invest in a diversified portfolio. The fund will be managed in a flexible manner and will use investment strategies and instruments beyond the reach of a typical mutual fund. The manager, on behalf of the fund, will make use of one or more skilled investment advisers not generally available to the broader public.

TERMS AND CONDITIONS

Fund style: Stock Selection	**RRSP eligibility:** No
Sub-style: Long Bias	**Asset size:** $12.3 million
Inception date: August 2001	**NAV:** $10.46
Management fee: 2.25%	**Early red'n period:**
Performance fee: 20%	**Early red'n fee:**
Hurdle rate: Yes	**High-water mark:** Yes
Liquidity: Weekly	**Redemption notice:**
* Min. investment: $150,000	**Max. leverage:**
Benchmark: S&P 500	

* or less based on provincial legislation

PERFORMANCE (AS OF DECEMBER 31, 2002)

	1 month	3 month	6 month	YTD	1 year	2 year	3 year	5 year	10 year	Since Inception
Fund:	6.51%	25.57%	14.43%	-5.63%	-5.63%					
S&P500	-5.48%	7.42%	-7.07%	-23.14%	-23.14%					

Year:		Jan	Feb	Mar	Apr	May	Jun	Jul	Aug	Sep	Oct	Nov	Dec
und:	2002	-5.63%	-2.64%	-3.93%	0.64%	-4.61%	-1.42%	-6.83%	-10.94%	5.10%	-2.65%	-3.85%	22.62%	6.51%
&P500	2002	-23.14%	-1.70%	-1.16%	3.33%	-7.67%	-3.25%	-7.77%	-3.73%	-0.98%	-9.25%	6.85%	6.36%	-5.48%
und:	2001	17.50%							2.20%	11.94%	3.41%	-2.71%	2.09%
&P500	2001	-0.92%							-5.18%	-6.42%	2.50%	6.63%	2.16%

PERFORMANCE COMPARISON

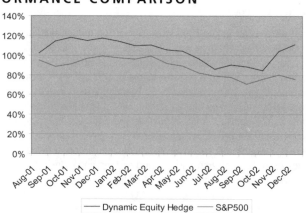

— Dynamic Equity Hedge — S&P500

RISK DATA (AS OF SEPTEMBER 30, 2002)

Alpha: 1.30%

Beta: 0.43

St. deviation (annualized): 27.85%

St. deviation (1 year): 9.57%

St. deviation (2 year): N\A

Sharpe Ratio: 0.20 (RFR=3.92%)

Sortino Ratio: 0.46 (MAR=0%)

Benchmark: S&P 500

Correlation to benchmark: 0.28

Maximum drawdown: -28.22%

Largest monthly drop: 10.94%

Percentage of negative months: 56.25%

Percentage of positive months: 43.75%

NAGY-BECK HEDGE RATING:

EPIC LIMITED PARTNERSHIP

Epic Capital Management Inc.   Telephone Number: (416) 703-4441
444 Adelaide Street West, Suite 202   Fax Number: (416) 703-4443
Toronto, ON • M5V 1S7   Web Site: www.epiccapital.ca

Similar funds: Arrow Epic Capital Fund

PORTFOLIO MANAGER(S)

Combined, the two portfolio managers have over 12 years' investment experience in Canada on the sell side. Both managers were nationally ranked equity research analysts.

David Fawcett, CFA, MA

David Fawcett started Epic in late 2000 after six years on the sell side, most recently at Deutsche Bank Securities, where he was a research analyst in charge of covering senior Canadian oil and gas companies with a global oil team. The Deutsche team was deemed to be one of the top five oil and gas research teams in 1999 by *Institutional Investor*. Fawcett was a nationally ranked analyst in the Brendan Woods institutional survey.

Prior to that, he covered oil and gas companies at First Marathon Securities (currently National Bank Financial). Analysis was weighted toward emerging international oil and gas companies. He also played a major role in numerous corporate finance deals.

Before that, Fawcett was employed by Middlefield Group, a merchant bank. His responsibilities included analyzing and offering recommendations on venture capital opportunities and assisting in managing a mutual fund.

He graduated from Wilfrid Laurier University with a master of arts degree in business economics and holds an honours bachelor of arts degree in economics from the University of Western Ontario. He is also a chartered financial analyst.

Tom Schenkel, CFA, MA

Tom Schenkel joined Epic in February 2001 after spending six years with the top-ranked research team at BMO Nesbitt Burns as a nationally ranked analyst in consumer products and special situations. His formal stock coverage universe consisted of 18 companies, in a variety of industries. He developed a strong institutional following on several companies, including Cott Corp., Rothmans Inc., and Finning International. Schenkel's broad-ranging analytical experience includes sectors such as consumer products, industrial products, telecommunications and media, mining, and special situations.

Prior to being appointed an analyst in 1997 at BMO Nesbitt Burns, Schenkel focused on the consumer product and media/communication sectors. He also has analytical experience in the mining sector, with a focus on gold and diamonds.

Schenkel graduated from Wilfrid Laurier University with a master of arts degree in business economics (1994) and holds an honours bachelor of arts degree in economics from Queen's University (1992). He received his chartered financial analyst designation in 1999 and has successfully completed his partners, directors and officers program (2001).

FUND DESCRIPTION

Epic Limited Partnership is a long/short equity hedge fund. Epic's goal is to achieve superior risk-adjusted returns. Individual stock selection is core to their strategy. They employ a bottom-up, value-driven approach. This approach is research intensive, including analyzing company-specific fundamentals, interviewing management, and studying industry dynamics. Equally important to stock selection is the portfolio strategy they implement to mitigate risk. Various strategies, including pairs trading, index hedging, short-selling, and merger arbitrage, materially contribute to lowering the risk of the fund.

Epic believes its investment strategy will allow the fund to deliver superior absolute and relative returns over the long term as demonstrated by the track record to date.

TERMS AND CONDITIONS

Fund style: Stock Selection

Sub-style: No Bias	***Min. investment:** $150,000	**Early red'n period:** 6 months
Inception date: December 2000	**Benchmark:** TSX	**Early red'n fee:** 5%
Management fee: 2.00%	**RRSP eligibility:** Yes	**High water mark:** Yes
Performance fee: 20%	**Asset size:** $6 million	**Redemption notice:**
Hurdle rate: 0%	**NAV:** $1,628.28	**Max. leverage:** 75%
Liquidity: Monthly		

* or less based on provincial legislation

PERFORMANCE (AS OF DECEMBER 31, 2002)

	1 month	3 month	6 month	YTD	1 year	2 year	3 year	5 year	10 year	Since Inception
Fund:	4.70%	8.39%	8.82%	19.88%	19.88%	25.76%				25.39%
TSX	0.67%	7.03%	-7.43%	-13.97%	-13.97%	-13.96%				-2.90%

Year:		Jan	Feb	Mar	Apr	May	Jun	Jul	Aug	Sep	Oct	Nov	Dec
und:	2002	19.88%	2.70%	0.00%	1.80%	1.60%	3.50%	0.20%	-0.60%	0.00%	1.00%	2.20%	1.30%	4.70%
'SX	2002	-13.97%	-0.52%	-0.14%	2.80%	-2.40%	-0.10%	-6.67%	-7.56%	0.10%	-6.53%	1.11%	5.15%	0.67%
und:	2001	31.94%	3.50%	1.60%	7.00%	2.30%	1.50%	2.40%	0.90%	2.40%	0.90%	1.10%	3.50%	1.10%
'SX	2001	-13.94%	4.35%	-13.34%	-5.83%	4.45%	2.71%	-5.21%	-0.60%	-3.78%	-7.58%	0.69%	7.84%	3.54%
und:	2000	1.30%												1.30%
'SX	2000	1.29%												1.29%

PERFORMANCE COMPARISON

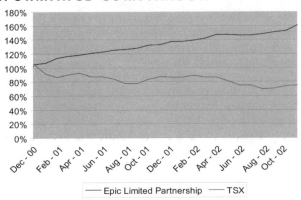

— Epic Limited Partnership — TSX

RISK DATA (AS OF DECEMBER 31, 2002)

Alpha:	Benchmark: TSX
Beta:	Correlation to benchmark: 0.15
St. deviation (annualized): 5.70%	Maximum drawdown: 0.60%
St. deviation (1 year):	Largest monthly drop: 0.60%
St. deviation (2 year):	Percentage of negative months: 4.00%
Sharpe Ratio: 3.43	Percentage of positive months: 96.00%
Sortino Ratio:	

NAGY-BECK HEDGE RATING:

FRIEDBERG TT EQU-HEDGE (US$)

Friedberg Commodity Mngmnt Inc.
181 Bay Street, Suite 250
Toronto, ON • M5J 2T3

Telephone Number: (416) 364-1171
Fax Number: (416) 364-5385
Toll-Free: 1-800-461-2700
Web Site: www.friedberg.com

PORTFOLIO MANAGER(S)

Albert D. Friedberg, MBA, Manager   **Friedberg Mercantile Group**

Both the Trading Manager and FMG were founded by Albert D. Friedberg, a recognized expert in foreign currencies and commodities. He was born in Lyon, France, raised in Uruguay, and educated at Johns Hopkins University and Columbia University, where he received an MBA in international banking. He served as chairman of the Toronto Futures Exchange from March 1985 to June 1988. Friedberg and his family indirectly beneficially own a controlling interest in each of FMG, the Trading Manager, and the General Partner.

FUND DESCRIPTION

The investment objective of the fund is to achieve capital appreciation. The fund will invest primarily in common stock, preferred stock, securities convertible into common or preferred stock, stock warrants and rights, limited partnership interests, units or shares of undertaking for collective investment and depositary receipts, engage in short sales of securities, and speculate in stock index futures contracts and related options traded on any exchange or through the OTC market.

TERMS AND CONDITIONS

Fund style: CTA

Sub-style:

Inception date: February 1998

Management fee: 2.50%

Performance fee:

Hurdle rate:

Liquidity: Daily

*Min. investment: $150,000

Benchmark: TSX

* (Not available in PQ, YK, NWT, NUV)

RRSP eligibility: Yes (Foreign Content)

Asset size: US$6 million

NAV: $16.33

Early red'n period:

Early red'n fee:

High water mark:

Redemption notice:

Max. leverage:

PERFORMANCE (AS OF DECEMBER 31, 2002)

	1 month	3 month	6 month	YTD	1 year	2 year	3 year	5 year	10 year	Since Inception
Fund:	11.12%	-13.17%	-15.08%	-0.07%	-0.07%	-2.34%	14.42%			10.49%
TSX	0.67%	7.03%	-7.43%	-13.97%	-13.97%	-13.96%	-7.71%			-0.26%

	Year:	Jan	Feb	Mar	Apr	May	Jun	Jul	Aug	Sep	Oct	Nov	Dec
Fund:	2002	-0.07%	0.39%	3.62%	-0.19%	7.49%	-0.08%	5.53%	-7.72%	-2.39%	8.58%	-14.19%	-8.94%	11.12%
TSX	2002	-13.97%	-0.52%	-0.14%	2.80%	-2.40%	-0.10%	-6.67%	-7.56%	0.10%	-6.53%	1.11%	5.15%	0.67%
Fund:	2001	-4.56%	-28.62%	21.11%	7.84%	-6.39%	5.56%	7.65%	-2.02%	8.56%	2.71%	-4.12%	-6.86%	-1.36%
TSX	2001	-13.94%	4.35%	-13.34%	-5.83%	4.45%	2.71%	-5.21%	-0.60%	-3.78%	-7.58%	0.69%	7.84%	3.54%
Fund:	2000	57.06%	1.74%	28.31%	-5.13%	5.56%	-1.61%	-0.14%	-4.79%	-0.90%	7.87%	-0.63%	14.83%	5.29%
TSX	2000	6.18%	0.80%	7.64%	3.65%	-1.21%	-1.02%	10.20%	2.07%	8.09%	-7.74%	-7.12%	-8.50%	1.29%
Fund:	1999	18.98%	-0.44%	-5.92%	-14.69%	-3.01%	1.55%	3.75%	9.49%	1.71%	1.44%	-5.09%	8.60%	25.14%
TSX	1999	29.71%	3.76%	-6.20%	4.52%	6.32%	-2.47%	2.46%	1.01%	-1.56%	-0.19%	4.29%	3.68%	11.84%
Fund:	1998	-8.37%		-4.10%	1.15%	-0.41%	3.42%	-1.00%	-3.64%	3.25%	-6.10%	-7.66%	1.41%	5.90%
TSX	1998	-3.20%		5.86%	6.57%	1.41%	-0.98%	-2.94%	-5.91%	-20.21%	1.51%	10.58%	2.18%	2.24%

PERFORMANCE COMPARISON

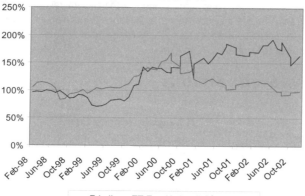

— Friedberg TT Equ-Hedge (US$) —— TSX

RISK DATA (AS OF SEPTEMBER 30, 2002)

Alpha (3 year): 0.71%	Sharpe Ratio: 0.13	Maximum drawdown: 28.62%
Beta: -0.67	Sortino Ratio:	Largest monthly drop: 28.62%
St. deviation (annualized): 10.49%	Benchmark: TSX	Percentage of negative months: 47.46%
St. deviation (1 year):	Correlation to benchmark:	Percentage of positive months: 52.54%
St. deviation (2 year):		

NAGY-BECK HEDGE RATING:

THE GOODWOOD FUND–A

Goodwood Fund
212 King Street West, Suite 201
Toronto, ON • M5H 1K5

Telephone Number: (416) 203-2022
Fax Number: (416) 203-0732
Toll-Free: (866) 681-4393
Web Site: www.goodwoodfunds.com

Similar funds:
The Goodwood Fund–B
Arrow Goodwood Fund

PORTFOLIO MANAGER(S)

Peter H. Puccetti, CFA, Chairman and Chief Investment Officer

Peter Puccetti is the founder and investment manager of the Goodwood Fund. The firm began in October 1996 with the sole focus being the investment management of a Canadian long/short fund.

In 1993 Puccetti founded the investment firm Puccetti Farell Capital Corporation, raising in excess of $100 million within a three-year period toward Canadian equity financings. In 1990 Puccetti joined Sprott Securities Limited as a special situation analyst, thereafter becoming a member of the firm's steering committee. He earned a bachelor of arts in economics, Dalhousie University, and has been awarded the chartered financial analyst (CFA) designation.

FUND DESCRIPTION

The investment objective of the Goodwood Fund is to maximize total return through the purchase and short sale of primarily Canadian exchange-listed and over-the-counter quoted securities. The manager selects long and short positions on the basis of a bottom-up, security-specific approach. The portfolio is relatively concentrated and does not currently exceed 35 holdings.

Goodwood's investment process and success can best be summarized as being bottom up, value oriented, and often event driven. The performance record is the result of intensive analysis of each company and industry in question. This serves as the starting point to understand both the risk and the opportunities present. Thereafter, a detailed accounting review coupled with an investment banking mindset has become the platform attributable to Goodwood's performance. Goodwood's mandate to their investors is simple—understand the risk to understand the return. Their performance benchmark is the TSX 300 Total Return Index; however, it is the stock selection and portfolio weightings versus an index exposure that results in their performance success.

TERMS AND CONDITIONS

Fund style: Stock selection

Sub-style: No Bias

Inception date: October 1996

Management fee: 1.90%

Performance fee: 20%

Hurdle rate: 10% (Class A unit)

Liquidity: Weekly

*Min. investment: $150,000

Benchmark: TSX

* or less based on provincial legislation

RRSP eligibility: Yes

Asset size (program): $200 million

NAV: $16.98 (Class A unit)

Early red'n period: 3 years

Early red'n fee: 1%

High-water mark: Yes

Redemption notice: Next available trade date

Max. leverage: 100%

PERFORMANCE (AS OF DECEMBER 31, 2002)

	1 month	3 month	6 month	YTD	1 year	2 year	3 year	5 year	10 year	Since Inception
Fund:	-1.78%	-2.25%	-16.56%	-18.53%	-18.53%	0.91%	15.51%	18.84%		21.44%
TSX	0.67%	7.03%	-7.43%	-13.97%	-13.97%	-13.96%	-7.71%	-0.26%		n/a

	Year:	Jan	Feb	Mar	Apr	May	Jun	Jul	Aug	Sep	Oct	Nov	Dec
Fund:	2002	-18.53%	2.01%	-2.37%	1.55%	-0.82%	1.01%	-3.63%	-8.07%	-4.61%	-2.66%	1.03%	-1.49%	-1.78%
TSX	2002	-13.97%	-0.52%	-0.14%	2.80%	-2.40%	-0.10%	-6.67%	-7.56%	0.10%	-6.53%	1.11%	5.15%	0.67%
Fund:	2001	24.98%	5.48%	-2.24%	0.28%	3.80%	3.60%	3.53%	1.43%	3.31%	-0.45%	1.73%	1.27%	1.02%
TSX	2001	-13.94%	4.35%	-13.34%	-5.83%	4.45%	2.71%	-5.21%	-0.60%	-3.78%	-7.58%	0.69%	7.84%	3.54%
Fund:	2000	51.37%	0.61%	11.47%	8.96%	-1.36%	1.89%	9.04%	-2.28%	1.40%	3.82%	-3.17%	0.50%	12.91%
TSX	2000	6.18%	0.80%	7.64%	3.65%	-1.21%	-1.02%	10.20%	2.07%	8.09%	-7.74%	-7.12%	-8.50%	1.29%
Fund:	1999	50.08%	2.29%	3.83%	1.23%	2.53%	4.44%	3.78%	-1.09%	8.93%	-0.76%	-1.87%	12.07%	6.82%
TSX	1999	29.71%	3.76%	-6.20%	4.52%	6.32%	-2.47%	2.46%	1.01%	-1.56%	-0.19%	4.29%	3.68%	11.84%
Fund:	1998	2.45%	-3.23%	1.61%	9.86%	1.75%	-5.98%	6.90%	4.54%	-2.61%	-9.51%	0.55%	-3.05%	3.26%
TSX	1998	-3.19%	0.01%	5.86%	6.57%	1.41%	-0.98%	-2.94%	-5.91%	-20.21%	1.51%	10.58%	2.18%	2.24%
Fund:	1997	41.09%	5.28%	-1.50%	-1.53%	-0.72%	9.38%	1.90%	7.76%	-2.69%	15.78%	12.47%	-8.42%	-0.15%
TSX	1997	0.00%												
Fund:	1996	-0.94%											2.72%	-3.56%
TSX	1996	0.00%												

PERFORMANCE COMPARISON

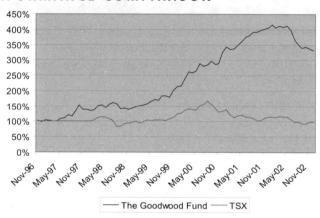

—— The Goodwood Fund ······ TSX

RISK DATA (AS OF DECEMBER 31, 2002)

Alpha:	Benchmark: TSX
Beta:	Correlation to benchmark: 0.37
St. deviation (annualized): 17.51%	Maximum drawdown: 20.14%
St. deviation (1 year):	Largest monthly drop: 9.50%
St. deviation (2 year):	Percentage of negative months: 37.84%
Sharpe Ratio: 1.05	Percentage of positive months: 63.89%
Sortino Ratio:	

NAGY-BECK HEDGE RATING:

HILLSDALE CANADIAN AGGRESSIVE HEDGED A

Hillsdale Investment Management Inc. Telephone Number: (416) 913-3900
100 Wellington Street West Fax Number: (416) 913-3901
CP Tower, Suite 2100 Web Site: www.hillsdaleinv.com
Toronto, ON • M5K 1J3

Similar funds: Hillsdale Canadian Aggressive Hedged I

PORTFOLIO MANAGER(S)

**Christopher Guthrie, BA, CFA President,
CEO, Portfolio Manager, Founding Partner**

Christopher Guthrie is responsible for establishing corporate strategy and leading its implementation and execution and is accountable to the Board of Directors. As portfolio manager, he has ultimate responsibility for all portfolio management decisions made by the firm. He has more than 15 years experience in investment management. Prior to founding Hillsdale in January 1996, Guthrie was employed as a Toronto-based investment counsellor specializing in quantitative equity management and was responsible for (i) assisting in the design and on-going development of quantitative equity management systems; (ii) training institutional money managers in the application of quantitative investment strategies; and (iii) supervising and managing in-house equity accounts.

Arun Kaul, BA, CFA, Portfolio Manager, COO, Partner

Arun Kaul is responsible for assisting in the establishment of corporate strategy and ensuring its implementation and execution. As portfolio manager, he shares responsibility with Guthrie for all portfolio management decisions. Prior to joining Hillsdale, Kaul was employed as a Toronto-based investment counsellor specializing in quantitative equity management and was responsible for (i) assisting in the design and on-going development of quantitative equity management systems; (ii) training institutional money managers in the application of quantitative investment strategies; (iii) managing in-house equity accounts. He was also previously employed as an auditor for the Prudential Insurance Company of America. Kaul joined Hillsdale in December 1996.

Tony Batek, BMath, CFA, Associate Portfolio Manager

Tony Batek is responsible for assisting in the design and implementation of the firm's proprietary research, providing equity market analysis, and assisting in the implementation of the firm's portfolio management decision-making process. Prior to joining Hillsdale, he was a quantitative analyst at Laketon Investment Management, and a foreign equity market manager and systems analyst at CPMS. Batek joined Hillsdale in July 2002.

FUND DESCRIPTION:

The fund is a directional equity hedge fund that invests in, and sells short, a long portfolio and a short portfolio of securities. In each portfolio the fund invests primarily in a diversified selection of mid-to-large-market-capitalization Canadian corporations trading on major Canadian exchanges. The investment objective is to provide a rate of return on capital in excess of Canadian equities over a three-year period with a low correlation to the S&P/TSX Composite Index and volatility equal to or less than that of other equity funds. Leverage limited to two times net assets and net market exposure will be between 50 and 90% at all times. A minimum of 80% of total assets will be invested in the capital of 50 to 100 selected Canadian corporations listed on major Canadian stock exchanges, primarily with market capitalization of at least CAD$100 million.

TERMS AND CONDITIONS

Fund style: Stock Selection

Sub-style: Long Bias	***Min. investment:** $150,000	**Early red'n period:**
Inception date: December 1999	**Benchmark:** TSX	**Early red'n fee:**
Management fee: 2.00%	**RRSP eligibility:** Yes	**High-water mark:** Yes
Performance fee: 20%	**Asset size (program):** $8 million	**Redemption notice:**
Hurdle rate: 0%	**NAV:** $14.47	**Max. leverage:** 200%
Liquidity: Daily		

* or less based on provincial legislation

PERFORMANCE (AS OF DECEMBER 31, 2002)

	1 month	3 month	6 month	YTD	1 year	2 year	3 year	5 year	10 year	Since Inception
Fund:	5.18%	-2.01%	-11.14%	-1.13%	-1.13%	2.56%	11.94%			11.94%
TSX	0.67%	7.03%	-7.43%	-13.97%	-13.97%	-13.96%	-7.71%			-7.71%

	Year:		Jan	Feb	Mar	Apr	May	Jun	Jul	Aug	Sep	Oct	Nov	Dec
d:	2002	-1.13%	5.32%	3.87%	3.21%	0.42%	2.34%	-4.11%	-10.41%	5.77%	-4.30%	-3.07%	-3.89%	5.18%
	2002	-13.97%	-0.52%	-0.14%	2.80%	-2.40%	-0.10%	-6.67%	-7.56%	0.10%	-6.53%	1.11%	5.15%	0.67%
d:	2001	6.38%	-11.01%	-2.33%	2.20%	3.74%	7.42%	-2.11%	4.99%	0.50%	-2.64%	-0.92%	5.56%	2.18%
:	2001	-13.94%	4.35%	-13.34%	-5.83%	4.45%	2.71%	-5.21%	-0.60%	-3.78%	-7.58%	0.69%	7.84%	3.54%
d:	2000	33.37%	0.00%	7.70%	-0.83%	-1.52%	2.83%	4.63%	3.08%	7.44%	4.54%	0.01%	-7.41%	9.93%
	2000	6.18%	0.80%	7.64%	3.65%	-1.21%	-1.02%	10.20%	2.07%	8.09%	-7.74%	-7.12%	-8.50%	1.29%

PERFORMANCE COMPARISON

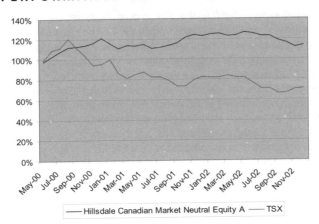

——— Hillsdale Canadian Market Neutral Equity A ——— TSX

RISK DATA (AS OF DECEMBER 31, 2002)

Alpha (annualized): 4.76%

Beta (3 year): 0.41

St. deviation (annualized): 16.80%

St. deviation (1 year):

St. deviation (2 year):

Sharpe Ratio (5% RF): 0.49

Sortino Ratio: 0.59

Benchmark: TSX

Correlation to benchmark: 0.42

Maximum drawdown: 19.00%

Largest monthly drop: 11.01%

Percentage of negative months: 36.11%

Percentage of positive months: 63.89%

NAGY-BECK HEDGE RATING:

HILLSDALE CANADIAN MARKET NEUTRAL EQUITY A

Hillsdale Investment Management Inc. Telephone Number: (416) 913-3900
100 Wellington Street West   Fax Number: (416) 913-3901
CP Tower, Suite 2100   Web Site: www.hillsdaleinv.com
Toronto, ON • M5K 1J3

Similar funds: Hillsdale Cndn Market Neutral Equity I

PORTFOLIO MANAGER(S)

**Christopher Guthrie, BA, CFA President,
CEO, Portfolio Manager, Founding Partner**

Christopher Guthrie is responsible for establishing corporate strategy and leading its implementation and execution and is accountable to the Board of Directors. As portfolio manager, he has ultimate responsibility for all portfolio management decisions made by the firm. He has more than 15 years experience in investment management. Prior to founding Hillsdale in January 1996, Guthrie was employed as a Toronto-based investment counsellor specializing in quantitative equity management and was responsible for (i) assisting in the design and on-going development of quantitative equity management systems; (ii) training institutional money managers in the application of quantitative investment strategies; and (iii) supervising and managing in-house equity accounts.

Arun Kaul, BA, CFA, Portfolio Manager, COO, Partner

Arun Kaul is responsible for assisting in the establishment of corporate strategy and ensuring its implementation and execution. As portfolio manager, he shares responsibility with Guthrie for all portfolio management decisions. Prior to joining Hillsdale, Kaul was employed as a Toronto-based investment counsellor specializing in quantitative equity management and was responsible for (i) assisting in the design and on-going development of quantitative equity management systems; (ii) training institutional money managers in the application of quantitative investment strategies; (iii) managing in-house equity accounts. He was also previously employed as an auditor for the Prudential Insurance Company of America. Kaul joined Hillsdale in December 1996.

Tony Batek, BMath, CFA, Associate Portfolio Manager

Tony Batek is responsible for assisting in the design and implementation of the firm's proprietary research, providing equity market analysis, and assisting in the implementation of the firm's portfolio management decision-making process. Prior to joining Hillsdale, he was a quantitative analyst at Laketon Investment Management, and a foreign equity market manager and systems analyst at CPMS. Batek joined Hillsdale in July 2002.

FUND DESCRIPTION

The fund is a market neutral equity hedge fund that invests in, and sells short, a long portfolio and a short portfolio of securities. In each portfolio the fund invests primarily in a diversified selection of mid- to large-market capitalization Canadian corporations trading on major Canadian exchanges. The investment objective is to provide a non-correlated rate of return on capital in excess of Canadian T-bills over a three-year period with volatility equal to or less than that of long-term bonds. Leverage limited to one times net assets and net market exposure will be between -20 and +20% at all times. A minimum of 80% of total assets will be invested in the capital of 50 to 200 selected Canadian corporations listed on major Canadian stock exchanges, primarily with market capitalization of at least CAD$100 million.

TERMS AND CONDITIONS

Fund style: Stock Selection

Sub-style: No Bias	***Min. investment:** $150,000	**Early red'n period:**
Inception date: May 2000	**Benchmark:** TSX	**Early red'n fee:**
Management fee: 0.20%	**RRSP eligibility:** Yes	**High-water mark:** Yes
Performance fee: 20%	**Asset size (program):** $1 million	**Redemption notice:**
Hurdle rate: 0%	**NAV:** $11.38	**Max. leverage:** 100%
Liquidity: Daily		

* or less based on provincial legislation

PERFORMANCE (AS OF DECEMBER 31, 2002)

	1 month	3 month	6 month	YTD	1 year	2 year	3 year	5 year	10 year	Since Inception
Fund:	1.67%	-4.22%	-9.10%	-7.41%	-7.41%	-5.74%				5.15%
TSX	0.67%	7.03%	-7.43%	-13.97%	-13.97%	-13.96%				-12.17%

	Year:	Jan	Feb	Mar	Apr	May	Jun	Jul	Aug	Sep	Oct	Nov	Dec
Fund:	2002	-7.41%	1.76%	0.46%	-2.09%	0.44%	2.53%	-1.19%	-1.76%	-0.12%	-3.27%	-2.35%	-3.53%	1.67%
TSX	2002	-13.97%	-0.52%	-0.14%	2.80%	-2.40%	-0.10%	-6.67%	-7.56%	0.10%	-6.53%	1.11%	5.15%	0.67%
Fund:	2001	1.8%	-4.5%	-3.7%	2.45%	-0.51%	1.42%	-3.73%	1.56%	1.25%	2.45%	4.4%	2.3%	-1.1%
TSX	2001	-13.94%	4.35%	-13.34%	-5.83%	4.45%	2.71%	-5.21%	-0.60%	-3.78%	-7.58%	0.69%	7.84%	3.54%
Fund:	2000	20.8%				-2.24%	4.95%	4.66%	4.24%	0.76%	0.80%	2.15%	3.99%
TSX	2000	-4.43%				-1.02%	10.20%	2.07%	8.09%	-7.74%	-7.12%	-8.50%	1.29%

PERFORMANCE COMPARISON

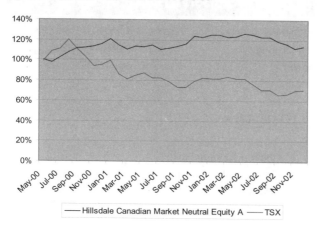

──── Hillsdale Canadian Market Neutral Equity A ──── TSX

RISK DATA (AS OF DECEMBER 31, 2002)

Alpha (annualized): 7.28%

Beta: 0.13

St. deviation (annualized): 9.20%

St. deviation (1 year):

St. deviation (2 year):

Sharpe Ratio (5% RF): 0.07

Sortino Ratio: 0.04

Benchmark: TSX

Correlation to benchmark: 0.27

Maximum drawdown: 11.65%

Largest monthly drop: 4.58%

Percentage of negative months: 41.94%

Percentage of positive months: 58.06%

NAGY-BECK HEDGE RATING:

HILLSDALE US AGGRESSIVE HEDGED EQUITY A

Hillsdale Investment Management Inc. Telephone Number: (416) 913-3900
100 Wellington Street West   Fax Number: (416) 913-3901
CP Tower, Suite 2100   Web Site: www.hillsdaleinv.com
Toronto, ON • M5K 1J3

PORTFOLIO MANAGER(S)

Christopher Guthrie, BA, CFA President,
CEO, Portfolio Manager, Founding Partner
Christopher Guthrie is responsible for establishing corporate strategy and leading its implementation and execution and is accountable to the Board of Directors. As portfolio manager, he has ultimate responsibility for all portfolio management decisions made by the firm. He has more than 15 years experience in investment management. Prior to founding Hillsdale in January 1996, Guthrie was employed as a Toronto-based investment counsellor specializing in quantitative equity management and was responsible for (i) assisting in the design and on-going development of quantitative equity management systems; (ii) training institutional money managers in the application of quantitative investment strategies; and (iii) supervising and managing in-house equity accounts.

Arun Kaul, BA, CFA, Portfolio Manager, COO, Partner
Arun Kaul is responsible for assisting in the establishment of corporate strategy and ensuring its implementation and execution. As portfolio manager, he shares responsibility with Guthrie for all portfolio management decisions. Prior to joining Hillsdale, Kaul was employed as a Toronto-based investment counsellor specializing in quantitative equity management and was responsible for (i) assisting in the design and on-going development of quantitative equity management systems; (ii) training institutional money managers in the application of quantitative investment strategies; (iii) managing in-house equity accounts. He was also previously employed as an auditor for the Prudential Insurance Company of America. Kaul joined Hillsdale in December 1996.

Debbie Chin, BComm, CFA, Associate Portfolio Manager
Ms. Chin is responsible for implementing the portfolio management decision-making process for all of the firm's U.S. products. Prior to joining Hillsdale, she was senior analyst and supervisor of fund analytics, investment management at AGF Funds Inc. and a consultant in executive compensation at William Mercer Ltd. Chin joined Hillsdale in October 2001.

FUND DESCRIPTION:

The fund is a directional equity hedge fund that invests in, and sells short, a long portfolio and a short portfolio of securities. In each portfolio the fund invests primarily in a diversified selection of mid-to-large-market-capitalization U.S. corporations trading on major U.S. exchanges. The investment objective is to provide a rate of return on capital in excess of U.S. equities over a three-year period with a low correlation to the S&P 500 Composite Index and volatility equal to or less than that of other equity funds. Leverage limited to two times net assets and net market exposure will be between 50 and 90% at all times. A minimum of 80% of total assets will be invested in the capital of 50 to 100 selected U.S. corporations listed on major U.S. stock exchanges, primarily with market capitalization of at least US$500 million.

TERMS AND CONDITIONS

Fund style: Stock Selection

Sub-style: Long Bias	***Min. investment:** US$110,000	**Early red'n period:**
Inception date: July 2000	**Benchmark:** S&P 500	**Early red'n fee:**
Management fee: 1.91%	**RRSP eligibility:** Yes (Foreign Content)	**High-water mark:** Yes
Performance fee: 20%	**Asset size (program):** $2 million	**Redemption notice:**
Hurdle rate: 0%	**NAV:** $7.45	**Max. leverage:** 100%
Liquidity: Daily		

* or less based on provincial legislation

PERFORMANCE (AS OF DECEMBER 31, 2002)

	1 month	3 month	6 month	YTD	1 year	2 year	3 year	5 year	10 year	Since Inception
Fund:	1.24%	-1.11%	-5.40%	-12.66%	-12.66%	-17.84%				-11.47%
S&P500	-5.48%	7.42%	-7.07%	-23.14%	-23.14%	-15.15%				-15.10%

Year:		Jan	Feb	Mar	Apr	May	Jun	Jul	Aug	Sep	Oct	Nov	Dec
Fund:	2002	-12.66%	8.30%	-1.59%	-7.51%	4.11%	-5.18%	-5.12%	-6.93%	7.89%	-4.74%	-3.38%	1.10%	1.24%
S&P500	2002	-23.14%	-1.70%	-1.16%	3.33%	-7.67%	-3.25%	-7.77%	-3.73%	-0.98%	-9.25%	6.85%	6.36%	-5.48%
Fund:	2001	-22.71%	-8.80%	-1.23%	2.67%	1.44%	0.90%	-2.89%	0.45%	-7.23%	-1.10%	-13.86%	1.74%	4.10%
S&P500	2001	-6.33%	3.51%	-6.78%	-3.95%	4.99%	0.87%	-3.94%	0.27%	-5.18%	-6.42%	2.50%	6.63%	2.16%
Fund:	2000	10.36%								16.59%	-3.13%	-9.74%	-0.14%	8.41%
S&P500	2000	-6.49%								5.20%	-3.27%	0.85%	0.93%	-9.72%

PERFORMANCE COMPARISON

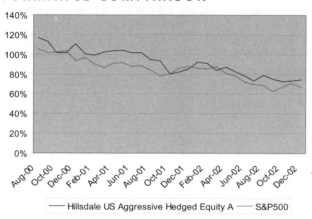

```
Hillsdale US Aggressive Hedged Equity A ——— S&P500
```

RISK DATA (AS OF DECEMBER 31, 2002)

Alpha (3 year):	Benchmark: S&P 500
Beta (3 year):	Correlation to benchmark:
St. deviation (annualized): 21.60%	Maximum drawdown: 20.70%
St. deviation (1 year):	Largest monthly drop: 13.86%
St. deviation (2 year):	Percentage of negative months: 51.72%
Sharpe Ratio:	Percentage of positive months: 63.89%
Sortino Ratio:	

NAGY-BECK HEDGE RATING:

HILLSDALE US MARKET NEUTRAL EQUITY

Hillsdale Investment Management Inc.
100 Wellington Street West
CP Tower, Suite 2100
Toronto, ON • M5K 1J3

Telephone Number: (416) 913-3900
Fax Number: (416) 913-3901
Web Site: www.hillsdaleinv.com

Similar funds:
Hillsdale Canadian Aggressive Hedged I

PORTFOLIO MANAGER(S)

Christopher Guthrie, BA, CFA President,
CEO, Portfolio Manager, Founding Partner

Christopher Guthrie is responsible for establishing corporate strategy and leading its implementation and execution and is accountable to the Board of Directors. As portfolio manager, he has ultimate responsibility for all portfolio management decisions made by the firm. He has more than 15 years experience in investment management. Prior to founding Hillsdale in January 1996, Guthrie was employed as a Toronto-based investment counsellor specializing in quantitative equity management and was responsible for (i) assisting in the design and on-going development of quantitative equity management systems; (ii) training institutional money managers in the application of quantitative investment strategies; and (iii) supervising and managing in-house equity accounts.

Arun Kaul, BA, CFA, Portfolio Manager, COO, Partner

Arun Kaul is responsible for assisting in the establishment of corporate strategy and ensuring its implementation and execution. As portfolio manager, he shares responsibility with Guthrie for all portfolio management decisions. Prior to joining Hillsdale, Kaul was employed as a Toronto-based investment counsellor specializing in quantitative equity management and was responsible for (i) assisting in the design and on-going development of quantitative equity management systems; (ii) training institutional money managers in the application of quantitative investment strategies; (iii) managing in-house equity accounts. He was also previously employed as an auditor for the Prudential Insurance Company of America. Kaul joined Hillsdale in December 1996.

Debbie Chin, BComm, CFA, Associate Portfolio Manager

Debbie Chin is responsible for implementing the portfolio management decision-making process for all of the firm's US products. Prior to joining Hillsdale, she was senior analyst and supervisor of fund analytics, investment management at AGF Funds Inc. and a consultant in executive compensation at William Mercer Ltd. Chin joined Hillsdale in October 2001.

FUND DESCRIPTION

The fund is a market neutral equity hedge fund that invests in, and sells short, a long portfolio and a short portfolio of securities. In each portfolio the Fund invests primarily in a diversified selection of mid- to large-market capitalization U.S. corporations trading on major U.S. exchanges. The fund's investment objective is to provide a non-correlated rate of return on capital in excess of U.S. T-bills over a three-year period with volatility equal to or less than that of long-term bonds. Leverage limited to one times net assets and net market exposure will be between -20 and +20% at all times. A minimum of 80% of total assets will be invested in the capital of 50 to 300 selected U.S. corporations listed on major U.S. stock exchanges, primarily with market capitalization of at least US$500 million.

TERMS AND CONDITIONS

Fund style: Stock Selection

Sub-style: No Bias	***Min. investment:** US$110,000	**Early red'n period:**
Inception date: March 1997	**Benchmark:** S&P 500	**Early red'n fee:**
Management fee: 2.00%	**RRSP eligibility:** Yes (Foreign Content)	**High-water mark:** Yes
Performance fee: 20%	**Asset size (program):** $2 million	**Redemption notice:**
Hurdle rate: 0%	**NAV:** $11.71	**Max. leverage:** 100%
Liquidity: Daily		

* or less based on provincial legislation

PERFORMANCE (AS OF DECEMBER 31, 2002)

	1 month	3 month	6 month	YTD	1 year	2 year	3 year	5 year	10 year	Since Inception
Fund:	0.93%	-2.79%	-0.49%	2.73%	2.73%	-5.56%	-0.55%	1.21%		5.31%
S&P500	-5.48%	7.42%	-7.07%	-23.14%	-23.14%	-15.15%	-12.23%	1.32%		N/A

	Year:	Jan	Feb	Mar	Apr	May	Jun	Jul	Aug	Sep	Oct	Nov	Dec
Fund:	2002	2.73%	3.42%	-2.98%	-1.26%	6.07%	-0.14%	-1.62%	0.93%	3.01%	-1.54%	-1.41%	-2.31%	0.93%
S&P500	2002	-23.14%	-1.70%	-1.16%	3.33%	-7.67%	-3.25%	-7.77%	-3.73%	-0.98%	-9.25%	6.85%	6.36%	-5.48%
Fund:	2001	-13.18%	-10.97%	-1.17%	1.01%	-0.76%	0.75%	1.40%	-1.01%	-1.60%	0.13%	-1.74%	-1.01%	1.57%
S&P500	2001	-6.33%	3.51%	-6.78%	-3.95%	4.99%	0.87%	-3.94%	0.27%	-5.18%	-6.42%	2.50%	6.63%	2.16%
Fund:	2000	10.27%	2.92%	-3.74%	1.20%	6.01%	-2.21%	3.59%	-1.78%	8.25%	1.53%	-6.05%	2.87%	-1.83%
S&P500	2000	-6.07%	-5.31%	-1.70%	9.80%	-0.87%	-1.01%	1.34%	-1.17%	5.20%	-3.27%	0.85%	0.93%	-9.72%
Fund:	1999	-16.00%	9.24%	-1.03%	-4.35%	-2.45%	-5.94%	-5.01%	4.78%	0.88%	-7.32%	-0.80%	-4.45%	0.37%
S&P500	1999	14.73%	2.85%	-3.27%	4.00%	0.32%	-1.19%	4.73%	-0.18%	-1.47%	-4.37%	6.56%	2.29%	4.19%
Fund:	1998	28.51%	-0.62%	2.37%	1.15%	-7.38%	3.68%	4.02%	-0.69%	3.08%	6.78%	-1.10%	1.28%	14.18%
S&P500	1998	37.59%	2.85%	4.96%	4.84%	1.78%	0.05%	4.78%	2.05%	-11.44%	3.97%	9.00%	5.39%	5.56%
Fund:	1997	27.4%			0.3%	3.4%	5.2%	2.4%	4.8%	-0.3%	3.7%	2.1%	1.8%	1.2%

PERFORMANCE COMPARISON

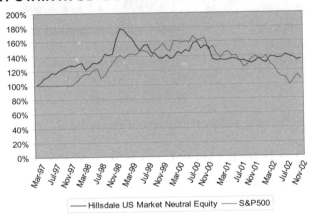

——— Hillsdale US Market Neutral Equity ——— S&P500

RISK DATA (AS OF DECEMBER 31, 2002)

Alpha (annualized): 6.48%

Beta: 0.05

St. deviation (annualized): 13.90%

St. deviation (1 year):

St. deviation (2 year):

Sharpe Ratio (5% RF): 0.11

Sortino Ratio:

Benchmark: S&P 500

Correlation to benchmark: 0.07

Maximum drawdown: 23.82%

Largest monthly drop: 10.97%

Percentage of negative months: 51.67% (based on past 5 years)

Percentage of positive months: 63.89% (based on past 5 years)

NAGY-BECK HEDGE RATING:

HORIZONS EQUITY LONG/SHORT FUND

First Horizon Capital Corp.
#230-375 Water Street
Vancouver, BC • V6B 5C6

Telephone Number: (604) 688-7333;
(416) 367-9333
Fax Number: (416) 601-1695
Toll-Free: 1-800-665-1158
Web Site: www.horizonsfunds.com

This fund will be re-branded under the Olympus United Group of Funds in 2003.

PORTFOLIO MANAGER(S)

SCI European Hedge Fund

The SCI European fund seeks to achieve capital appreciation by investing, on the long and short side, in mid- and large-cap European equities while actively managing risk to reduce volatility. At any point in time, the fund is invested in 40 to 60 publicly traded equities selected from a universe of approximately 600 stocks. Stock selection is driven by fundamentals and each position is assigned an absolute price target. Derivatives are used only in exceptional market circumstances. Normally the beta adjusted net market exposure will range between 50% net long and 20% net short, with gross exposure never exceeding 150%.

Okumus Market Neutral Funds

Okumus utilizes a bottom-up approach in security selection and does not place major bets on the direction of the market. It invests in a concentrated number of stocks, both long and short. The primary objective of the funds is to achieve consistent capital growth while strictly emphasizing risk management and capital preservation. Market Neutral Fund uses Okumus portfolio management style while seeking to eliminate market risk with a dollar neutral exposure. This 0% market exposure helps minimize downside deviation while still generating the solid returns. The Market Neutral Fund targets 0% net exposure by maintaining equal dollar exposures on the long side and the short side at any given time.

Sprott Asset Management

This manager invests in opportunities that provide the best reward per unit of risk at the time of investment. Some of the core techniques employed are making long investments in securities believed to be undervalued, short-selling securities believed to be overvalued, and managing the relative weightings of long and short positions depending on their view of the domestic and international economy and market trends, including liquidity flows within the U.S. financial system.

Horizons Hedge Overlay

This program combines four derivatives-based managers into a single portfolio component designed to deliver consistently non-correlated performance to the traditional fund managers. Allocations to the four managers are weighted according to their historic performance volatility, the least volatile manager receiving the larger allocation.

FUND DESCRIPTION

The fund utilizes the expertise of (basically) three managers: SCI European Hedge Fund, Okomus Market Neutral Fund, and Sprott Asset Management. Combined, these funds offer investors a fund of hedge funds allocation with little correlation to any market, low volatility, and consistent relatively high return.

TERMS AND CONDITIONS

Fund style: Fund of Hedge Funds

Sub-style: Stock Selection/Market Neutral	*** Min. investment:** $150,000	**Early red'n period:** N/A
Inception date: September 2002	**Benchmark:** MSCI	**Early red'n fee:** None
Management fee: 1.75%	**RRSP eligibility:** Yes (Foreign Content)	**High-water mark:** Yes
Performance fee: 20%	**Asset size:** $4 million	**Redemption notice:**
Hurdle rate: N/A	**NAV:** $9.12	**Max. leverage:**
Liquidity: Weekly		

* or less based on provincial legislation

PERFORMANCE (AS OF DECEMBER 31, 2002)

	1 month	3 month	6 month	YTD	1 year	2 year	3 year	5 year	10 year	Since Inception
Fund:	-2.32%	0.28%								
MSCI	-4.83%	7.74%								

Year:		Jan	Feb	Mar	Apr	May	Jun	Jul	Aug	Sep	Oct	Nov	Dec
Fund:	2002	-0.92%								-1.20%	-1.00%	3.70%	-2.32%
MSCI	2002	-4.08%								-10.97%	7.40%	5.41%	-4.83%

PERFORMANCE COMPARISON

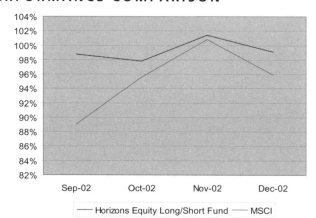

— Horizons Equity Long/Short Fund   — MSCI

RISK DATA (AS OF DECEMBER 31, 2002)

Alpha:	Benchmark: MSCI
Beta:	Correlation to benchmark:
St. deviation (annualized):	Maximum drawdown: 2.32%
St. deviation (1 year):	Largest monthly drop: 2.32%
St. deviation (2 year):	Percentage of negative months: 75.00%
Sharpe Ratio:	Percentage of positive months: 25.00%
Sortino Ratio:	

NAGY-BECK HEDGE RATING:

HORIZONS MONDIALE HEDGE FUND

First Horizon Capital Corp.   Telephone Number: (416) 601-2228
71 King Street East, Second Floor   Fax Number: (416) 601-1695
Toronto, ON   Toll-Free: 1-877-450-0722
M5G 1C3   Web Site: www.horizonsfunds.com

PORTFOLIO MANAGER(S)

Mondiale Asset Management Ltd.

Mondiale is a Canadian firm that specializes in quantitative hedge fund management, actively investing in securities and derivatives on a global basis. Mondiale, currently comprised of three professionals and one support staff, has been managing both public and private capital for more than six years. The firm currently manages CDN$ 138 million of assets, acting as portfolio manager to the Horizons Mondiale Hedge Fund and the Mondiale Performance Hedge Program.

The Horizons Mondiale Hedge Fund is an RRSP-eligible (as Canadian content), full-prospectus retail mutual fund available in all provinces except Quebec. The Mondiale Performance Hedge Program can currently be accessed by retail investors in Canada through a product under offering memorandum: the Horizons Strategic Fund.

FUND DESCRIPTION:

The Horizons Mondiale Hedge Fund uses a trend-following investment strategy to produce consistent returns regardless of the direction of global equity markets. Investment decisions are determined by the firm's systematic trading rules, initiating long positions as the market trends higher and allocating to cash or short positions as the market sells off. This creates a very defensive portfolio.

TERMS AND CONDITIONS

Fund style: Directional Trading

Sub-style: System Trading	**Min. investment:** $5,000	**Early red'n period:** N/A
Inception date: September 1997	**Benchmark:** S&P 500	**Early red'n fee:** None
Management fee: 2.50%	**RRSP eligibility:** Yes	**High-water mark:** Yes
Performance fee: 20%	**Asset size:** $125 million	**Redemption notice:**
Hurdle rate: 90 days Cdn. T-Bill	**NAV:** $9.70	**Max. leverage:** None
Liquidity: Daily		

PERFORMANCE (AS OF DECEMBER 31, 2002)

	1 month	3 month	6 month	YTD	1 year	2 year	3 year	5 year	10 year	Since Inception
Fund:	-3.73%	-2.00%	2.03%	-0.73%	-0.73%	2.66%	10.26%	10.55%		10.94%
S&P500	-5.48%	7.42%	-7.07%	-23.14%	-23.14%	-15.15%	-12.23%	1.32%		n/a

Year:		Jan	Feb	Mar	Apr	May	Jun	Jul	Aug	Sep	Oct	Nov	Dec
Fund:	2002	-0.73%	-1.10%	-1.19%	2.84%	-2.28%	-2.41%	1.52%	5.99%	0.80%	-2.55%	0.56%	1.23%	-3.73%
S&P500	2002	-23.14%	-1.70%	-1.16%	3.33%	-7.67%	-3.25%	-7.77%	-3.73%	-0.98%	-9.25%	6.85%	6.36%	-5.48%
Fund:	2001	6.17%	1.78%	-1.88%	0.73%	2.05%	1.37%	0.18%	-2.51%	-3.39%	4.31%	-0.95%	2.89%	1.71%
S&P500	2001	-6.33%	3.51%	-6.78%	-3.95%	4.99%	0.87%	-3.94%	0.27%	-5.18%	-6.42%	2.50%	6.63%	2.16%
Fund:	2000	27.20%	0.81%	4.19%	3.11%	3.85%	0.68%	-0.48%	0.90%	1.94%	-1.25%	4.09%	2.04%	4.63%
S&P500	2000	-6.07%	-5.31%	-1.70%	9.80%	-0.87%	-1.01%	1.34%	-1.17%	5.20%	-3.27%	0.85%	0.93%	-9.72%
Fund:	1999	-4.87%	-1.98%	-1.21%	-1.42%	1.55%	-0.34%	0.84%	-0.58%	-2.16%	-2.07%	-0.60%	1.51%	1.59%
S&P500	1999	14.73%	2.85%	-3.27%	4.00%	0.32%	-1.19%	4.73%	-0.18%	-1.47%	-4.37%	6.56%	2.29%	4.19%
Fund:	1998	29.46%	3.49%	4.81%	2.84%	0.97%	0.42%	-0.53%	0.26%	2.54%	-0.18%	6.47%	1.65%	3.61%
S&P500	1998	37.59%	2.85%	4.96%	4.84%	1.78%	0.05%	4.78%	2.05%	-11.44%	3.97%	9.00%	5.39%	5.56%
Fund:	1997	5.38%									1.88%	0.62%	-0.37%	3.18%
S&P500	1997	0.00%												

PERFORMANCE COMPARISON

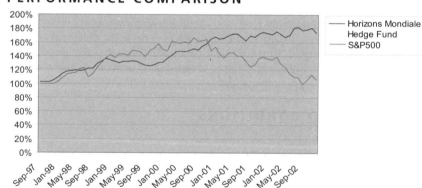

Horizons Mondiale Hedge Fund
S&P500

RISK DATA (AS OF DECEMBER 31, 2002)

Alpha (5 year): 6.28%	Sortino Ratio: 1.24%	Percentage of negative months: 35.94%
Beta (5 year): 0.11	Benchmark: S&P 500	Percentage of positive months: 64.06%
St. deviation (annualized): 7.97%	Correlation to benchmark: 0.26	
St. deviation (5 year):	Maximum drawdown: 7.75%	
Sharpe Ratio: 0.85%	Largest monthly drop: 3.73%	

NAGY-BECK HEDGE RATING:

HORIZONS STRATEGIC FUND

First Horizon Capital Corp.   Telephone Number: (416) 601-2228
71 King Street East, Second Floor   Fax Number: (416) 601-1695
Toronto, ON • M5G 1C3   Toll-Free: 1-877-450-0722
                                      Web Site: www.horizonsfunds.com

This fund will be re-branded under the Olympus United Group of Funds in 2003.

PORTFOLIO MANAGER(S)

Mondiale Asset Management Ltd.

Mondiale is a Canadian firm that specializes in quantitative hedge fund management, actively investing in securities and derivatives on a global basis. Mondiale, currently made up of three professionals and one support staff, has been managing both public and private capital for more than six years. The firm currently manages CDN$132.5 million of assets, acting as portfolio manager to the Horizons Mondiale Hedge Fund and the Mondiale Performance Hedge Program.

The Horizons Mondiale Hedge Fund is an RRSP-eligible (as Canadian content), full-prospectus retail mutual fund available in all provinces except Quebec. The Mondiale Performance Hedge Program can currently be accessed by retail investors in Canada through a product under offering memorandum: the Horizons Strategic Fund.

FUND DESCRIPTION

Mondiale's investment methodology, characterized by its systematic nature, is predominantly reactive, with price movements determining market positions. The focus of Mondiale's style is to generate consistently attractive risk-adjusted returns through both rising and falling markets. Using only computer-driven strategies both within and across multiple domestic and international markets, Mondiale exploits trends to generate returns while at the same time always acting to minimize drawdowns.

Mondiale's two investment products are differentiated by the degree of leverage they employ. The Mondiale Performance Hedge Program has a target risk weighting approximately 1.6 times the Horizons Mondiale Hedge Fund.

TERMS AND CONDITIONS

Fund style: Directional Trading

Sub-style: System Trading	* Min. investment: $150,000	Early red'n period: N/A
Inception date: April 2000	Benchmark: S&P 500	Early red'n fee: None
Management fee: 1.75%	RRSP eligibility: Yes (Foreign Content)	High water mark: Yes
Performance fee: 20%	Asset size: $3 million	Redemption notice:
Hurdle rate: N/A	NAV: $11.36	Max. leverage: 60%
Liquidity: Daily		

* $150,000 or less based on provincial legislation

PERFORMANCE (AS OF DECEMBER 31, 2002)

	1 month	3 month	6 month	YTD	1 year	2 year	3 year	5 year	10 year	Since Inception
Fund:	-5.66%	-2.35%	4.18%	-4.62%	-4.62%	2.27%	15.84%	16.86%		18.95%
S&P500	-5.48%	7.42%	-7.07%	-23.14%	-23.14%	-15.15%	-12.23%	-6.15%		n/a

Year:		Jan	Feb	Mar	Apr	May	Jun	Jul	Aug	Sep	Oct	Nov	Dec
Fund:	2002	-4.62%	-2.15%	-2.47%	5.54%	-5.37%	-5.33%	1.46%	10.13%	1.96%	-4.99%	1.80%	1.68%	-5.66%
S&P500	2002	-23.14%	-1.70%	-1.16%	3.33%	-7.67%	-3.25%	-7.77%	-3.73%	-0.98%	-9.25%	6.85%	6.36%	-5.48%
Fund:	2001	9.65%	3.72%	-4.26%	0.91%	3.70%	2.01%	0.29%	-4.57%	-6.53%	6.82%	-0.43%	5.28%	3.27%
S&P500	2001	-6.33%	3.51%	-6.78%	-3.95%	4.99%	0.87%	-3.94%	0.27%	-5.18%	-6.42%	2.50%	6.63%	2.16%
Fund:	2000	48.64%	2.35%	6.23%	5.42%	6.17%	0.42%	-0.09%	1.65%	4.15%	-2.40%	5.55%	2.98%	8.40%
S&P500	2000	-6.07%	-5.31%	-1.70%	9.80%	-0.87%	-1.01%	1.34%	-1.17%	5.20%	-3.27%	0.85%	0.93%	-9.72%
Fund:	1999	-10.79%	-6.52%	-1.96%	-3.22%	3.15%	-1.11%	-0.05%	-1.57%	-0.15%	-3.01%	-1.02%	1.76%	2.75%
S&P500	1999	14.73%	2.85%	-3.27%	4.00%	0.32%	-1.19%	4.73%	-0.18%	-1.47%	-4.37%	6.56%	2.29%	4.19%
Fund:	1998	57.14%	3.99%	5.73%	5.13%	2.16%	-2.06%	0.00%	2.06%	8.42%	0.30%	14.09%	2.69%	4.49%
S&P500	1998	37.59%	2.85%	4.96%	4.84%	1.78%	0.05%	4.78%	2.05%	-11.44%	3.97%	9.00%	5.39%	5.56%
Fund:	1997	15.78%								6.17%	2.89%	0.09%	5.89%
S&P500	1997	0.00%											

PERFORMANCE COMPARISON

— Horizons Strategic Fund   — S&P500

RISK DATA (AS OF DECEMBER 31, 2002)

Alpha:	Benchmark: S&P 500
Beta:	Correlation to benchmark:
St. deviation (annualized):	Maximum drawdown: 14.67%
St. deviation (1 year):	Largest monthly drop: 6.53%
St. deviation (2 year):	Percentage of negative months: 34.38%
Sharpe Ratio:	Percentage of positive months: 65.63%
Sortino Ratio:	

NAGY-BECK HEDGE RATING:

HORIZONS UNIVEST II

First Horizon Capital Corp.
71 King Street East, Second Floor
Toronto, ON • M5G 1C3

Telephone Number: (416) 601-2228
Fax Number: (416) 601-1695
Toll-Free: 1-877-450-0722
Web Site: www.firsthorizon.com

Similar funds:
Horizons Univest II (US$)
Horizons Univest DPP
Horizons Univest DPP (US$)

Norshield Univest Class B
Norshield Univest Class C
National Life, Multi Strategy Univest

This fund will be re-branded under the Olympus United Group of Funds in 2003.

PORTFOLIO MANAGER(S)

Norshield Financial Group

Horizons Univest II is based on Norshield's Univest product, first introduced in April 1991. Horizons Univest II differs somewhat from Norshield's Univest in that only 92 to 95% of the money goes to Univest II and the balance is invested in a overlay program run by First Horizon Bank in Barbados. This overlay program allows the fund to qualify as an active business and therefore take advantage of the Canada Barbados Tax Treaty.

Norshield was founded by John Xanthoudakis, whose interests in both financial services and technology encouraged him to formulate a pioneering approach to investing and managing risk. In the 1980s, his firm created Tactical Market Timing for U.S. stock indices, a proprietary product that has consistently outperformed the S&P 500 over the past 10 years. During this same decade, Xanthoudakis broadened his investment skills by developing an expertise in risk management and hedge funds.

Norshield is a firm with global reach and resources, maintaining offices in Montreal, Toronto, South Florida, and Athens. The company currently employs 40 people and has assets approaching three-quarters of a billion dollars under management and advisement. Its multidisciplinary team of financial experts advise on alternative investment strategies and value-added products that diversify traditional equity and bond portfolios and address the particular needs of sophisticated clients.

FUND DESCRIPTION

Horizon Univest II is 92 to 95% based on Norshield's Univest product. Univest is a fund of hedge funds product combining the expertise of 14 different hedge fund managers across different hedge fund styles and managers. The fund is actively managed by Norshield and has built a solid reputation since 1991.

TERMS AND CONDITIONS

Fund style: Fund of Hedge Funds

Sub-style: Well Diversified Across Styles   *** Min. investment:** $1,000   **Early red'n period:** N/A

Inception date: April 1991 (Norshield Univest) **Benchmark:** MSCI   **Early red'n fee:** None

Management fee: 1.75%	RRSP eligibility: Yes (Foreign Content)	High-water mark: Yes
Performance fee: 10%	Asset size: $107 million	Redemption notice:
Hurdle rate: N/A	NAV: $11.36	Max. leverage: 100%
Liquidity: Weekly		

* assuming buying National Life, Multi Strategy Univest

PERFORMANCE (AS OF DECEMBER 31, 2002) OF NORSHIELD'S UNIVEST CLASS "B" SHARES (US$)

	1 month	3 month	6 month	YTD	1 year	2 year	3 year	5 year	10 year	Since Inception
Fund:	0.99%	1.77%	4.03%	7.25%	7.25%	6.74%	8.82%	11.77%	15.48%	16.28%
MSCI	-4.83%	7.74%	-11.97%	-19.55%	-19.55%	-18.04%	-16.37%	-7.49%	6.69%	5.96%

	Year:	Annual	Jan	Feb	Mar	Apr	May	Jun	Jul	Aug	Sep	Oct	Nov	Dec
und:	2002	7.25%	0.31%	-0.20%	0.54%	0.77%	0.65%	0.99%	0.55%	0.86%	0.80%	-0.03%	0.80%	0.99%
ISCI	2002	-19.55%	-3.02%	-0.85%	4.44%	-3.36%	0.23%	-6.05%	-8.42%	0.21%	-10.97%	7.40%	5.41%	-4.83%
und:	2001	6.24%	1.41%	-0.99%	0.07%	1.79%	3.38%	0.03%	-0.44%	0.20%	-0.08%	0.15%	0.32%	0.30%
SCI	2001	-16.51%	2.00%	-8.43%	-6.61%	7.37%	-1.37%	-3.11%	-1.26%	-4.67%	-8.80%	1.93%	5.93%	0.64%
und:	2000	13.10%	1.01%	1.37%	0.89%	1.42%	1.57%	1.54%	0.78%	1.30%	0.99%	0.81%	0.25%	0.45%
SCI	2000	-12.93%	-5.72%	0.28%	6.92%	-4.22%	-2.52%	3.38%	-2.80%	3.27%	-5.31%	-1.66%	-6.06%	1.63%
und:	1999	17.05%	1.08%	1.45%	1.78%	1.61%	1.24%	2.31%	-0.39%	0.58%	1.90%	1.01%	1.58%	1.72%
ISCI	1999	25.23%	2.19%	-2.65%	4.16%	3.97%	-3.67%	4.66%	-0.29%	-0.17%	-0.96%	5.21%	2.82%	8.11%
und:	1998	15.65%	2.07%	1.47%	1.38%	1.14%	1.41%	1.28%	1.32%	1.30%	0.07%	0.97%	0.92%	1.31%
ISCI	1998	24.83%	2.82%	6.78%	4.23%	0.99%	-1.25%	2.38%	-0.14%	-13.32%	1.80%	9.07%	5.97%	4.90%
und:	1997	14.65%	0.90%	0.01%	3.03%	-1.57%	1.17%	2.25%	1.31%	3.65%	0.99%	0.59%	0.45%	1.07%
ISCI	1997	16.10%	1.24%	1.15%	-1.99%	3.29%	6.19%	5.01%	4.63%	-6.76%	5.45%	-5.24%	1.77%	1.23%
und:	1996	18.93%	-0.50%	3.81%	2.28%	1.63%	1.48%	1.23%	1.66%	0.59%	-0.53%	1.25%	0.75%	3.92%
ISCI	1996	14.04%	1.88%	0.62%	1.67%	2.36%	0.09%	0.54%	-3.53%	1.19%	3.93%	0.69%	5.64%	-1.57%
und:	1995	16.71%	0.84%	0.37%	1.43%	2.27%	1.45%	1.78%	1.34%	2.24%	0.97%	1.66%	0.40%	0.82
ISCI	1995	21.37%	-1.50%	1.50%	4.84%	3.51%	0.91%	-0.02%	5.02%	-2.22%	2.95%	-1.55%	3.49%	2.94%
und:	1994	16.92%	0.88%	0.63%	0.38%	0.68%	1.04%	1.40%	1.04%	1.53%	1.67%	2.37%	1.74%	2.40%
ISCI	1994	5.57%	6.57%	-1.31%	-4.30%	3.15%	0.29%	-0.27%	1.93%	3.04%	-2.61%	2.88%	-4.32%	0.97%
und:	1993	29.92%	2.94%	2.94%	2.94%	2.91%	2.91%	2.91%	0.57%	0.57%	0.57%	2.42%	2.42%	2.42%
ISCI	1993	23.19%	0.34%	2.39%	5.81%	4.65%	2.34%	-0.83%	2.08%	4.62%	-1.83%	2.81%	-5.67%	4.94%
und:	1992	12.91%	0.50%	0.50%	0.50%	1.14%	1.14%	1.14%	1.40%	1.40%	1.40%	1.03%	1.03%	1.03%
ISCI	1992	-4.63%	-1.87%	-1.69%	-4.74%	1.42%	3.99%	-3.32%	0.29%	2.52%	-0.88%	-2.71%	1.78%	0.85%
und:	1991	23.53%				2.60%	2.60%	2.60%	1.81%	1.81%	1.81%	2.72%	2.72%	2.72%
ISCI	1991	8.34%				0.84%	2.26%	-6.15%	4.73%	-0.28%	2.70%	1.69%	-4.36%	7.32%

PERFORMANCE COMPARISON

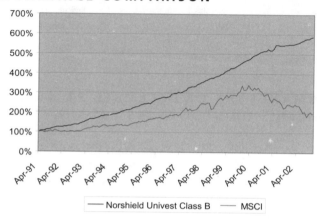

—— Norshield Univest Class B —— MSCI

RISK DATA (AS OF DECEMBER 31, 2002)

Alpha (compared to S&P 500): 16.28%

Beta (to S&P 500 TR): 0.009

St. deviation (annualized): 3.31%

St. deviation (1 year): 1.32%

St. deviation (2 year): 2.94%

Sharpe Ratio: 3.12

Sortino Ratio (5%): 10.93

Benchmark: MSCI

Correlation to S&P 500: 0.039

Maximum drawdown: 1.57%

Largest monthly drop: 1.57%

Percentage of negative months: 6.38%

Percentage of positive months: 93.62%

NAGY-BECK HEDGE RATING:

BLUMONT CANADIAN OPPORTUNITIES

BluMont Capital
220 Bay Street
Suite 1500, P.O. Box 23
Toronto, ON • M53 2W4

Telephone Number: (416) 216-3566
Fax Number: (416) 360-1102
Toll-Free: 1-866-473-7376
Web Site: www.blumontcapital.com

PORTFOLIO MANAGER(S)

Veronika Hirsch (B.Comm., FLMI)

Veronika Hirsch is chief investment officer of BluMont Capital Corporation and lead portfolio manager of the BluMont Canadian Opportunities Fund and of the BluMont Hirsch Long/Short Fund. Hirsch, who has been in the investment management industry for over 20 years, is recognized as one of Canada's premier equity investment managers. In 1997, she was named Gordon Pape's Mutual Fund Manager of the Year.

Hirsch has managed funds at Prudential (now Mackenzie), AGF and Fidelity. While at Prudential, all funds under her management were top-quartile performers and she continues to post impressive results as a top performer. Hirsch is a frequent guest on prominent Canadian business programs, regularly appearing on ROB TV's "The Bottom Line," and CBC Newsworld. She also contributes articles to various industry publications.

In an effort to minimize fund volatility, 50% of the management responsibilities are allocated to Hillsdale Investment Management, a disciplined Toronto-based quantitative modeling firm.

FUND DESCRIPTION:

The fund's objective is to achieve above-average, long-term capital growth by investing primarily in Canadian corporations with superior growth profiles while mitigating the overall market risk of the portfolio through various hedging strategies. The fund's investment approach is designed to deliver consistent returns by combining two complementary strategies managed 50% by BluMont Capital Corporation (Veronika Hirsch) and 50% by Hillsdale Investment Management Inc.

Hirsch's style is a qualitative, research-intensive, bottom-up approach to long/short portfolio construction combined with event-driven trading. The Hillsdale portion of the fund uses a quantitative , multi-factor, bottom-up approach to long/short stock selection employed across market capitalization, style, and sector.

TERMS AND CONDITIONS

Fund style: Stock Selection

Sub-style: Long Bias

Inception date: January 2001

Management fee: 3.16%

Performance fee: 20%

Hurdle rate: 0%

Liquidity: Weekly

* or less based on provincial legislation

*Min. investment: $150,000

Benchmark: TSX

RRSP eligibility: Yes

Asset size: $62 million

NAV: $124.27

Early red'n period: 6 months

Early red'n fee: 5%

High-water mark: Yes

Redemption notice:

Max. leverage: 100%

PERFORMANCE (AS OF DECEMBER 31, 2002)

	1 month	3 month	6 month	YTD	1 year	2 year	3 year	5 year	10 year	Since Inception
Fund:	2.61%	-1.29%	-6.94%	2.85%	2.85%	12.21%				12.21%
TSX:	0.67%	7.03%	-7.43%	-13.97%	-13.97%	-13.96%				-13.96%

Year:		Jan	Feb	Mar	Apr	May	Jun	Jul	Aug	Sep	Oct	Nov	Dec
Fund:	2002	2.85%	1.17%	3.38%	4.67%	0.59%	4.85%	-4.28%	-9.86%	6.94%	-2.19%	-2.32%	-1.51%	2.61%
TSX:	2002	-13.97%	-0.52%	-0.14%	2.80%	-2.40%	-0.10%	-6.67%	-7.56%	0.10%	-6.53%	1.11%	5.15%	0.67%
Fund:	2001	22.42%	3.71%	0.81%	3.07%	4.31%	3.47%	-2.05%	1.99%	0.26%	-1.45%	-1.11%	4.36%	3.32%
TSX:	2001	-13.94%	4.35%	-13.34%	-5.83%	4.45%	2.71%	-5.21%	-0.60%	-3.78%	-7.58%	0.69%	7.84%	3.54%

PERFORMANCE COMPARISON

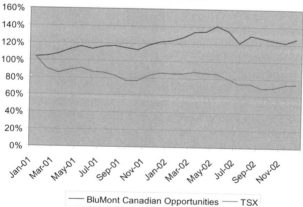

BluMont Canadian Opportunities ——— TSX

RISK DATA (AS OF DECEMBER 31, 2002)

Alpha (annualized): 1.41%

Beta: 0.39

St. deviation (annualized): 12.76%

St. deviation (1 year):

St. deviation (2 year):

Sharpe Ratio: 0.61

Sortino Ratio:

Benchmark: TSX

Correlation to benchmark: 0.52

Maximum drawdown: 13.72%

Largest monthly drop: 9.86%

Percentage of negative months: 33.33%

Percentage of positive months: 66.67%

NAGY-BECK HEDGE RATING:

BLUMONT HIRSCH LONG/SHORT

BluMont Capital
220 Bay Street
Suite 1500, P.O. Box 23
Toronto, ON • M53 2W4

Telephone Number: (416) 216-3566
Fax Number: (416) 360-1102
Toll-Free: 1-866-473-7376
Web Site: www.blumontcapital.com

PORTFOLIO MANAGER(S)

Veronika Hirsch (B.Comm., FLMI)

Veronika Hirsch is chief investment officer of BluMont Capital Corporation and lead portfolio manager of the BluMont Canadian Opportunities Fund and of the BluMont Hirsch Long/Short Fund. Hirsch, who has been in the investment management industry for over 20 years, is recognized as one of Canada's premier equity investment managers. In 1997, she was named Gordon Pape's Mutual Fund Manager of the Year.

Hirsch has managed funds at Prudential (now Mackenzie), AGF and Fidelity. While at Prudential, all funds under her management were top-quartile performers and she continues to post impressive results as a top performer. Hirsch is a frequent guest on prominent Canadian business programs, regularly appearing on ROB TV's "The Bottom Line," and CBC Newsworld. She also contributes articles to various industry publications.

FUND DESCRIPTION

The fund's objective is to achieve above-average returns each year independent of the performance of the S&P/TSX Total Return Index by investing primarily in Canadian issuers and mitigating the overall market risk of the portfolio through various hedging strategies. Hirsch's style is a qualitative, research-intensive, bottom-up approach to long/short portfolio construction combined with event-driven trading.

TERMS AND CONDITIONS

Fund style: Stock Selection

Sub-style: Long Bias	***Min. investment:** $150,000	**Early red'n period:** 6 months
Inception date: August 2002	**Benchmark:** TSX	**Early red'n fee:** 5%
Management fee: 2.50%	**RRSP eligibility:** Yes	**High-water mark:** Yes
Performance fee: 20%	**Asset size:** $12 million	**Redemption notice:**
Hurdle rate: 0%	**NAV:** $105.54	**Max. leverage:** 100%
Liquidity: Weekly		

* or less based on provincial legislation

PERFORMANCE (AS OF DECEMBER 31, 2002)

	1 month	3 month	6 month	YTD	1 year	2 year	3 year	5 year	10 year	Since Inception
Fund:	1.66%	1.78%								5.50%
TSX:	0.67%	7.03%								0.14%

Year:		Jan	Feb	Mar	Apr	May	Jun	Jul	Aug	Sep	Oct	Nov	Dec
Fund:	2002	5.50%							2.63%	1.00%	-0.41%	0.53%	1.66%
TSX:	2002	0.14%							0.10%	-6.53%	1.11%	5.15%	0.67%

PERFORMANCE COMPARISON

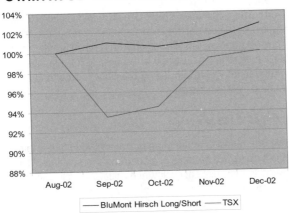

— BluMont Hirsch Long/Short —— TSX

RISK DATA (AS OF DECEMBER 31, 2002)

Alpha (annualized): 1.09%

Beta: -0.05

St. deviation (annualized): 3.98%

St. deviation (1 year):

St. deviation (2 year):

Sharpe Ratio: 2.23

Sortino Ratio:

Benchmark: TSX

Correlation to benchmark: -0.17

Maximum drawdown: 0.41%

Largest monthly drop: 0.41%

Percentage of negative months: 20.00%

Percentage of positive months: 80.00%

NAGY-BECK HEDGE RATING:

BLUMONT GABELLI GLOBAL FUND

BluMont Capital
220 Bay Street
Suite 1500, P.O. Box 23
Toronto, ON • M53 2W4

Telephone Number: (416) 216-3566
Fax Number: (416) 360-1102
Toll-Free: 1-866-473-7376
Web Site: www.blumontcapital.com

PORTFOLIO MANAGER(S)

The fund's advisor is Gabelli & Partners LLC, a subsidiary of Gabelli Asset Management. This prestigious firm was founded in 1976 by chairman Mario Gabelli, who is recognized as one of the greatest stock-pickers of our time and is a prominent member of the Alternative Asset Management investment team.

The Fund's lead portfolio manager is Marc Gabelli, managing director at Gabelli & Partners and a member of the portfolio management team at Gabelli Asset Management. Prior to his present position, Gabelli worked with Lehman Brothers in their equity research and arbitrage departments. Gabelli is responsible for a number of separate account portfolios and mutual funds, including the Gabelli Growth Fund, which has earned a five-star rating by Morningstar.

FUND DESCRIPTION:

The fund's objective is to outperform the Morgan Stanley World Index, through event-driven investment in a diversified portfolio of global long/short equities. Stock selection is based on fundamentals, management quality, and valuation levels. There is an emphasis on purchasing companies at less than 50% of their private market value and, more importantly, with a catalyst in place to realize that value within six months.

TERMS AND CONDITIONS

Fund style: Stock Selection

Sub-style: No Bias, Event Driven

Inception date: January 2001

Management fee: 3.56%

Performance fee: 20%

Hurdle rate: 0%

Liquidity: Weekly

*Min. investment: $150,000

Benchmark: MSCI

* or less based on provincial legislation

RRSP eligibility: Yes (Foreign Content)

Asset size: $15 million

NAV: $81.15

Early red'n period: 6 months

Early red'n fee: 5%

High-water mark: Yes

Redemption notice:

Max. leverage: 100%

PERFORMANCE (AS OF DECEMBER 31, 2002)

(Performance figures between July 1999 and December 2000 show strategy performance.)

	1 month	3 month	6 month	YTD	1 year	2 year	3 year	5 year	10 year	Since Inception
Fund:	4.16%	-0.65%	2.13%	-7.53%	-7.53%	-9.28%	-5.16%			9.28%
MSCI:	-4.83%	7.74%	-11.97%	-19.55%	-19.55%	-18.04%	-16.37%			-18.04%

Year:		Jan	Feb	Mar	Apr	May	Jun	Jul	Aug	Sep	Oct	Nov	Dec
Fund:	2002	-7.53%	3.32%	-0.99%	-2.20%	0.07%	-2.35%	-7.31%	5.54%	-0.31%	-2.37%	2.13%	-6.61%	4.16%
MSCI:	2002	-19.55%	-3.02%	-0.85%	4.44%	-3.36%	0.23%	-6.05%	-8.42%	0.21%	-10.97%	7.40%	5.41%	-4.83%
Fund:	2001	-10.99%	0.31%	1.89%	-1.67%	-1.45%	0.17%	-2.81%	-0.89%	0.42%	-0.64%	-10.45%	-5.57%	6.75%
MSCI:	2001	-16.51%	2.00%	-8.43%	-6.61%	7.37%	-1.37%	-3.11%	-1.26%	-4.67%	-8.80%	1.93%	5.93%	0.64%
Fund:	2000	3.65%	-1.20%	0.36%	-0.19%	4.44%	1.29%	3.12%	1.31%	-1.65%	-1.72%	-5.63%	4.93%	-0.99%
MSCI:	2000	-12.93%	-5.72%	0.28%	6.92%	-4.22%	-2.52%	3.38%	-2.80%	3.27%	-5.31%	-1.66%	-6.06%	1.63%
Fund:	1999	41.32%							1.45%	-2.30%	3.70%	9.53%	9.24%	14.91%
MSCI:	1999	15.30%							-0.29%	-0.17%	-0.96%	5.21%	2.82%	8.11%

PERFORMACE COMPARISON

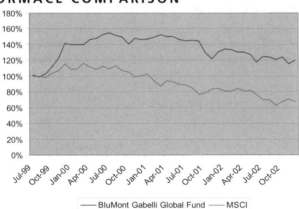

—— BluMont Gabelli Global Fund —— MSCI

RISK DATA (AS OF DECEMBER 31, 2002)

(Since fund's inception, January 2001)

Alpha (annualized): -1.05%	Sharpe Ratio: N/A	Maximum drawdown: 23.96%
Beta: -0.21	Sortino Ratio:	Largest monthly drop: 8.19%
St. deviation (annualized): 13.87%	Benchmark: MSCI	Percentage of negative months: 54.17%
St. deviation (1 year):	Correlation to benchmark: -0.27	Percentage of positive months: 45.83%
St. deviation (2 year):		

NAGY-BECK HEDGE RATING:

BLUMONT SELECT LEADERS FUND

BluMont Capital	Telephone Number: (416) 216-3566
220 Bay Street	Fax Number: (416) 360-1102
Suite 1500, P.O. Box 23	Toll-Free: 1-866-473-7376
Toronto, ON • M53 2W4	Web Site: www.blumontcapital.com

Similar funds: BluMont Select Leaders (US$)

PORTFOLIO MANAGER(S)

The BluMont Select Leaders Fund utilizes the skills of individual managers from some of the world's leading asset management companies, in a powerful combination that enables investors to access them all via a "multi-manager" strategy.

The fund combines the experience of Marc Gabelli (BluMont Gabelli Global Fund), Veronika Hirsch and Hillsdale Investment Management (BluMont Canadian Opportunities Fund), and Dr. John Schmitz (BluMont Market Neutral Fund). Their specializations, when united into one fund, capitalize on their individual strengths and each manager contributes a different investment strategy to give investors a diversified product offering designed to deliver consistent returns.

FUND DESCRIPTION

The fund's objective is to achieve superior returns while limiting the overall volatility of the fund. The investment approach weights all new allocations among all of the funds. The fund weightings are reviewed on a quarterly basis to ensure adequate diversification.

TERMS AND CONDITIONS

Fund style: Fund of Hedge Funds

Sub-style: Stock Selection	**RRSP eligibility:** Yes (Foreign content)
Inception date: January 2001	**Asset size:** $8 million
Management fee: 0.48% (excl. fees for the underlining funds)	**NAV:** $79.45
Performance fee: 20%	**Early red'n period:** 6 months
Hurdle rate: 0%	**Early red'n fee:** 5%
Liquidity: Weekly	**High-water mark:** Yes
*Min. investment: $150,000	**Redemption notice:**
Benchmark: MSCI	**Max. leverage:** 100%

* or less based on provincial legislation

PERFORMANCE (AS OF DECEMBER 31, 2002)

	1 month	3 month	6 month	YTD	1 year	2 year	3 year	5 year	10 year	Since Inception
Fund:	3.14%	-2.67%	-9.38%	-21.98%	-21.98%	-10.85%				-10.85%
MSCI	-4.83%	7.74%	-11.97%	-19.55%	-19.55%					-18.04%

Year:		Jan	Feb	Mar	Apr	May	Jun	Jul	Aug	Sep	Oct	Nov	Dec
und:	2002	-21.98%	-1.80%	-4.25%	2.28%	-3.88%	-0.24%	-6.64%	-6.47%	1.02%	-1.46%	-1.26%	-4.43%	3.14%
ISCI	2002	-19.55%	-3.02%	-0.85%	4.44%	-3.36%	0.23%	-6.05%	-8.42%	0.21%	-10.97%	7.40%	5.41%	-4.83%
und:	2001	1.87%	3.82%	-2.36%	-1.68%	3.46%	2.45%	-3.31%	0.74%	-3.98%	-4.24%	1.02%	2.33%	4.15%
ISCI	2001	-16.51%	2.00%	-8.43%	-6.61%	7.37%	-1.37%	-3.11%	-1.26%	-4.67%	-8.80%	1.93%	5.93%	0.64%

PERFORMANCE COMPARISON

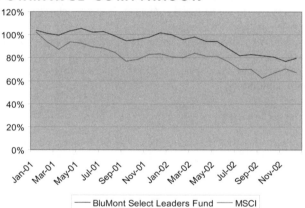

— BluMont Select Leaders Fund — MSCI

RISK DATA (AS OF NOVEMBER 30, 2002)

Alpha (annualized): -0.42%	Benchmark: MSCI
Beta: 0.32	Correlation to benchmark: 0.51
St. deviation (annualized): 11.47%	Maximum drawdown: 27.06%
St. deviation (1 year):	Largest monthly drop: 6.64%
St. deviation (2 year):	Percentage of negative months: 58.33%
Sharpe Ratio (risk free rate=5%): N/A	Percentage of positive months: 41.67%
Sortino Ratio:	

NAGY-BECK RATING:

iPERFORM STRATEGIC PARTNERS HEDGE FUND

Blumont Capital
220 Bay Street
Suite 1500, P.O. Box 23
Toronto, ON • M53 2W4

Telephone Number: (416) 216-3566
Fax Number: (416) 360-1102
Toll-Free: 1-866-473-7376
Web Site: www.blumontcapital.com

PORTFOLIO MANAGER(S)

The iPerform Strategic Partners Hedge Fund brings together five separate investment advisors from some of the world's leading asset management companies, in a unique combination that provides investors with access to them all via a "multi-manager" long/short hedge fund strategy.

The fund combines the experience of Eric Sprott (Sprott Asset Management Inc.), Marc Gabelli (Gabelli Securities International Ltd.), Christopher Guthrie (Hillsdale Investment Management Inc.), John Clark (J.C. Clark Ltd.), and Dr. John Schmitz (Scivest Capital Management Inc.).

Each investment advisor brings his/her own unique investment style and strategy and when combined the fund has the potential to provide investors with a well diversified product that will attempt to yield consistent returns with lower volatility than the comparable equity indexes.

FUND DESCRIPTION:

The fund aims to achieve capital appreciation while mitigating risk through a diversified hedged equity investment program. It will also strive to achieve these returns with less volatility than returns of the major market indexes. Up to 30% of the assets of the fund may be invested in securities of non-Canadian issuers.

TERMS AND CONDITIONS

Fund style: Fund of Hedge Funds

Sub-style: Stock Selection (Neutral to Long Bias)	***Min. investment:** None	**Early red'n period:** None
Inception date: May 2002	**Benchmark:** TSX	**Early red'n fee:** None
Management fee: 3.16%	**RRSP eligibility:** Yes	**High-water mark:** Yes
Performance fee: 20%	**Asset size:** $195 million	**Redemption notice:** None
Hurdle rate: 0%	**NAV:** $8.51	**Max. leverage:** 50%
Liquidity: Weekly	**Market value:** $8.18	

* This is a closed-end fund traded on the TSX with symbol ISH.UN

PERFORMANCE (AS OF DECEMBER 31, 2002)

	1 month	3 month	6 month	YTD	1 year	2 year	3 year	5 year	10 year	Since Inception
Fund:	7.72%	-4.92%	-5.76%							-9.37%
TSX:	0.67%	7.03%	-7.43%							-13.69%

Year:		Jan	Feb	Mar	Apr	May	Jun	Jul	Aug	Sep	Oct	Nov	Dec
Fund:	2002 -9.37%					0.64%	-4.44%	-4.43%	2.55%	1.13%	-6.26%	-5.84%	7.72%
TSX:	2002 -13.69%					-0.10%	-6.67%	-7.56%	0.10%	-6.53%	1.11%	5.15%	0.67%

PERFORMANCE COMPARISON

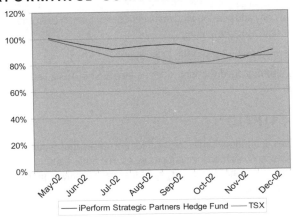

—— iPerform Strategic Partners Hedge Fund —— TSX

RISK DATA (AS OF DECEMBER 31, 2002)

Alpha (annualized):	Benchmark: TSX
Beta:	Correlation to benchmark:
St. deviation (annualized):	Maximum drawdown: 16.40%
St. deviation (1 year):	Largest monthly drop: 6.26%
St. deviation (2 year):	Percentage of negative months: 50.00%
Sharpe Ratio:	Percentage of positive months: 50.00%
Sortino Ratio:	

NAGY-BECK HEDGE RATING:

THE PRESERVATION TRUST

J.C. Clark Ltd.   Telephone Number: (416) 361-6144
BCE Place, 161 Bay Street   Fax Number: (416) 361-0128
Toronto, Ontario • M5J 2S1   Toll-Free: 1-800-480-0002
                                         Web Site: www.jcclark.com

PORTFOLIO MANAGER(S)

John Clark, Portfolio Manager

John Clark has managed the fund since its inception in 1999 and has managed similar long/short equity funds since 1982. He is the co-founder of wealth management firm Connor Clark & Company and pension fund manager Connor Clark & Lunn and a former chairman of the Toronto Stock Exchange.

Colin Stewart, CFA, Associate Portfolio Manager

Colin Stewart has also managed the fund since its inception in 1999. He is a former investment banker.

FUND DESCRIPTION

J.C. Clark Ltd. serves institutional investors and family offices that require thorough transparency, liquidity, and risk management processes. The firm's flagship hedge fund, the Preservation Trust, is a long/short equity fund that invests only in publicly traded Canadian and U.S. securities.

By employing one of the more straightforward approaches in the hedge fund industry, the fund derives its returns from security selection and not from arbitrage or directional market bets. Investment decisions are based on proprietary fundamental analysis conducted by an internal team of analysts (e.g., balance sheet analysis, cash flow forecasts, forensic accounting, and reviews of management strength).

The fund holds a range of long and short positions across a wide variety of sectors. Strict limits are placed on individual position sizes and overall sector exposure. The fund maintains a variable bias with net market exposure ranging between -20% and +40%. Portfolio liquidity is also carefully managed to ensure the greatest level of investing flexibility. Low correlation (-0.20) with the broader markets and with other hedge funds makes the Preservation Trust attractive to institutions and family offices seeking diversification.

Due to its focused investment strategy, the fund has limited capacity and is currently closed to new investors.

TERMS AND CONDITIONS

Fund style: Stock Selection
Sub-style: Variable Bias
Inception date: May 1999
Management fee: 2.00%
Performance fee: 20%
Hurdle rate: N/A
Liquidity: Monthly

Min. investment:
Benchmark: S&P 500
RRSP eligibility: None
Asset size: $220 million
NAV:

Early red'n period: N/A
Early red'n fee: None
High water mark: Yes
Redemption notice:
Max. leverage: 200%

PERFORMANCE (AS OF DECEMBER 31, 2002)

	1 month	3 month	6 month	YTD	1 year	2 year	3 year	5 year	10 year	Since Inception
Fund:	N/A	0.29%	0.50%	19.95%	19.95%	39.88%	38.54%			31.99%
S&P500	N/A	7.42%	-7.07%	-23.14%	-23.14%	-15.15%	-12.23%			-7.63%

Year:		Jan	Feb	Mar	Apr	May	Jun	Jul	Aug	Sep	Oct	Nov	Dec
Fund:	2002	19.95%		8.74%			9.76%			0.21%			0.29%
S&P500	2002	-23.14%	-1.70%	-1.16%	3.33%	-7.67%	-3.25%	-7.77%	-3.73%	-0.98%	-9.25%	6.85%	6.36%	-5.48%
Fund:	2001	63.12%		31.75%			5.23%			27.03%			-7.38%
S&P500	2001	-6.33%	3.51%	-6.78%	-3.95%	4.99%	0.87%	-3.94%	0.27%	-5.18%	-6.42%	2.50%	6.63%	2.16%
Fund:	2000	35.91%		-5.99%			35.68%			5.34%			1.15%
S&P500	2000	-6.07%	-5.31%	-1.70%	9.80%	-0.87%	-1.01%	1.34%	-1.17%	5.20%	-3.27%	0.85%	0.93%	-9.72%
Fund:	1999	4.03%					11.85%			4.32%			-10.84%
S&P500	1999	10.54%				-1.19%	4.73%	-0.18%	-1.47%	-4.37%	6.56%	2.29%	4.19%

PERFORMANCE COMPARISON

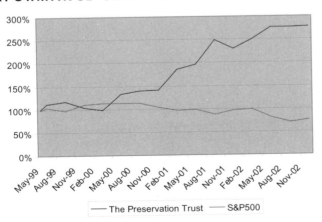

— The Preservation Trust — S&P500

RISK DATA (AS OF DECEMBER 31, 2002)

Alpha:

Beta:

St. deviation (annualized): 21.40%

St. deviation (1 year): 11.70%

St. deviation (2 year):

Sharpe Ratio: 1.36

Sortino Ratio:

Benchmark: S&P 500

Correlation to Dow Jones: -0.23

Maximum drawdown: 16.18%

Largest quarterly drop: 10.84%

Percentage of negative months: 35.00%

Percentage of positive months: 65.00%

NAGY-BECK HEDGE RATING:

LEEWARD BULL & BEAR FUND L.P.

Leeward Hedge Funds Inc.
1099A Yonge Street
Toronto, ON • M4W 2L7

Telephone Number: (416) 482-0242
Fax Number: (416) 482-3067
Toll-Free: 1-866-533-9273
Web Site: www.leewardhedgefunds.ca

PORTFOLIO MANAGER(S)

Brendan Kyne, CFA, Manager
Leeward Capital Management Inc.

Brendan Kyne established Leeward Hedge Funds Inc. in April 2001. Prior to starting his own firm he had accumulated 14 years' experience in the money management field with experience working in both the United States and Canada.

Kyne graduated from McMaster University and began his investment career at Hughes, King & Company in 1988 as an investment analyst. He received the chartered financial analyst designation (CFA) in 1992. After four years he joined Acuity Investment Management Inc. of Toronto with responsibility for equity research. In February of 1995, Driehaus Capital Management Inc. hired him to research Canadian securities for the firm's clients. During that year he was promoted to vice president and was responsible for increasing the firm's Canadian business and managing its Canadian portfolios.

Kyne has an impressive track record as a portfolio manager in the investment industry. While with the prestigious Chicago-based firm Driehaus Capital Management Inc., he increased the organization's Canadian asset management business from $45 million to more than $800 million in assets in five years. Kyne became known as one of the leading small to mid-cap investment managers in North America. He has frequently appeared as a commentator on Canadian markets in print and TV media, including the *New York Times*, *Wall Street Journal*, CBC Businessworld, ROBTV, and all major Canadian business papers.

FUND DESCRIPTION

The primary objective of the fund is to provide consistent positive absolute returns. The partnership will focus on achieving superior returns by utilizing a bottom-up growth strategy for security selection for both long and short positions. The fund will have a small to mid cap bias in its long positions, while short positions will have no bias in terms of market capitalization. The partnership will have no sector bias, or be required to be fully invested at all times. The partnership is excluded from investing in futures, currencies, and real estate, and will limit options to 5% of total assets. The partnership intends to hold 35 to 40 stocks split between long and short positions. The manager intends to make extensive use of risk arbitrage opportunites in order to add incremental returns to the partnership.

TERMS AND CONDITIONS

Fund style: Stock Selection
Sub-style: Variable Bias
Inception date: June 2001
Management fee: 2.00%
Performance fee: 20%
Hurdle rate: 10%
Liquidity: Monthly
* not available in Quebec

*Min. investment: $150,000
Benchmark: TSX
RRSP eligibility: None
Asset size: $28 million
NAV: $1,315.00

Early red'n period: Yes
Early red'n fee: None
High-water mark: Yes
Redemption notice: 30 days in writing
Max. leverage: None

PERFORMANCE (AS OF DECEMBER 31, 2002)

	1 month	3 month	6 month	YTD	1 year	2 year	3 year	5 year	10 year	Since Inception
Fund:	4.15%	7.96%	-0.75%	4.78%	4.78%					20.03%
TSX	0.67%	7.03%	-7.43%	-13.97%	-13.97%					-9.92%

	Year:		Jan	Feb	Mar	Apr	May	Jun	Jul	Aug	Sep	Oct	Nov	Dec
Fund:	2002		3.18%	7.32%	-1.32%	-5.59%	3.00%	6.01%	-3.30%	-9.15%	11.74%	-9.44%	1.25%	2.38%	2.56%
TSX	2002	-13.97%	-0.52%	-0.14%	2.80%	-2.40%	-0.10%	-6.67%	-7.56%	0.10%	-6.53%	1.11%	5.15%	0.67%
Fund:	2001	25.50%							1.19%	0.00%	3.59%	9.72%	0.08%	9.03%
TSX	2001	-0.62%							-0.60%	-3.78%	-7.58%	0.69%	7.84%	3.54%

PERFORMANCE COMPARISON

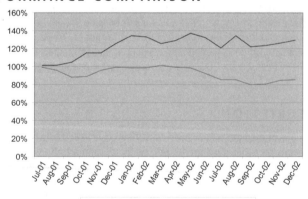

Leeward Bull & Bear Fund L.P. ——— TSX

RISK DATA (AS OF DECEMBER 31, 2002)

Alpha:
Beta:
St. deviation (annualized):
St. deviation (1 year):
St. deviation (2 year):

Sharpe Ratio:
Sortino Ratio:
Benchmark: TSX
Correlation to benchmark:

Maximum drawdown: 12.15%
Largest monthly drop: 9.44%
Percentage of positive months: 72.22%
Percentage of negative months: 27.78%

NAGY-BECK HEDGE RATING:

MACKENZIE ALTERNATIVE STRATEGIES

Mackenzie Financial Corp.
150 Bloor Street West, Suite M111
Toronto, ON • M5S 3B5

Telephone Number: (416) 922-5322
Fax Number: (416) 922-5660
Toll-Free: 1-800-387-0614
Web Site: www.mackenziefinancial.com

PORTFOLIO MANAGER(S)

Tremont Investment Mgmt. Team
Tremont Investment Management

Founded in 1984, Tremont is the largest adviser to multi-manager hedge fund portfolios worldwide with $12 billion under management. Tremont's clients include major financial institutions, funds of funds, pensions, endowments, and high-net-worth families. It employs over 70 full-time staff providing rigorous quantitative and qualitative research, search, and oversight. Tremont is the only major hedge fund specialist with substantial operations in both the U.S. and Europe.

FUND DESCRIPTION

The investment objective of the fund is to achieve an attractive risk-adjusted return through the use of a "multi-manager" investment approach by investing with a variety of hedge fund managers. The fund will invest directly in specialized hedge funds and may also retain hedge fund managers to manage segregated accounts for it. The fund's objective emphasizes total return, not current income. The fund invests in a number of specialized hedge funds that employ a variety of strategies. These include long and short techniques in equities and fixed-income markets as well as arbitrage of corporate mergers, convertible bonds, mortgage-backed securities, and fixed-income securities. They may also employ leverage and short selling to enhance returns. Initially, the fund will invest in a small number of hedge funds. Once the fund's assets reach a reasonable size, the fund will further diversify its holdings so that no one hedge fund will represent, at the time of purchase, more than 10% of the net assets of the fund.

TERMS AND CONDITIONS

Fund style: Fund of Funds

Sub-style: Stock Selection (Long Bias)	RRSP eligibility: Yes (Foreign Content)
Inception date: January 2001	Asset size: $146 million
Management fee: 3.87%	NAV: $10.51
Performance fee: 20%	Early red'n period: 6 months
Hurdle rate: 0%	Early red'n fee: 2%
Liquidity: Monthly	High-water mark: Yes
* Min. investment: $150,000	Redemption notice:
Benchmark: S&P 500	Max. leverage: 100.00%

* or less based on provincial legislation

PERFORMANCE (AS OF DECEMBER 31, 2002)

	1 month	3 month	6 month	YTD	1 year	2 year	3 year	5 year	10 year	Since Inception
Fund:	1.07%	0.55%	-0.05%	-2.66%	-2.66%	1.95%				1.95%
S&P500	-5.48%	7.42%	-7.07%	-23.14%	-23.14%	-15.15%				-15.15%

	Year:	Jan	Feb	Mar	Apr	May	Jun	Jul	Aug	Sep	Oct	Nov	Dec
Fund:	2002	-2.66%	-0.34%	-0.72%	0.73%	-0.70%	-0.67%	-0.93%	-0.45%	-0.19%	0.04%	-1.50%	1.00%	1.07%
S&P500	2002	-23.14%	-1.70%	-1.16%	3.33%	-7.67%	-3.25%	-7.77%	-3.73%	-0.98%	-9.25%	6.85%	6.36%	-5.48%
Fund:	2001	6.78%	0.00%	3.35%	2.85%	-2.20%	1.85%	-2.49%	0.81%	0.97%	-0.98%	0.77%	0.58%	1.24%
S&P500	2001	-6.33%	3.51%	-6.78%	-3.95%	4.99%	0.87%	-3.94%	0.27%	-5.18%	-6.42%	2.50%	6.63%	2.16%

PERFORMANCE COMPARISON

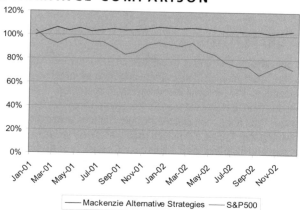

—— Mackenzie Alternative Strategies —— S&P500

RISK DATA (AS OF DECEMBER 31, 2002)

Alpha:

Beta:

St. deviation (annualized):

St. deviation (1 year):

St. deviation (2 year):

Sharpe Ratio:

Sortino Ratio:

Benchmark: S&P 500

Correlation to benchmark:

Maximum drawdown: 4.65%

Largest monthly drop: 2.49%

Percentage of negative months: 50.00%

Percentage of positive months: 50.00%

NAGY-BECK HEDGE RATING:

MACKENZIE LONG/SHORT EQUITY

Mackenzie Financial Corp.
150 Bloor Street West, Suite M111
Toronto, ON • M5S 3B5

Telephone Number: (416) 922-5322
Fax Number: (416) 922-5660
Toll-Free: 1-800-387-0614
Web Site: www.mackenziefinancial.com

PORTFOLIO MANAGER(S)

Mackenzie Financial Mgmt. Team

FUND DESCRIPTION

The investment objective of this fund is to achieve an attractive risk-adjusted return through the use of a multi-manager investment approach by investing with a variety of hedge fund managers who employ primarily long/short equity strategies. The fund invests directly in specialized hedge funds and may also retain hedge fund managers to manage segregated accounts for it. The fund may, from time to time, hold cash and money market instruments, securities of fixed-income mutual funds managed by Mackenzie, foreign exchange derivative instruments, and derivative instruments based on the securities of the hedge fund. The fund's objective emphasizes total return, not current income.

TERMS AND CONDITIONS

Fund style: Fund of Funds

Sub-style: Stock Selection (Long Bias)

Inception date: December 2001

Management fee: 3.46%

Performance fee: 20%

Hurdle rate: 0%

Liquidity: Monthly

* Min. investment: $150,000

Benchmark: S&P 500

* or less based on provincial legislation

RRSP eligibility: Yes (Foreign Content)

Asset size: $11 million

NAV: $9.38

Early red'n period: 6 months

Early red'n fee: 2%

High-water mark: Yes

Redemption notice:

Max. leverage: 100%

PERFORMANCE (AS OF DECEMBER 31, 2002)

	1 month	3 month	6 month	YTD	1 year	2 year	3 year	5 year	10 year	Since Inception
Fund:	0.87%	-1.97%	-1.35%	-8.18%	-8.18%					-5.93%
S&P500										-10.13%

Year:		Jan	Feb	Mar	Apr	May	Jun	Jul	Aug	Sep	Oct	Nov	Dec
Fund:	**2002**	-8.18%	-0.40%	-2.22%	-0.15%	-0.89%	-2.79%	-0.65%	3.49%	-2.62%	-0.15%	-1.73%	-1.10%	0.87%
S&P500	2002	-23.14%	-1.70%	-1.16%	3.33%	-7.67%	-3.25%	-7.77%	-3.73%	-0.98%	-9.25%	6.85%	6.36%	-5.48%
Fund:	**2001**	1.93%												
S&P500	2001	2.16%												2.16%

PERFORMANCE COMPARISON

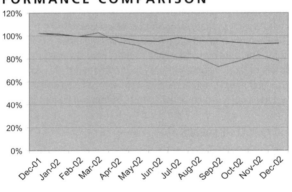

 Mackenzie Long/Short Equity ——— S&P500

RISK DATA (AS OF DECEMBER 31, 2002)

Alpha:	Benchmark: TSX
Beta:	Correlation to benchmark:
St. deviation (annualized):	Maximum drawdown: 8.97%
St. deviation (1 year):	Largest monthly drop: 2.79%
St. deviation (2 year):	Percentage of negative months: 76.92%
Sharpe Ratio:	Percentage of positive months: 23.08%
Sortino Ratio:	

NAGY-BECK HEDGE RATING:

MAPLE KEY MARKET NEUTRAL LP

Maple Financial Group Inc.
Maritime Life Tower
Toronto Dominion Centre, Suite 3500
P.O. Box 328
Toronto, ON • M5K 1K7

Telephone Number: (416) 350-8200
Fax Number: (416) 350-8222
Toll-Free: 1-800-275-5897
Web Site: www.maplefinancial.com

PORTFOLIO MANAGER(S)

Fund of Funds

FUND DESCRIPTION

Maple Key is a portfolio of market-neutral hedge funds assembled and managed by Maple Financial. Qualified Canadian investors are eligible to invest in Maple Key Market Neutral LP, which provides a return that is based on the returns of Maple Key. Qualified non-Canadian investors are eligible to invest in Maple Key Market Neutral Cayman Islands LP, which indirectly holds the Maple Key portfolio of funds. Investments in Maple Key Market Neutral LP and Maple Key Market Neutral Cayman Islands LP involve a high degree of risk and are suitable only for a sophisicated investor who can afford to lose some or all of its investment in such funds. An investment in either Maple Key Market Neutral LP or Maple Key Market Neutral Cayman Islands LP may be offered on a private placement basis only, pursuant to the confidential offering memorandum of the applicable fund. Maple Key is also available in a leveraged form.

TERMS AND CONDITIONS

Fund style: Fund of Funds
Sub-style: Various Market-Neutral Strategies
Inception date: January 1999
Management fee: 1.00%–1.50%
Performance fee: 10%
Hurdle rate: 3-month T-bill
Liquidity: Quarterly
Min. investment: US$150,000
Benchmark: S&P 500

RRSP eligibility: No
Asset size:
NAV:
Early red'n period: N/A
Early red'n fee: None
High water mark: Yes
Redemption notice: 100 days
Max leverage: None in fund of funds

PERFORMANCE (AS OF DECEMBER 31, 2002)

	1 month	3 month	6 month	YTD	1 year	2 year	3 year	5 year	10 year	Since Inception
Fund:	1.05%	2.13%	3.70%	6.29%	6.29%	6.92%	8.55%			9.21%
S&P500	-5.48%	7.42%	-7.07%	-23.14%	-23.14%	-15.15%	-12.23%			-6.15%

	Year:	Jan	Feb	Mar	Apr	May	Jun	Jul	Aug	Sep	Oct	Nov	Dec
Fund:	2002	6.04%	0.96%	0.30%	0.56%	0.62%	0.41%	-0.38%	0.24%	0.65%	0.64%	0.30%	0.77%	1.05%
S&P500	2002	-23.14%	-1.70%	-1.16%	3.33%	-7.67%	-3.25%	-7.77%	-3.73%	-0.98%	-9.25%	6.85%	6.36%	-5.48%
Fund:	2001	7.55%	2.00%	1.03%	0.62%	0.82%	1.12%	-0.55%	0.42%	0.78%	-0.11%	1.01%	0.23%	-0.04%
S&P500	2001	-6.33%	3.51%	-6.78%	-3.95%	4.99%	0.87%	-3.94%	0.27%	-5.18%	-6.42%	2.50%	6.63%	2.16%
Fund:	2000	11.87%	1.21%	1.43%	0.88%	1.42%	1.12%	0.83%	1.12%	1.14%	0.89%	0.68%	0.25%	0.31%
S&P500	2000	-6.07%	-5.31%	-1.70%	9.80%	-0.87%	-1.01%	1.34%	-1.17%	5.20%	-3.27%	0.85%	0.93%	-9.72%
Fund:	1999	11.21%	1.18%	0.95%	0.58%	1.25%	1.10%	1.09%	1.09%	0.52%	0.88%	0.71%	0.47%	0.86%
S&P500	1999	14.73%	2.85%	-3.27%	4.00%	0.32%	-1.19%	4.73%	-0.18%	-1.47%	-4.37%	6.56%	2.29%	4.19%

PERFORMANCE COMPARISON

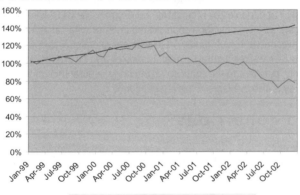

— Maple Key Market Neutral LP —— S&P500

RISK DATA (AS OF DECEMBER 31, 2002)

Alpha: 5.59%

Beta: 0.02

St. deviation (annualized): 1.64%

St. deviation (1 year):

St. deviation (2 year):

Sharpe Ratio: 3.18

Sortino Ratio:

Benchmark: S&P 500

Correlation to benchmark: 0.17

Maximum drawdown: 0.55%

Largest monthly drop: 0.55%

Percentage of negative months: 8.33%

Percentage of positive months: 91.67%

NAGY-BECK HEDGE RATING:

FOCUS ABSOLUTE RETURN GLOBAL FUND (C$)

Montrusco Bolton
1250 Réné Levesque Blvd. W., Suite 4600
Montreal, PQ • H3B 5J5

Telephone Number: (514) 282-2910
Fax Number: (514) 282-2973
Web Site: www.montruscobolton.com

PORTFOLIO MANAGER(S)

A fund of hedge funds managed by Montrusco Bolton.

FUND DESCRIPTION

The Montrusco Bolton Focus Absolute Return Global Fund seeks to achieve appreciation with low volatility. The fund will invest in a diversified portfolio of alternative investment managers whose expertise varies by both strategy and geographical region. The fund seeks to generate consistent absolute returns between 6% and 12% per annum.

TERMS AND CONDITIONS

Fund style: Directional Trading

Sub-style: System Trading

Inception date: April 1998

Management fee: 1.50%

Performance fee: 10%

Hurdle rate: 0%

Liquidity: Monthly

Min. investment: $150,000

Benchmark: MSCI

RRSP eligibility: No (except for periodic principal protected notes)

Asset size: $112 million

NAV: $100.24

Early red'n period:

Early red'n fee: None

High-water mark: Permanent high-water mark

Redemption notice: 35 days

Max. leverage: 100% (200% on Convertible Arbitrage strategies)

PERFORMANCE (AS OF NOVEMBER 30, 2002)

	1 month	3 month	6 month	YTD	1 year	2 year	3 year	5 year	10 year	Since Inception
Fund:	1.13%	1.38%	-1.17%	1.18%	1.18%	5.07%	9.58%			11.23%
MSCI	6.36%	3.13%	-9.33%	-18.68%	-18.31%	-17.08%	-9.33%			0.81%

Year:		Jan	Feb	Mar	Apr	May	Jun	Jul	Aug	Sep	Oct	Nov	Dec
und:	2002	1.18%	0.93%	0.17%	0.61%	0.44%	0.21%	-1.22%	-1.77%	0.46%	0.10%	0.15%	1.13%	
MSCI	2002	-18.68%	-1.70%	-1.16%	3.33%	-7.67%	-3.25%	-7.77%	-3.73%	-0.98%	-9.25%	6.85%	6.36%	
und:	2001	7.87%	1.73%	1.15%	0.62%	0.52%	1.05%	0.63%	0.16%	0.96%	-0.73%	0.47%	0.60%	0.46%
MSCI	2001	-6.33%	3.51%	-6.78%	-3.95%	4.99%	0.87%	-3.94%	0.27%	-5.18%	-6.42%	2.50%	6.63%	2.16%

Fund:	2000	15.39%	1.93%	3.64%	1.59%	-0.56%	1.44%	1.65%	0.79%	2.14%	0.24%	0.35%	0.11%	1.15%
MSCI	2000	-6.07%	-5.31%	-1.70%	9.80%	-0.87%	-1.01%	1.34%	-1.17%	5.20%	-3.27%	0.85%	0.93%	-9.72%
Fund:	1999	21.71%	1.25%	-0.56%	3.75%	3.21%	1.57%	1.14%	0.98%	-0.25%	0.53%	0.98%	2.87%	4.47%
MSCI	1999	14.73%	2.85%	-3.27%	4.00%	0.32%	-1.19%	4.73%	-0.18%	-1.47%	-4.37%	6.56%	2.29%	4.19%
Fund:	1998	2.55%									-2.12%	0.07%	2.80%	1.85%
MSCI	1998	26.08%									3.97%	9.00%	5.39%	5.56%

PERFORMANCE COMPARISON

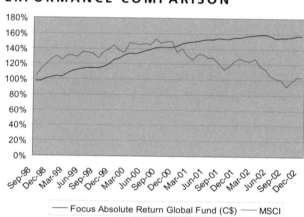

—— Focus Absolute Return Global Fund (C$) —— MSCI

RISK DATA (AS OF NOVEMBER 30, 2002)

Alpha:

Beta:

St. deviation (annualized): 4.46%

St. deviation (1 year):

St. deviation (2 year):

Sharpe Ratio: 1.96

Sortino Ratio: 7.46

Benchmark: MSCI

Correlation to benchmark: 0.41

Maximum drawdown: 2.97%

Largest monthly drop: 2.12%

Percentage of negative months: 13.73%

Percentage of positive months: 86.27%

NAGY-BECK HEDGE RATING:

BTR GLOBAL ARBITRAGE FUND

Salida Capital Corp.
2200 Yonge Street, Suite 605
Toronto, ON • M4S 2C6

Telephone Number: (416) 322-7607
Fax Number: (416) 322-7610
Web Site: www.salidacapital.com

PORTFOLIO MANAGER(S)

Daniel Guy, President and Chief Investment Officer

Daniel Guy, along with a core group of professionals from Banfield Capital Management, founded Salida Capital in 2001.

He brings with him over 10 years of investment management experience, with a background in equity research followed by a transition to equity trading. He has been managing alternative management portfolios since 1996 and has the full range of experience necessary to successfully execute all portfolio mandates. Guy is responsible for North American investments and risk management within the firm. In 1998 he joined Banfield Capital Management as a portfolio manager and trader, and was a key factor in that firm's successful track record. In addition, he helped to build the firm's research and trading group and also established their U.S. merger arbitrage business. While managing the firm's long/short portfolio from its inception in 1998, he achieved superior results.

In 1996, Guy joined the Merger Arbitrage group at First Marathon Securities, and was responsible for trading liability positions and co-running the firm's merger-arbitrage book. This assignment included covering hedge funds on a global basis, both from a sales and a trading perspective. Guy started his investment career with Richardson Greenshields in 1993 as an oil and gas analyst, moving to First Marathon in 1995, also as an analyst, before joining its Merger Arbitrage group in 1996.

Brad White, CFA, VP, North American Equities
Patrick McGuire, VP, Credit & Volatility Arbitrage, Senior Portfolio Manager
Terry Bell, VP, Global Mining
Malcom Smith, Investment Analyst

FUND DESCRIPTION

The investment process at Salida Capital incorporates three core strategies: long/short investing, convertible arbitrage, and merger arbitrage.

Long/Short Investments

The process starts with a fundamental decision regarding net market exposure. Do they choose to be net long, net short, or market neutral? The aggregate market exposure will depend on whether they are finding better investment opportunities on the long or the short side of the market.

The stock selection criteria incorporate characteristics such as the dynamic within the sector, the management team, relative valuations appropriate to the sector, fundamental outlook, and the business plan/model. They look for investment ideas, and then look for a catalyst that will focus the investment community's attention on the company.

In order to mitigate systemic risk they will examine the correlation of long/short positions within the same sector. In addition, they monitor diversification across sectors to mitigate specific industry risk.

Convertible Arbitrage

The process begins with screening the universe of convertible bonds in order to identify bonds that are mispriced or undervalued relative to their underlying stock. The process involves looking at company and industry fundamentals in order to identify the potential future impacts of the various characteristics of the bond. Important factors are premium to conversion ratio, call provisions, creditworthiness of the issuer, yield advantage, and the company's earnings momentum.

The number of underlying shares sold short depends on the market exposure they want. The hedge ratio will be determined by yield curve shifts, dividend yield, volatility of the stock, and the stock's price.

Merger Arbitrage

Often their fundamental stock selection takes into account a potential takeover or merger situation, although they do not try to anticipate possible mergers.

When a deal is announced, they research the situation thoroughly in an effort to reduce the uncertainty about possible outcomes. Before taking a position they will consider public corporate documents, analyst reports, and conversations with company and industry contacts. If the rewards outweigh the risks of the deal failing, they may invest. In addition, they may add to positions as more information becomes available and the outcome becomes more certain. Normally, they will take long and short positions in the ratio of the proposed transaction in order to lock in the spread.

On the other hand, they will liquidate a position if the risk-reward relationship deteriorates or when the deal is consummated.

TERMS AND CONDITIONS

Fund style: Multi-Strategy

Sub-style: Long/Short; Conv. Arb., Merger Arb.

Inception date: April 2000

Management fee: 2.00%

Performance fee: 20%

Hurdle rate: 0%

Liquidity: Monthly

Min. Investment: $150,000

Benchmark: S&P 500

RRSP eligibility: No

Asset size: US$45 million

NAV: US$155.09 (Sept 30, 2002)

Early red'n period: 1 year

Early red'n fee:

High-water mark: Yes

Redemption notice: 20 days

Max. leverage:

PERFORMANCE (AS OF DECEMBER 31, 2002)

	1 month	3 month	6 month	YTD	1 year	2 year	3 year	5 year	10 year	Since Inception
Fund:	5.64%	7.08%	8.55%	23.02%	23.02%	15.31%				20.27%
S&P500:	-5.48%	7.42%	-7.07%	-23.14%	-23.14%	-15.15%				-13.95%

Year:		Jan	Feb	Mar	Apr	May	Jun	Jul	Aug	Sep	Oct	Nov	Dec
nd:	2002	23.02%	3.05%	0.41%	6.01%	-1.66%	4.32%	0.71%	-4.23%	5.39%	0.44%	1.09%	0.27%	5.64%
P500	2002	-23.14%	-1.70%	-1.16%	3.33%	-7.67%	-3.25%	-7.77%	-3.73%	-0.98%	-9.25%	6.85%	6.36%	-5.48%
nd:	2001	8.09%	1.23%	0.74%	-1.55%	2.49%	4.44%	0.24%	-1.66%	-1.70%	-0.42%	2.14%	-0.42%	2.48%
P500	2001	-6.33%	3.51%	-6.78%	-3.95%	4.99%	0.87%	-3.94%	0.27%	-5.18%	-6.42%	2.50%	6.63%	2.16%
nd:	2000	24.93%			10.46%	0.66%	2.87%	-0.15%	5.27%	1.71%	0.67%	0.17%	1.31%
P500	2000	-8.10%			-0.87%	-1.01%	1.34%	-1.17%	5.20%	-3.27%	0.85%	0.93%	-9.72%

PERFORMANCE COMPARISON

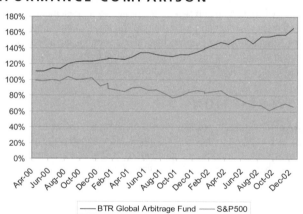

———BTR Global Arbitrage Fund ———S&P500

RISK DATA (AS OF DECEMBER 31, 2002)

Alpha (annualized): 23.97%

Beta: 0.16

St. deviation (annualized): 9.92%

St. deviation (1 year):

St. deviation (2 year):

Sharpe Ratio (5.0%): 1.43

Sortino Ratio (0%): 3.59

Benchmark: S&P 500

Correlation to benchmark: 0.42

Maximum drawdown: 4.23%

Largest monthly drop: 4.23%

Percentage of negative months: 24.24%

Percentage of positive months: 75.76%

NAGY-BECK HEDGE RATING:

SCIVEST MARKET NEUTRAL EQUITY FUND

SciVest Alternative Strategies Inc.
1 First Canadian Place
Suite 6960
P.O. Box #12
Toronto, ON • M5X 1A9

Telephone Number: (416) 304-3800
Fax Number: (416) 304-6832
Toll-Free: 1-866-599-2400
Web Site: www.scivest.com

Similar funds:
SciVest Market Neutral Equity US$
BluMont Market Neutral
BluMont Market Neutral US$

PORTFOLIO MANAGER(S)

Dr. John J. Schmitz

Schmitz is a recognized expert in the research, development, and implementation of quantitative investment management processes. He has extensive practical experience, including financial consulting and several senior money management positions. He has also done extensive research and publishing in the areas of investments and portfolio management. Schmitz holds a BESc (Mechanical Engineering) and a BA (Economics) from the University of Western Ontario, an MA (Economics) from the University of Toronto, a PhD (Finance) from the Ivey School of Business, and a CFA.

FUND DESCRIPTION

The objective of the fund is to produce returns meaningfully higher than equity with low volatility risk as compared to the S&P 500 Index. More importantly, the fund is to meet these objectives while being fully independent of the general movements of the equity markets. It is managed using highly sophisticated quantitative investment models that harness the power of today's computer systems and the availability of large high-quality databases. The strategy is cash neutral (i.e., equal dollars long and short), market neutral (i.e., forecasted beta equal to 0.0), close to sector and industry neutral (i.e., maximum 2% net exposures) with leverage of 1.6:1 (i.e., $160 long and $160 short, for every $100 of capital).

Stock selection is driven by dynamic, fundamental, quantitative models that forecast the expected return of every stock in the eligible universe of liquid stocks. The expected return models are dynamic in the sense that they adapt to the current market environment, focusing on only those return-generating factors that appear to be working the best in the current environment. Risk management is rigorous and viewed as at least as important as return generation. Risk management combines highly sophisticated risk models, as well as over 100 "common sense" based risk management constraints. Transaction costs and market impact is explicitly modelled and forecasted for each position.

Portfolios are ultimately formed using a sophisticated integrated optimization process that incorporates expected returns, risks, and trading costs of every stock in the eligible universe. The result is a highly diversified portfolio of over 360 stock positions across all sectors and most industries. Average stock-holding periods tend to range between two and four months. The portfolio is also diversified internationally, with 82% of capital allocated to the liquid U.S. markets and 18% of capital allocated to the Canadian markets.

TERMS AND CONDITIONS

Fund style: Stock Selection

Sub-style: Market Neutral Equity

Inception date: May 2001

Management fee: 2.50%

Performance fee: 20%

Hurdle rate: Canadian Treasury Bill rate

Liquidity: Daily

*Min. investment: $150,000

Benchmark: S&P 500

* or less based on provincial legislation

RRSP eligibility: Yes (Foreign Content)

Asset size: $22 million

NAV: $101.05 (January 17, 2003)

Early red'n period: Within 120 days of initial purchase

Early red'n fee: 5%

High-water mark: Yes

Redemption notice:

Max. leverage: 60%

PERFORMANCE (AS OF DECEMBER 31, 2002)

	1 month	3 month	6 month	YTD	1 year	2 year	3 year	5 year	10 year	Since Inception
Fund:		2.00%	-8.63%	-5.44%	7.67%	7.67%				
Benchmark:		-5.48%	7.42%	-7.07%	-23.14%	-23.14%				

Year:		Jan	Feb	Mar	Apr	May	Jun	Jul	Aug	Sep	Oct	Nov	Dec
und:	2002	7.67%	7.3%	-2.4%	4.3%	-0.1%	2.6%	1.7%	-3.1%	3.1%	3.6%	-4.30%	-6.40%	2.00%
&P500	2002	-23.14%	-1.70%	-1.16%	3.33%	-7.67%	-3.25%	-7.77%	-3.73%	-0.98%	-9.25%	6.85%	6.36%	-5.48%
und:	2001	16.05%					1.1%	-1.8%	4.0%	3.5%	6.8%	-3.5%	3.4%	1.9%
&P500	2001	-3.74%					0.87%	-3.94%	0.27%	-5.18%	-6.42%	2.50%	6.63%	2.16%

PERFORMANCE COMPARISON

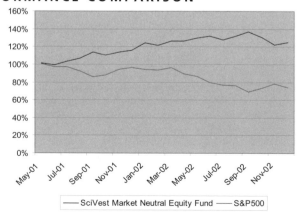

SciVest Market Neutral Equity Fund —— S&P500

RISK DATA (AS OF DECEMBER 31, 2002)

Alpha (annualized): 0.84%

Beta: -0.06

St. deviation (annualized): 10.70%

St. deviation (1 year):

St. deviation (2 year):

Sharpe Ratio: 1.07

Sortino Ratio: 1.54

Benchmark: S&P 500

Correlation to benchmark:-0.13

Maximum drawdown: 10.50%

Largest monthly drop: 10.50%

Percentage of negative months: 30.00%

Percentage of positive months: 70.00%

NAGY-BECK HEDGE RATING:

SPROTT BULL/BEAR RSP FUND

Sprott Asset Management Inc.
Royal Bank Plaza, South Tower
Suite 3450
Toronto, ON • M5J 2J2

Telephone Number: (416) 943-6707
Fax Number: (416) 943-6497
Toll-Free: 1-866-299-9906
Web Site: www.sprottassetmanagement.com

PORTFOLIO MANAGER(S)

Eric Sprott, CA

Eric Sprott is CEO and chief investment officer of Sprott Asset Management Inc. After earning his designation as a chartered accountant, he entered the investment industry working in research as well as institutional sales. In 1981 he founded Sprott Securities Limited (now Sprott Securities Inc.) which, under his leadership, has become one of the most successful investment firms in Canada.

Sprott has established himself as a clear leader in Canada's investment community. With over 30 years of industry experience, his expertise at making predictions on the market and recognizing investment opportunities with superior growth potential have been proven many times over. His investment abilities are clearly demonstrated by the excellent performance track record of Sprott Managed Accounts, Sprott Canadian Equity Fund, and the Sprott Hedge Fund L.P.

FUND DESCRIPTION

The objective of the fund is to maximize absolute returns on investments. The fund intends to accomplish its set objective through superior securities selection by taking both long and short investment positions.

The investment manager intends to invest in opportunities that provide what the investment manager, at the time of investment, believes to be the best reward per unit of risk. The investment manager also intends to optimize the reward per unit of risk of the investment portfolio by varying the allocation of long and short positions depending on the investment manager's view of the domestic and international economy, market trends, and other considerations. The fund's portfolio will be positioned in accordance with the investment manager's market view. Generally, a bearish market view would increase emphasis on short positions and defensive long positions such as cash and gold. A bullish market view would generally increase emphasis on long positions with high growth prospects. The fund will overweight certain industry sectors and asset classes, such as cash and gold, when deemed appropriate by the investment manager. In executing this strategy, the following core techniques will be employed:

1. making long investments in securities that the investment manager believes are undervalued, typically in companies with improving fundamentals, strong balance sheets, superior earnings growth potential, and solid business models; and

2. short selling of securities that the investment manager believes are overvalued, especially those with deteriorating fundamentals, weak balance sheets, and other factors that merit a determination of overvaluation by the investment manager.

TERMS AND CONDITIONS

Fund style: Stock Selection

Sub-style: Variable Bias

Inception date: November 2002

Management fee: 2.00%

Performance fee: 20%

Hurdle rate: 0%

Liquidity: Monthly

*Min. investment: $150,000

Benchmark: S&P 500

RRSP eligibility: No

* or less based on provincial legislation

Asset size: $35 million

NAV: $5.26

Early red'n period: 6 months

Early red'n fee: 3%

High-water mark: yes

Redemption notice: Monthly, with 7 days notice
  (minimum 6 months lock-up period)

Lock-up period: 6 month

Max. leverage: 100%

PERFORMANCE (AS OF DECEMBER 31, 2002)

	1 month	3 month	6 month	YTD	1 year	2 year	3 year	5 year	10 year	Since Inception
Fund:	15.96%									5.20%
Benchmark:	-5.48%									0.53%

Year:	Jan	Feb	Mar	Apr	May	Jun	Jul	Aug	Sep	Oct	Nov	Dec
Fund: 2002	5.20%										-9.28%	15.96%
S&P500 2002	0.53%										6.36%	-5.48%

PERFORMANCE COMPARISON

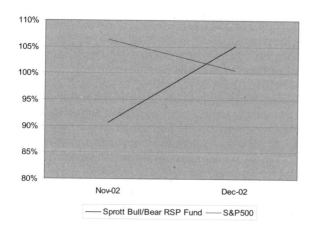

Sprott Bull/Bear RSP Fund ——— S&P500

RISK DATA (AS OF DECEMBER 31, 2002)

Alpha:

Beta:

St. deviation (annualized):

St. deviation (1 year):

St. deviation (2 year):

Sharpe Ratio:

Sortino Ratio:

Benchmark: S&P 500

Correlation to benchmark:

Maximum drawdown: 9.28%

Largest monthly drop: 9.28%

Percentage of negative months: 50.00%

Percentage of positive months: 50.00%

NAGY-BECK HEDGE RATING:

SPROTT HEDGE FUND L.P.

Sprott Asset Management Inc.   Telephone Number: (416) 943-6707
Royal Bank Plaza, South Tower   Fax Number: (416) 943-6497
Suite 3450   Toll-Free: 1-866-299-9906
Toronto, ON • M5J 2J2   Web Site: www.sprottassetmanagement.com
Similar funds: Sprott Hedge Fund L.P. II

PORTFOLIO MANAGER(S)

Eric Sprott, CA

Eric Sprott is CEO and chief investment officer of Sprott Asset Management Inc. After earning his designation as a chartered accountant, he entered the investment industry working in research as well as institutional sales. In 1981 he founded Sprott Securities Limited (now Sprott Securities Inc.) which, under his leadership, has become one of the most successful investment firms in Canada.

Sprott has established himself as a clear leader in Canada's investment community. With over 30 years of industry experience, his expertise at making predictions on the market and recognizing investment opportunities with superior growth potential have been proven many times over. His investment abilities are clearly demonstrated by the excellent performance track record of Sprott Managed Accounts, Sprott Canadian Equity Fund, and the Sprott Hedge Fund L.P.

FUND DESCRIPTION

The fund's investment objective is to maximize absolute returns on investments while attempting to mitigate market risk. The fund intends to accomplish its set objective through superior securities selection by taking both long and short investment positions. The fund's managers may also execute arbitrage strategies, seek spin-off opportunities, and participate in select private placements in order to maximize investment returns. The investment team will vary the allocation of long and short positions depending on their view of the domestic and international economy and market trends, including liquidity flows within the U.S. financial system.

TERMS AND CONDITIONS

Fund style: Stock Selection

Sub-style: Variable Bias	*Min. investment: $150,000	Early red'n fee:
Inception date: November 2000	Benchmark: S&P 500	High-water mark: yes
Management fee: 2.35%	RRSP eligibility: No	Lock-up period: 6 month
Performance fee: 20%	Asset size: $440 million	Redemption notice: Monthly, with
Hurdle rate: 10%	NAV: 30.42	90 days notice (minimum 1 year lock-up period)
Liquidity: Monthly	Early red'n period:	Max. leverage: 100%

* or less based on provincial legislation

PERFORMANCE (AS OF DECEMBER 31, 2002)

	1 month	3 month	6 month	YTD	1 year	2 year	3 year	5 year	10 year	Since Inception
Fund:	13.25%	-8.37%	6.06%	73.97%	73.97%	69.05%				67.13%
S&P 500:	-5.48%	7.42%	-7.07%	-23.14%	-23.14%	-15.15%				-17.68%

Year:		Jan	Feb	Mar	Apr	May	Jun	Jul	Aug	Sep	Oct	Nov	Dec
Fund:	2002	73.97%	12.33%	13.37%	8.21%	11.44%	8.15%	-1.24%	4.12%	4.67%	6.21%	-11.05%	-9.04%	13.25%
S&P500	2002	-23.14%	-1.70%	-1.16%	3.33%	-7.67%	-3.25%	-7.77%	-3.73%	-0.98%	-9.25%	6.85%	6.36%	-5.48%
Fund:	2001	64.27%	3.52%	16.52%	3.71%	1.40%	1.17%	11.32%	5.73%	5.63%	8.48%	-0.53%	-5.38%	0.84%
S&P500	2001	-6.33%	3.51%	-6.78%	-3.95%	4.99%	0.87%	-3.94%	0.27%	-5.18%	-6.42%	2.50%	6.63%	2.16%
Fund:	2000	6.47%										4.90%	1.50%
S&P500	2000	-8.88%										0.93%	-9.72%

PERFORMANCE COMPARISON

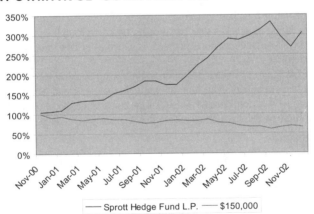

—— Sprott Hedge Fund L.P.   —— $150,000

RISK DATA (AS OF DECEMBER 31, 2002)

Alpha:	Benchmark: S&P 500
Beta:	Correlation to benchmark:
St. deviation (annualized):	Maximum drawdown: 19.09%
St. deviation (1 year):	Largest monthly drop: 11.05%
St. deviation (2 year):	Percentage of negative months: 19.23%
Sharpe Ratio:	Percentage of positive months: 80.77%
Sortino Ratio:	

NAGY-BECK HEDGE RATING:

STRATEGICNOVA MANAGED FUTURES HEDGE FUND

Dynamic
Scotia Plaza, 55th Floor
40 King Street West
Toronto, ON • M5H 4A9

Telephone Number: (514) 908-3212
Fax Number: 1-800-419-5119
Toll-Free: 1-800-268-8186
Web Site: www.strategicnova.com

PORTFOLIO MANAGER(S)

**Doug Sereda, Matisse Investment Management Ltd.
(an indirect subsidiary of Dynamic)**

Doug Sereda has over 20 years of experience in the derivatives industry and has worked closely with Dynamic to build a pre-eminent managed futures product for Canadian investors.

FUND DESCRIPTION

The manager of the fund has selected a handful of CTAs from a universe of over 700 to manage the fund's assets. The selection process, based on computerized analytic techniques and well-defined investment criteria, is aimed at achieving optimum portfolio diversification.

The CTAs utilize systematic trend-following trading applications. These programs eliminate the discretionary input from the portfolio managers and have demonstrated superior long-term performance as a result of the consistent application of well-defined modelling. These models pursue capital growth within the limits of defined risk tolerances.

Fund Highlights

This alternative investment opportunity, which is 100% eligible for registered plans, provides investors with unprecedented global exposure using exchange-traded derivatives representing global stock indexes, foreign currencies, interest rate instruments, precious and industrial metals, energy products, and various agricultural markets such as grains, coffee, sugar, and cocoa. The addition of managed futures to a traditionally diversified portfolio has historically enhanced returns and reduced volatility.

TERMS AND CONDITIONS

Fund style: CTA (Commodity Trading Advisors)

Sub-style: Systematic Trend Following	**RRSP eligibility:** Yes
Inception date: October 1999	**Asset size:** $21.1 million
Management fee: 1.50% (other fees apply)	**NAV:** $11.93
Performance fee: 10% to 25%	**Early red'n period:** 90 days
Hurdle rate: Yes	**Early red'n fee:** Short-term trading fee of 2% within 90 days applies
Liquidity: Daily	**High-water mark:** Yes
Min. investment: $3,000	**Redemption notice:** None
Benchmark: TSX	**Max. leverage:** None

PERFORMANCE (AS OF DECEMBER 31, 2002)

	1 month	3 month	6 month	YTD	1 year	2 year	3 year	5 year	10 year	Since Inception
Fund:	9.10%	-6.40%	19.40%	26.46%	26.46%	4.24%	11.05%			5.79%
TSX	0.67%	7.03%	-7.43%	-13.97%	-13.97%	-13.96%	-7.71%			-1.55%

Year:		Jan	Feb	Mar	Apr	May	Jun	Jul	Aug	Sep	Oct	Nov	Dec
und:	2002	26.46%	-1.48%	-4.44%	2.10%	-5.16%	3.24%	12.54%	11.21%	5.22%	9.02%	-8.58%	-6.16%	9.10%
SX	2002	-13.97%	-0.52%	-0.14%	2.80%	-2.40%	-0.10%	-6.67%	-7.56%	0.10%	-6.53%	1.11%	5.15%	0.67%
und:	2001	-14.07%	6.06%	-2.13%	7.32%	-12.35%	-0.37%	-10.42%	-4.14%	4.46%	6.92%	10.84%	-17.13%	0.27%
SX	2001	-13.94%	4.35%	-13.34%	-5.83%	4.45%	2.71%	-5.21%	-0.60%	-3.78%	-7.58%	0.69%	7.84%	3.54%
und:	2000	26.02%	4.22%	-0.11%	-8.43%	-9.33%	-6.86%	-2.69%	1.75%	5.01%	-3.54%	6.07%	18.78%	23.88%
SX	2000	6.18%	0.80%	7.64%	3.65%	-1.21%	-1.02%	10.20%	2.07%	8.09%	-7.74%	-7.12%	-8.50%	1.29%
und:	1999	-12.30%										-6.80%	-0.43%	-5.50%
SX	1999	20.93%										4.29%	3.68%	11.84%

PERFORMANCE COMPARISON

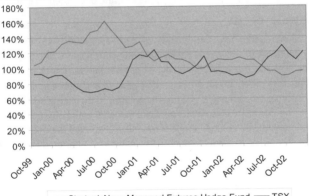

StrategicNova Managed Futures Hedge Fund —— TSX

RISK DATA (AS OF DECEMBER 31, 2002)

Alpha: 0.83%

Beta: -0.54

St. deviation (annualized): 29.64%

St. deviation (1 year): 26.19%

St. deviation (2 year): 26.09%

Sharpe Ratio: 0.20 (RFR=3.92%)

Sortino Ratio: 0.32 (MAR=0%)

Benchmark: TSX

Correlation to benchmark: -0.36

Maximum drawdown: -31.30%

Largest monthly drop: -17.13%

Percentage of negative months: 51.28%

Percentage of positive months: 48.72%

NAGY-BECK HEDGE RATING:

VERTEX FUND

Vertex One Asset Management   Telephone Number: (604) 681-5359
1920-1177 West Hastings Street   Fax Number: (604) 681-5146
Vancouver, BC • V6E 2K3   Toll-Free: 1-866-681-5787
                                     Web Site: www.vertexone.com

PORTFOLIO MANAGER(S)

John Thiessen, Director

John Thiessen is a founding partner and director of Vertex One Asset Management and has overall responsibility for the investment and trading decisions affecting the Vertex Fund's investment portfolio. He has been the lead manager since the fund's inception on February 6, 1998. Thiessen has significant experience in the investment field, with more than 15 years of equity, fixed income, and arbitrage experience. He began his career with the Alberta Treasury Investment Management Division, moving on to an investment officer with National Trust. He was a portfolio manager with HSBC Asset Management before starting with Vertex One. Thiessen holds the professional designation of chartered financial analyst (CFA) and is a member of the Institute of Chartered Financial Analysts.

Matthew Wood, Director

Matthew Wood is a founding partner and director of Vertex One Asset Management. He is the lead manager of the Vertex Balanced Fund and is responsible for the investment and trading decisions that affect the fund. He has been the lead manager since the fund's inception on April 3, 1998. Wood has over 14 years of experience in dealing with equities, fixed income, and derivatives. He began his career as an analyst and became a financial adviser with Royal Trust. He was a portfolio manager with HSBC Asset Management before starting with Vertex One. Wood holds the professional designation of chartered financial analyst (CFA) and is a member of the Institute of Chartered Financial Analysts.

FUND DESCRIPTION

Often hedge funds will concentrate on one specific strategy. Experience has taught Vertex One that opportunities in any one strategy may become scarce from time to time, therefore many strategies are used to drive performance. The strategy chosen is based on the relative risk-return tradeoff against others. Their investment style can best be described as opportunistic.

TERMS AND CONDITIONS

Fund style: Various

Sub-style:

Inception date: February 1998

Management fee: 1.00%

Performance fee: 20%

Hurdle rate: 0%

Liquidity: Monthly

*Min. investment: $150,000

Benchmark: S&P 500

* or less based on provincial legislation

RRSP eligibility: Yes (Foreign Content)

Asset size: $82 million

NAV: $24.09

Early red'n period:

Early red'n fee:

High-water mark:

Redemption notice:

Max. leverage:

PERFORMANCE (AS OF DECEMBER 31, 2002)

	1 month	3 month	6 month	YTD	1 year	2 year	3 year	5 year	10 year	Since Incception
Fund:	5.16%	1.56%	-7.84%	-2.43%	-2.43%	2.38%	13.61%			21.69%
Benchmark:	-5.48%	7.42%	-7.07%	-23.14%	-23.14%	-15.15%	-12.23%			0.76%

Year:		Jan	Feb	Mar	Apr	May	Jun	Jul	Aug	Sep	Oct	Nov	Dec
Fund:	2002	-2.43%	1.82%	0.96%	3.26%	-2.13%	4.23%	-2.23%	-11.93%	4.01%	-0.94%	-1.54%	-1.91%	5.16%
&P500	2002	-23.14%	-1.70%	-1.16%	3.33%	-7.67%	-3.25%	-7.77%	-3.73%	-0.98%	-9.25%	6.85%	6.36%	-5.48%
Fund:	2001	7.42%	0.12%	0.10%	-2.42%	2.78%	2.62%	-0.11%	1.09%	1.95%	-0.27%	0.13%	-1.50%	2.85%
&P500	2001	-6.33%	3.51%	-6.78%	-3.95%	4.99%	0.87%	-3.94%	0.27%	-5.18%	-6.42%	2.50%	6.63%	2.16%
Fund:	2000	39.91%	3.95%	18.90%	-0.10%	-0.88%	3.21%	2.54%	1.67%	5.29%	2.07%	-3.30%	-0.85%	3.11%
&P500	2000	-6.07%	-5.31%	-1.70%	9.80%	-0.87%	-1.01%	1.34%	-1.17%	5.20%	-3.27%	0.85%	0.93%	-9.72%
Fund:	1999	69.26%	9.36%	-3.46%	6.26%	10.53%	3.04%	3.47%	3.86%	0.78%	0.23%	2.72%	7.82%	10.19%
&P500	1999	14.73%	2.85%	-3.27%	4.00%	0.32%	-1.19%	4.73%	-0.18%	-1.47%	-4.37%	6.56%	2.29%	4.19%
Fund:	1998	5.77%		0.53%	16.62%	10.59%	-4.29%	-4.47%	-1.57%	-18.40%	-1.08%	-4.54%	10.97%	6.01%
&P500	1998	33.78%		4.96%	4.84%	1.78%	0.05%	4.78%	2.05%	-11.44%	3.97%	9.00%	5.39%	5.56%

PERFORMANCE COMPARISON

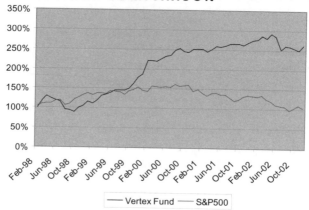

Vertex Fund ——— S&P500

RISK DATA (AS OF DECEMBER 31, 2002)

Alpha (annualized):

Beta (3 year): 0.36

St. deviation (annualized):

St. deviation (1 year):

St. deviation (3 year): 14.82%

Sharpe Ratio (risk free rate=5%): 0.83

Sortino Ratio:

Benchmark: S&P 500

Correlation to benchmark:

Maximum drawdown: 30.65%

Largest monthly drop: 18.40%

Percentage of negative months: 35.59%

Percentage of positive months: 64.41%

NAGY-BECK HEDGE RATING:

Glossary of Terms

1 day Return   Percentage change of the hedge fund NAV over 1 day adjusted to distribution.

1 mth   Percentage change of the hedge fund NAV over 1 month adjusted to distributions.

1 yr   The hedge fund's 1 year performance.

10 yr   The hedge fund's annualized rate of return over 10 years.

15 yr   The hedge fund's annualized rate of return over 15 years.

3 mth   Percentage change of the hedge fund NAV over 3 month adjusted to distributions.

3 yr   The hedge fund's annualized rate of return over 3 years.

6 mth   Percentage change of the hedge fund NAV over 6 month adjusted to distributions.

7 day Return   Percentage change of the hedge fund NAV over 7 day adjusted to distributions.

Alpha   The abnormal (or manager specific) rate of return on the hedge fund in excess of what would be predicted by the market return and risk measure (beta).

Beta   The measure of the systematic risk of the hedge fund. The tendency of the hedge fund's returns to respond to swings in the broad market.

Compound Annual Return   Annualized rate of return of the hedge fund (provided that the fund is at least 1 year "old").

Convergence Arbitrage   The manager focuses on obtaining returns with low or no correlation to the market. The manager buys different securities of the same issuer (e.g., the common stock and convertibles) and "works the spread" between them. For example, within the same company the manager buys one form of security that he/she believes is undervalued and sells short another security of the same company.

Correlation   A statistic that scales the covariance to a value between minus one (perfect negative correlation) and plus one (perfect positive correlation).

CTA   Commodity trading advisor. A CTA runs separate commodity accounts.

Current Exposure—Long   Current percentage of long exposure.

Current Exposure—Net   Current percentage of net exposure.

Current Exposure—Short   Current percentage of short exposure.

Daily Change   Dollar change of the hedge fund's NAV.

Directional Trading   Based upon speculation of market direction in multiple asset classes. Both model-based systems and subjective judgement are used to make trading decisions.

Discretionary Trading   The manager of these types hedge fund rotates investment selection to different sectors of the economy as he/she sees fit.

Distressed Securities   Buying the equity or debt of companies that are in or facing bankruptcy. The manager hopes to buy company securities at a low price and hopes that company will come out of bankruptcy and securities will appreciate.

Distribution   Dates of distributions with dollar values (of distributions).

Early redemption fee   Percentage fee (usually 5%) applied in case of redemption of the hedge fund investment within a certain period of time (often 6 months).

Fund of funds   Fund containing more than 1 hedge fund. Hedge funds used in fund of funds could be classified in one or more main styles. Often a diversified portfolio of generally uncorrelated hedge funds.

Fund Size   Size of the Hedge Fund in millions of US or Can dollars.

High Water Mark   The high water mark is either the previous highest value of an investor's investment for which incentive fees were paid already or in case of no previous incentive fees paid his original investment in a particular hedge fund adjusted to purchases and redemptions since the first buy. The high water mark value marks the point below the fund cannot charge a performance fee to the particular investor even in case of over hurdle rate performance in the year. Should the high water mark value be higher than the beginning of year value of the investment (adjusted to cash flows) the performance fees will only be calculated and paid based on the difference of the high water mark and the end of the year value of the particular hedge fund investment.

Hurdle rate   A set calendar year rate of return over which performance fees are charged.

Inception Date   Month and year when the particular hedge fund was launched.

Long Bias   Long Bias substyle hedge funds have usually more exposure to "long" financial instruments than to "short" financial instruments. Managers of these funds assume that the market goes up in the long run.

Macro Trading   The investment philosophy is based on shifts in global economies. Derivatives are often used to speculate on currency and interest rate moves.

Management fee   Set annual fee the hedge fund company charges its fund for providing investment management services (usually ranges between 1.5% to 3% similar to Mutual Funds).

Maximum Drawdown   Maximum percentage loss from the hedge fund's "peak to valley".

Merger Arbitrage   Managers seek to capture the price spread between current market prices and the value of securities upon successful completion of a take-over or a merger. The price spread is due to the time value of money and a risk premium on the deal not closing. Returns in merger arbitrage arise from the correct anticipation of relative movements in stock prices.

Minimum Investment   Minimum initial investment to the particular hedge fund (normally $150,000 in Ontario for a non accredited investor).

Monthly Rate of Return   Month by month performances of the hedge fund.

Month-to-Date   Percentage change of the hedge fund NAV since the last date of the previous month adjusted to distributions.

NAV   Net Asset Value per share (of hedge fund).

No Bias   No Bias substyle hedge funds have usually equal exposure to "long" financial instruments and to "short" financial instruments. Managers of these funds do not assume anything about the market direction in the long run.

Performance fee   The performance fee is a certain percentage what a particular hedge fund charges per year over and above the management fee. Performance fee usually is 20% over a threshold performance (hurdle rate) in a calendar year. Many hedge funds' threshold performance for incentive fee is 0% however some charge over +10% or the T-Bill rate of return in the calendar year.

Positive Carry   Positive carry exploits investment opportunities when the cost of borrowed funds is lower than the return earned on investments.

Possible Exposure range—Long   Percentage range of possible long "exposures".

Possible Exposure range—Net   Percentage range of possible net "exposures".

Possible Exposure range—Short   Percentage range of possible short "exposures".

Private Placements   Managers of this type of hedge fund try to take advantage of the short term opportunities represented by investing in firms that need to raise capital quickly.

Relative Value   A focus on the spread relationship between pricing components of financial assets. Market risk is kept to a minimum. Many managers use leverage to enhance returns.

RRSP Eligibility   Indicates whether the particular hedge fund is eligible for RRSP investment. In case of RRSP eligibility it can be either classified as Canadian or foreign content.

Sharpe Ratio   Reward-to-volatility ratio. Ratio of the hedge fund's excess return to standard deviation.

Short Bias   Short Bias substyle hedge funds have usually more exposure to "short" financial instruments than to "long" financial instruments. Managers of these funds do not assume that the market goes up in the long run.

Specialist Credit   Based on lending to credit-sensitive issuers. Funds in this style conduct a high level of due diligence in order to identify relatively inexpensive securities.

Standard deviation   Statistical measure of volatility measuring the difference between the hedge fund actual performance and average performance.

Statistical Arbitrage   Believing that equities behave in a way that is mathematically describable, managers perform a low risk, market neutral analytical equity strategy. This approach captures momentary pricing aberrations in the stocks being monitored. The strategy's profit objective is to exploit mis-pricing in as risk-free a manner as possible.

Stock Selection   Combining long and short positions, primarily in equities, in order to exploit under or overvalued securities. Market exposure can vary substantially.

Systems Trading   A proprietary computer program system that makes most or all decisions about the positions of the fund.

Valuation Frequency   It shows how often the particular hedge fund is valued (normally weekly).

Variable Bias   Variable Bias substyle hedge funds frequently rotate their bias about the direction of the market and their exposure to "long" and "short" financial instruments. Managers of these funds assume either a bullish or bearish bias at different times and change their net exposure accordingly.

YTD   Percentage change of the hedge fund NAV since December 31 of last year adjusted to distributions.

Resources

RELATED OR SIMILAR BOOKS ON
THE CANADIAN MARKET:

Up until now, there has been no publication dedicated solely to the
Canadian Hedge Fund Industry. While some of the rules and regulations differ between Canadian and U.S. hedge funds, their strategies
and styles are similar. The books below are available in Canada, but
were all published in the USA.

Author	Title	Publisher
Peter Temple	*Hedge Funds: Courtesans of Capitalism*	John Wiley & Sons 2001
Mark Boucher	*The Hedge Fund Edge: Maximum Profit/Minimum Risk Global Trend Trading Strategies*	John Wiley & Sons, 1998
Joseph G. Nicholas Kristen M. Fox	*Investing in Hedge Funds*	Bloomberg Press 1999
Francois-Serge L'Habitant	*Hedge Funds: Risks and Returns*	John Wiley & Sons 2001

Author	Title	Publisher
Lars Jaeger	*Managing Risk in Alternative Investment Strategies: Successful Investing in Hedge Funds and Managed Funds*	Prentice Hall 2002
Gordon de Brouwer	*Hedge Funds in Emerging Markets*	Cambridge University Press 2002
James P. Owen	*The Prudent Investors Guide to Hedge Funds*	Wiley Trade Publishing 2000
Daniel A. Strachman	*Getting Started in Hedge Funds*	John Wiley & Sons, 1999
Beverly Chandler	*Investing with Hedge Fund Giants: Financial Times Profit Whether Markets Rise or Fall*	Financial Times Prentice Hall 2001
Stefano Lavinio	*The Hedge Fund Handbook*	McGraw-Hill Ryerson Ltd 1999
Jess Lederman Robert Klein	*Hedge Funds: Investment & Portfolio Strategies for the Institutional Investor*	Irwin Professional Publishing 1995
William J. Crerend Robert A. Jaeger	*Fundamentals of Hedge Fund Investing: A Professional Investors's Guide*	McGraw-Hill (Health Professional Division) 1998
Laurence A. Connors	*Investment Secrets of a Hedge Fund Manager: Breakthrough Techniques Beat the Market*	Irwin Professional Publishing 1995
Carl C. Peters	*Handbook of Managed Futures & Hedge Funds: Performance, Evaluation & Analysis*	Irwin Professional 1996
Sarah Barhan	*Starting a Hedge Fund— A U.S. Perspective*	ISI Publications 2001
Sarah Barham Ian Hallsworth	*Starting a Hedge Fund— A European Perspective*	ISI Publications 1999
Ron Lake	*Evaluating & Implementing Hedge Strategies*	American Educational Systems 1996

INTERNET RESOURCES:

There are a number of excellent sources of information on hedge funds available through the Internet. Some of the most comprehensive are listed below.

In Canada:

http://www.canadianhedgewatch.com

http://hedgefunds.ca

http://www.fundlibrary.com

http://www.globefund.com

http://www.hedge.ca/

In the United States:

http://www.thehfa.org (has a Canadian Chapter)

http://www.hedgefund.net

http://www.e-hedge.com

http://www.hedgeworld.com

Index of Hedge Funds

Index

MIKLOS NAGY

Miklos Nagy is President, co-founder and CEO of Canadian Hedge Watch Inc., a Toronto based publishing and educational firm focusing on the Canadian hedge fund industry, and a Partner at NS Alternative Wealth Management. Mr. Nagy has 16 years of financial industry experience in Canada including Senior Partner at York Financial Group, financial planning at Money Concepts (Newmarket) and credit analysis at Credit Suisse Canada in Toronto.

Mr. Nagy studied Math and Computer Science in Hungary, and graduated with a B.Sc.(Hons.) degree from the University of Toronto in Economics and Statistics. He holds the CFA (Chartered Financial Analyst) and CFP (Certified Financial Planner) professional designations.

A leading authority on alternative investments and hedge funds in Canada, Mr. Nagy has been featured extensively on national television and in newspapers speaking about hedge funds. He has also been a speaker at financial seminars and conferences for numerous organizations.

He is a member of AIMR (Association of Investment Management and Research), the Toronto Society of Financial Analysts and a founding member of the Hungarian Society of Investment Professionals, Budapest.

PETER BECK

Peter Beck is a well-known financial expert and President of Swift Trade Securities, Canada's leading direct-access trading firm.

A true entrepreneur, Peter started his colorful career as a chef in Hungary. He immigrated to Canada in 1979 where he started a number of successful businesses, including the country's first long distance company in 1988, competing directly with Bell Canada. When he sold the company in 1993, there were offices coast to coast making it one of the leaders in the industry.

In 1997 Peter read an article about a US Day Trading firm and decided to bring the concept to Canada. In just four years, Swift Trade Securities grew from one office to 10 across Canada, used by over 400 full-time traders. Swift Trade Securities remains Canada's premier Direct Access Electronic Trading Centre, and was named one of the Top 10 Hottest Startups in Canada by *Profit Magazine* in 2001 for its remarkable two-year growth rate of almost 4000%.

Mr. Beck has been featured in media across the country, including *The Globe and Mail*, *The Toronto Star*, CTV News, ROB TV and Canadian Business. He regularly appears on television to offer commentary on the US markets.